# LIES OF OMISSION

## Algorithms Versus Democracy

CATHERINE DESOTO

Skyhorse Publishing

All Rights Reserved. No part of this book may be reproduced in any manner without the express written consent of the publisher, except in the case of brief excerpts in critical reviews or articles. All inquiries should be addressed to Skyhorse Publishing, 307 West 36th Street, 11th Floor, New York, NY 10018.

Skyhorse Publishing books may be purchased in bulk at special discounts for sales promotion, corporate gifts, fund-raising, or educational purposes. Special editions can also be created to specifications. For details, contact the Special Sales Department, Skyhorse Publishing, 307 West 36th Street, 11th Floor, New York, NY 10018 or info@skyhorsepublishing.com.

Skyhorse® and Skyhorse Publishing® are registered trademarks of Skyhorse Publishing, Inc.®, a Delaware corporation.

Visit our website at www.skyhorsepublishing.com.

10 9 8 7 6 5 4 3 2 1

Library of Congress Cataloging-in-Publication Data is available on file.

ISBN: 978-1-5107-7228-1
eBook ISBN: 978-1-5107-7229-8

Cover design by Kai Texel
Cover photograph by Getty Images

Printed in the United States of America

*To my late father, Jerry, and to all the lives he touched, especially those who followed his teaching and have taken steps on the Road Less Travelled, for whom it made a difference.*

# Contents

# PART ONE

# CHAPTER ONE

# A Frame for the Lies

When a condition afflicts an individual, doctors call it idiopathic. It means an ailment has arisen with spontaneity, as if out of thin air. A term of lacking, a cop out, a way to say unknown. If a nation develops an unknown problem, it may be called a curse, or a blight. If the blight has begun to be understood, if some insight into its cause has been observed, then names are proposed, ramifications are discussed, and, books are written.

A lie of omission is to dishonestly withhold crucial information needed to correct false beliefs. These lies have been multiplying. Many people paying close attention observe that we, as a society, have become increasingly tainted over the past decade, our institutions have become blighted with mistrust, and, the promise of social media has become a curse. There is a lack of curiosity about, and even intolerance for, opposing views. Somehow, collectively, we are simultaneously both more fragmented and more certain we are right. It is no longer an isolated relative who rants politics over holiday turkey. It is the whole table, the town, humanity. Not just the quirky, not just the fanatics, not just the fringes: the core. The core has gone rogue, except it's not rogue anymore. It is the new normal. Dox those blind to your truth. It is an affliction on society.

Divisiveness has consequences. As Google ex-CEO Eric Schmidt has said, "We have a problem with our information technology in that targeting engines are being used to take what is worst about human behavior and make it even worse." The modern algorithms behind social media hide parts of truths, building islands of ignorance while simultaneously departing a sense of being well informed.

Technological modernity has made a perfect storm. While diverse opinions are certainly integral to American culture, it is the thesis of this book that we are in trouble. The book is divided into two parts, plus a test yourself appendix. The first part, chapters one through five, describes the modern blight and conveys what science has to say about it. The chapters spell out the nature of the divisiveness, the lure of social media, the supplying of agreeable content, and why we like it so much. In this section, I draw upon social psychology and a bit of neuroscience, with a smidge of historical jurisprudence for good measure. Next, in part two, eight issues that American citizens have trouble seeing the other side of are tackled. Similar in style to a set of pro and con, opposing view chapters, but with a goal to bridge the disinformation gap in a way our smart phones will never do. Thus, it is also a reminder that physically written words, books, have value.

The book begins with an overview of the extent of the growing divide, drawing upon polls and the decades-long shift of media's role in society. There is mention of evolving laws and regulations; the extent of the problem becomes clear.

Next, it is explained that humans have an innate love to be right, that social media is telling us we are right. There is a reason why we respond with growing conformity to the narrative we are fed. The social media experience is really a perfect storm, and the human response can be understood as rooted in our neurochemistry.

Chapter four tells some history of social media and the use of algorithms. The research that investigates associated effects is explored. Chapter five is devoted to critical thinking, extolling the formerly accepted truisms of good logic. The once accepted tenet, that one only knows an issue when they can convincingly articulate the opposition, is the guiding star. The opposing viewpoints section is introduced and the approach explained.

As a result of the book, trying to give a fair accounting of views I do not hold, I learned some things. Some things really surprised me, and I felt some anger. I felt lied to as I learned more about the issues: lies of omission from sources I had trusted to inform me. Many of the surprising things ended up in The Test, at the end of the book. No shame in being wrong about some of them—if they are in the book, it probably means I found them surprising too.

Each essay is written to be a strong and persuasive argument for the given position. Do not kill the messenger. Social media has not been honest with you. The cause of the scourge on society, the polarization and the hate are the pocket portal's lies of omission. The world of social media, held in the palm of your hand, exploits our neural circuitry; as research documents, it makes us angry.

If this book, and the polarizing issues explained from at least two opposing sides, causes anger that's okay, but I hope we will direct the anger where it belongs. Our seductive little pocket portal and its sweet song of confirmation, using the dislike of opposition to increase its advertising dollars. If you have been an avid user of social media, or if you get your news from Facebook, YouTube, or a chosen set of information sites, you are not used to having strong contra-arguments presented. Buckle up. I have endeavored to write respectable explanations of viewpoints I do not have. Doing so was kind of a test for myself, too. I don't want to be part of the problem. Before I trust my own opinions, I want to be sure I know, really know, what the other side has to say.

Critical Race Theory, Covid Mandates, Kyle Rittenhouse, Police Brutality, and the Second Amendment. Transsexuality, Moon Landing Conspiracies, Election Fraud 2020, and Tax Policy. It's all right here.

Like a snowball that is becoming an avalanche, a kind of rigid polarization has spread and gained momentum. Today, in 2022, it feels like a majority of Americans cannot begin to fathom why other humans see things differently than they themselves do. It is as though the majority of humans imagine that a given assessment of facts, that seems obvious from their viewpoint, must therefore be the only reasonable interpretation to have. One might even say militant ignorance is the national zeitgeist of the 2020s.

# CHAPTER TWO

# Breaking Up with the Left

Of course, the divide has always been there. The Federalists versus the Anti-Federalists, the Confederates versus the Union, and sixty years ago the Vietnam War and then Civil Rights again threatened to tear apart the United States of America. The idealized melting pot never blended, and the States have never had the unifying national identity that comes from sharing a common history. The divide is again accelerating. In 2020, a whopping 77 percent of US citizens said the country was more divided than before the pandemic. This literally means that the USA was decidedly *less* divided pre-pandemic.

Who would have thought we would ever look at the Obama and Trump years as comparatively unified? And yet, the Pew Research Center survey results suggest that when Ted Nugent was saying the then-president was a piece of shit who could suck on his machine gun, or Kathy Griffin was holding a decapitated head model of the then-president, were the *good old days*. Ominously, this same question was posed in 2021, just one year later. It had worsened more still: 88 percent (up from 77 percent) felt the split in the country had grown even larger. In 2021, strong partisans were more likely to declare themselves to have a "Very Unfavorable" view of citizens from the other party (66 percent and 59 percent). Comparatively, just five years prior in 2017, the number of Americans who selected "Very Unfavorable" was about 17 percent. That is a shift of impressive magnitude.

Teachers, nurses, students, executives, and waiters, we all seem to individually behave as if there is a chance we are correct about everything. That of all the people in the world—it might be that *our* personal opinions (the current ones as opposed to the now discarded myriad opinions we have held in the past) are the ones that are *all* correct . . . what are the odds? Can we calculate an estimate? If we assume that no two people agree on everything and if there *is* an individual human who is right on everything they believe to be true—what are the odds it is you? Or me?

There are 8 billion living human beings, that makes the odds about one in 8 billion. Not a good bet. Yet the hallmark of the 2020s is that taking time to listen to others, with the goal of understanding opposing assessments, not only lacks value but is disloyal and repellant. Slow and mutually respectful debate among neighbors is passé when we can hop into the metaverse and easily find confirming viewpoints.

## Lonely Out in Left Field

I feel it. As a tenured academic I feel a disconcerting intolerance of opposing views within the once authority-questioning ivory tower of liberalism. One definition for liberal is "willing to respect or accept behavior or opinions different from one's own." Merriam-Webster (online) defines a liberal as "a supporter of a political and social philosophy that promotes individual rights, civil liberties, democracy, and free enterprise."

Has something fundamental shifted among liberalism? Certainly, the sides are sharpening and today, who one votes for predicts all manner of opinions. Liberalism and tolerance seem scarce on both sides, but promotion of individual rights and broadmindedness were formerly *the defining features* of liberalism. A white leader of the democratic party recently said, you can't be Black if you consider voting Republican. That is quite a statement. As a life-long liberal, that statement worried me. What has happened to respect for dissenting viewpoints? From top to bottom, on all sides, it has mostly disappeared. This is a sharp change.

David Golberger was a legislative director of the American Civil Liberties Union in the 1970s. His hallowed defense of the Nazi's right to march with their swastikas, right smack in the middle of a community of aging holocaust survivors in Skokie, Illinois, was once lauded by liberals who simultaneously detested the Nazi's message. The march happened in 1978. I have a clear memory of learning about the case in my Introduction to the Legal Process course as an undergraduate. What would happen today? Would the ACLU defend this right today? The reason the marcher's rights were defended was not because Nazis were thought to have had something valuable to say, but because having a human in the position to decide what is, and is not, valuable represents the demise of democracy.

I feel that if I were to advocate for an unpopular person like Milo Yiannopoulus's right to speak at a public university in Iowa, or express that anti-Black Lives Matter flyers should not be systematically removed from a university campus, I would be met with disagreement from my fellow liberal professors. I feel this way because I did express these opinions, and that's literally what happened. Unlike in 1978, one can sense it has become suspect to promote the peculiar but charming ideas of yesterday's liberalism, the protection of unpopular speech.

In-group conformity and derision for those with opposing views is at an all-time high. The United States of America, with its world changing Declaration of Independence may be falling. Is it possible for a country to be united with this much polarized divisiveness? It is not trivial to try and contemplate how it is possible that people, living side by side in the same communities, have come to exist with such diametrically opposing viewpoints.

## The Fall of Fairness

Perhaps the saga begins with the Fairness Doctrine. This was a helpful rule by the Federal Communication Commission (FCC) that, until 1987, formally required broadcasters to provide their viewers or listeners with information that fairly covered both sides of an issue of public concern, if the issue was covered at all. In effect, it was not legal to present the public with partial information designed to make one side of a policy question triumph. How far we have moved. It is interesting and largely unappreciated that the decisive case, *Red Lion Broadcasting v. FCC*, technically was never overturned, even though the Fairness Doctrine (on which it partially stood) and the related FCC rule are no more.

The Red Lion legal case was triggered by a radio station criticism of the author of a political book, followed by said author demanding air time to respond. The case went all the way to the US Supreme Court. Overall, the resulting ruling of the court centered on the following key tenet: the right of the citizen to be informed was tantamount to a functioning democracy. In essence, jurisprudence has held that this right trumped any competing right of broadcasters to present one-sided information. "It is the right of the viewers and listeners, not the right of the broadcasters, which is paramount,"

(*Red Lion v. FCC*). The simple beauty of that sentence attests to the prudence that has been lost.

The court affirmed that speech relating to policy and politics was not just communication, but was indeed the foundation of self-governing democracies. Nonetheless, as the 1980s ended, the FCC itself repealed the Fairness Doctrine, over the objections of Congress. Many legal experts felt that the repeal flouted both reason and the will of Congress. Congress even united to pass a law to clarify the importance of fairness and balance in media, but it was vetoed. The door was open for news to become non-news. Dissemination of propaganda as a form of entertainment ensued.

Fox News Network may have been first to embrace calling opinions and fact selection "news," but they have not been the last. This unhelpful turn against the rights of viewers in favor of the rights of broadcasters set the table, and the modern broadcasters and advertisers feasted. The demise of the objective, Walter Cronkite style, evening news about the world and national affairs was in full force as the new Millennium arrived. Today, in the 2020s, citizens from across the various political spectrums find themselves perplexed, "How can she not see that the narcissist fired his best generals and allies, and turns on anyone who disagrees with his uneducated views, views that are formed based primarily from watching TV shows?" Or, "How can my nephew trust an authority figure that has been wrong about Covid so many times, and has openly lied to Congress?" In truth, it can be vexing to comprehend others' views that are miles apart from one's own: Whose Kool-Aid are they drinking?

I know the answer, and I know why diametrically opposite realities have become more common. We know who is pouring the Kool-Aid. Although I intend to offer some research and explanation from history, neuroscience, and psychology, here is the spoiler: it doesn't look good for us. The momentum breaking us apart is very strong. To step back from the precipice, to move away from the fracture, would mean to overcome several forces working against even baby steps in that direction. It would need to overcome the biggest corporations' natural desire (and legal requirement) to make more money. It would need to push against the trends in jurisprudence of the past twenty years. It would need to stand against the human dopamine-based reward system that loves confirmation. These are the things that are widening the divide. Modern social media and their information algorithms select information for the individual which they are going to like, to click upon, to read, and to see the advertisements. Advertisements pay: Articles that get clicks and reads earn money. Jurisprudence says corporations have rights. In the end, we users are all delivered sweet stories that whisper, "you are right!" and splash yummy dopamine molecules right onto our brain's nucleus accumbens. And those comments! It is naturally delightful to behold the throngs of support.

But I am getting ahead of myself.

# CHAPTER THREE

# Confirmation and Dopamine

In 2016, the *Wall Street Journal* published side by side samples of social media feeds, referred to as *Blue Feed Red Feed,* for two hypothetical users: one very liberal, one very conservative. As noted, the difference in the information was striking. Consider a young man, with his Gadsden flag proudly nailed to the wall behind his desk, clicking on an article from his social media feed about immigration. At the exact same moment, his social justice warrior aunt consults her social media feed a few miles away. The aunt finds a story about a wide-eyed child, with braids, softly crying in a detention center and an interview with a mother of two from Honduras, now working on a farm for twelve-hour shifts, picking strawberries and fleeing a history of unimaginable abuse, abuse which is carefully described. Meanwhile, in the alternative, the young man is fed a story about an illegal immigrant who was just convicted of murdering beautiful Molly Tibbits, a university student, in the formerly safe cornfields of Iowa. Do not underestimate the importance of this information segregation. It is like geographical neighbors inhabit different realities.

The divergent feeding began in earnest around 2010, and by the year 2016, Twitter, Facebook, YouTube, and Instagram were all using automatized algorithms to guide which content is received by a user. TikTok has since joined the fray. Since at least 2016, major social media and newsfeeds have individually promoted stories a given individual is most likely to click upon, based on their past viewing and sharing behavior. The underlying reason makes economic sense and does not require an assumption of nefarious intent. The goal is to entice users to stay longer on the platform, to give information they want to see, that they will click upon, and ultimately to increase advertising revenue. More views equal more advertising revenue. But the result is that we all sip from individualized tea; neighbors no longer receive a common set of informative facts. The device in our pocket or purse delivers information based on what we like. The background system learns about our views, and reacts, and recommends. Neutrality in news, with a goal of sharing objective information that former generations took for granted, is passé.

In thinking about why the country is dividing, consider the effect of today's media. If you followed (clicked and consumed) the political conspiracy centered on satanic activities of the Left and were interested in the Pizzagate stories, you probably were therefore recommended the most tantalizing information about the mysterious QAnon. If you went ahead and clicked on a Q-drop, then you almost certainly did *not* have information in your feed about how some of the drops (most) had been proven wrong. It goes both ways. On the other hand, if you browsed information about why some of the Q conspiracy ideas were absurd and proven wrong, you may have missed information about actual and documented voting problems. Objective information that exists to service Democracy's needs, rather than to generate ad revenue, is challenging to find.

## Human Nature

Let me commit a little psychology here. Decades of study into human thought processes suggest human beings are not the logical assimilators of incoming data we assume ourselves to be. Analyzing data is hard and humans are lazy when it comes to cognitive resources. Mental short cuts (we psychologists call them heuristics) are relied upon because humans cannot always use their vast reasoning abilities to fully and carefully process information; it is sometimes necessary to take shortcuts due to the complexity of the world we live in. It causes some problems. One short cut that matters to broadcasters, internet providers, and advertisers trying to hold consumers attention is called "confirmation bias." It has played a major role in the success of the algorithms that lasso our attention and help us avoid opposing views.

### Humans Love to Be Right

According to the psychology book I rely upon to teach a couple hundred Introduction to Psychology students each year, confirmation bias is "the tendency to search for and use information that supports rather than refutes one's ideas," (King, 2022). Most students are able to learn the definition, and appreciate that this happens. Many possess enough insight to realize they probably discount opposing information occasionally. Few fully grasp the overwhelming pull of this tendency. Let's take a stroll back in time, forty years ago, when confirmation bias and the tendency for opinions to persevere in spite of opposing information was not investigated to document how party politics can ruin us, but as a general feature of human thinking.

Craig Anderson was finishing his doctorate at Stanford and was observing that people will form strongly held beliefs based on minimal evidence. Investigating this further, his work showed that beliefs can be manipulated and even randomly assigned. Here's how it worked: people were given some information about how individual firefighters scored on a personality test measuring willingness to take risks. They were also told about the lives of the firefighters and whether they were successful as firefighters, or not. Unbeknownst to the people, it was made up; the information given was total fiction. In fact, it was set up so that some received information that strongly suggested riskiness *was probably a dangerous trait* in firefighters, and others had information that conveyed the opposite: that avoiding risky decisions was associated with *success* as a firefighter. Next—and perhaps importantly—the people had to write a few sentences on their discovery. Essentially, people were asked to state and justify their conclusion on the relationship between riskiness and firefighting.

They no doubt came up with some good reasons. Perhaps willingness to take risks allowed firefighters to put their own safety aside to save others. Conversely, perhaps conservatively following protocol leads to better outcomes via avoiding risking the lives of fellow firefighters. After all of this was finished, the participants in the research study were informed it was all fabricated information. Checks were made to make meticulously sure the people understood it had been all fictional data. They understood. But guess what? Once they had written that justifying essay, it didn't matter that the original data was made up, and it didn't matter that they know it was made up. Apparently, once they persuaded themselves it was true, and professed it in writing, they desired it to be true, and their belief persisted.

As Dr. Craig Anderson explained it, even after they were debriefed regarding the true nature of the research, "subjects initially exposed to data indicative of a positive relationship continued to believe that a positive relationship existed, whereas subjects in the negative relationship condition continued to believe in a negative relationship," (p. 1041–42). Does this frighten you? If not, make sure it is clear. It should be startling. People were randomly (just luck of a coin toss) assigned to discover a made-up relationship between risk taking and success as a firefighter. It worked, the belief was formed and articulated. Straight up telling them it was bogus did not make them discard their now professed beliefs.

What hope do we have regarding opinions on gun laws, Russia, Covid policy, or anything else? As the authors of the above research spelled out in black and white, perseverance of beliefs occurs "even when subjects' theories are initially based on minimal, and indeed logically inadequate evidence—even when their beliefs are of exactly the tentative, hastily-formed, and ill-founded variety most likely to face subsequent logical or evidential discrediting in everyday experience," they persist. It isn't just right-wingers, nor just left-wingers. This is how *humans* work. To summarize, this is the story science tells on the Establishment of Beliefs.

1. Provide people flimsy, or even made-up, information.
2. Let them discover a connection implanted in the information.
3. Ask them to write about their discovery.
4. Watch them adhere to their new belief.
5. Step four lasts and lasts.

Typically, nothing changes after the fourth step. No incoming information, even to the extreme of telling people that you provided them fake information in the first place, has an impact. Indeed, step four appears to be permanent.

Let us consider this research by the light of modern times: the omnipresent computer screen. Twitter. Facebook. TikTok. Instagram. Pull out your portal. Post a picture. Share a link. Check your friends. Learn what happened in the world today. There are several common features to all social media. The totality of the experience in relation to the research on belief adherence and confirmation is significant. All social media experiences feed personalized, somewhat differentiated content, all allow users to review and then comment (favorably or unfavorably) on posts, tweets, and stories. Users can even simply publicly express support via likes and thumbs ups to other posts, comments or tweets.

1. Users are provided information, which is sometimes bogus or flimsy.
2. The information is considered by the person.

3. Users profess their views via comments and likes.
4. The views are clung to.
5. There is no five. Users are unlikely to ever change their mind.

The point is, there is research that carefully documents what we all can observe: people generally do not change their minds once they discover evidence, form an opinion, and profess it. Science tells us information received does not have to be high quality to persuade, it just has to be believed for a bit and professed. Click, Consider, Comment, Cling. No fifth step.

## Dopamine's Reason to Be

Imagine you have posted, commented, or tweeted something. Maybe you read this new interesting book, or you made a connection related to a new movie and some experience you had, or you tweeted the current president is doing a bad job in some particular way. Then you go to sleep. Next morning (or probably during the night) you go ahead and check your personal portal to the world. You are wondering what *other* people are thinking about the president, the movie, the book. You discover with astonishment your comment has three hundred likes. Moreover, at least thirty people have commented favorably about your insight. Question: How do you *feel*? That pleasantly surprised satisfied feeling is brought to you by dopamine. Another aspect of the social media experience is encountered.

### *Enhancing Survival Yesterday and Today*

Dopamine is a brain chemical that one neuron sends across the synapse to another neuron. It carries this message: "Good! We want to do that more." It accomplishes this feat by imparting a feeling of satisfaction. If one contemplates the mechanisms required for survival, Nature's need to have a way to encourage some kinds of behaviors over others becomes apparent. In other words, we need built-in mechanisms to get us to do things that would keep us alive. Consider the alternative: Animal nervous systems that did not make an animal repeat survival enhancing behavior probably didn't survive as well. If eating high calorie food was not enjoyable, animals might not work to get it, and they might starve during times of famine. What works well is whenever a behavior is survival-enhancing, the nervous system releases a morsel of dopamine in the part of your brain that make you feel nice. This circuit runs between the ventral tegmental area and nucleus accumbens, deep in the brain. Dopamine here feels good.

Sneakily, this part of your brain connects directly to your best-planning pre-frontal cortex: the part that plans ahead and can figure out how to get things done. Get that dopamine releasing thing again. Here are some things neuroscientists know release dopamine into your ventral tegmental and nucleus accumbens: sex, sweet and fatty food, winning at gambling, drug use, and certain kinds of social interactions. In fact, dopamine in this brain area is what makes addictions possible. An activity that doesn't produce any dopamine zing is not going to produce the craving that underlies addiction. For most of human history, this all worked well. Dopamine splashes made us recall the taste, and thus work to again obtain the high value delicious food (insert the smell of bacon here) or remember where to find those super sweet strawberries. Dopamine made us put effort into the goal of having sex. It made us motivated to act in ways that caused us to be liked in our social group. All of these things are survival enhancing. All is satisfactory for tens of thousands of years.

Now enter modern society. Scientists have discovered how dopamine works, and we can use our frontal cortex gray matter to contemplate how it can be used. Flashy marketing and modern supply chains make it trivially easy to engineer cravings and for us to get more chocolate, juicy hamburgers, and bright colored, fruity tasting cereals. Although we no longer benefit from more calories to avoid starvation, the dopamine areas still direct us to seek them. Our hunter gatherer minds within our modern society cause us to get diabetes, heart attacks, and grow fat. Our brains are designed to love and crave these things, but our brains aren't expecting the ease and ubiquity and constant glitzy enticements.

When you feel that distracting crave for the familiar taste of pizza, or to see if people are liking your post, that is the expectancy created neurochemically from past reward urging you to repeat. It's eerie to ponder—but that is how your brain is working. You have circuitry that evolved to keep you alive. Today the human brain works basically the same as it did ten thousand years ago.

## Likes: The Neurochemistry of Social Interaction

The dopamine activity in the ventral tegmental to nucleus accumbens circuit has actually been measured while animals are interacting. The techniques of optogenetics are complicated, but are able to measure activity of dopamine producing neurons in real time. Dr. Lisa Gunaydin and colleagues at Stanford have firmly established that for mammals, social interaction itself increases the dopamine activity. Moreover, the amount of the dopamine activity predicts subsequent desire to socially interact. This is what dopamine is for: it makes one want it again. And Gunaydin's team made sure: it doesn't work this way with just *anything* interesting. For example, exploring cool new inanimate objects didn't release dopamine that predicted later behavior, only social explorations. We know that the dopamine system likes social interactions.

Social likes matter to humans. We want to be liked. Agreement and affirmation feel neurochemically good. They call us back. They keep us going. You have collided with another layer of the social media trap.

It is hard to not spend hours a day staring into the portal. Neurochemistry from yesteryear is stacked against us.

# CHAPTER FOUR

# Lies of Omission

In a 2015, "Exposure to Ideologically Diverse News," was published in the journal *Science*. In this article, the effect of algorithms was formally investigated by Eytan Bakshy and two other employees of Facebook. Setting aside some valid criticisms of the methods and conclusions (scholars like Christian Sandvig noting the authors' tendency to soften the faults of Facebook pejoratively calling the research the "not my fault" study), there were indeed interesting *mea culpas* within the results. First, if there was a question, it was verified that stories at the top of one's feed are clicked on more often than information lower in the feed. The algorithm employed, at least at that time, also removed some news stories, but never news the user was likely to agree with (details are found on p. 23 of supplementary materials associated with Bakshy's article). The removal matters and place in the feed matters; the result is that people do not have uniform access to information. Are citizens using media like Facebook to inform them of the world? Yes. Among people in their mid-twenties to about forty, Facebook is the top source for political news. Generation X is similar, but the Baby Boom Generation differs: that generation always has, and still does, rely upon television news and legacy media.

The social media portal as the world news source is new, it is a generational shift. We have given our smart phones the power to change our knowledge base. As Google wrote in their blog (2009) when describing the Faustian bargain they were offering, "Now when you search using Google, we will be able to better provide you with the most relevant results possible. For example, since I always search for recipes and often click on results from epicurious, Google might rank epicurious.com higher on the results page the next time I look for recipes." Same for Covid dangers versus Covid hoax. Same for Black Lives Matter protests versus Black Lives Matter riots. Election Fraud versus election results. The stories served are not unified and sections of truth are omitted. Reality is curated.

Today's Google algorithms do not work the same today, and Google confirms that it is constantly changing how search results work. A list of the dates of algorithm updates is available at Search Engine Journal; there are a few every year. For example, in January of 2022, Google announced an algorithm update that changed website rankings for 14 percent of searches, but Google doesn't specify exactly what the changes are. The constant tweaking has itself led to concerns that censorship and bias in results are being encoded. As psychologist and expert on artificial intelligence Robert Epstein wrote in 2016, "Google, Inc., isn't just the world's biggest purveyor of information; it is also the world's biggest censor. . . . When Google's employees or algorithms decide to block our access to information about a news item, political candidate or business, opinions and votes can shift, reputations can be ruined and businesses can crash and burn," (U.S. News, online).

The changes are dizzying. Censorship and affirming social media blend together and prevent anything like objectively authoritative, fair news via social media. Books and card catalogs of the Baby Boomers were unchanging: the same last year as this year, and the same for Betty as for Shirley. It is not like that anymore. It may be subtle, but there is a constant manipulation of every single smart phone user's attention.

We are living this change, it is naturally challenging to perceive the full effect of a wave one is in. Perhaps it is not unlike the revolution of ten thousand years ago transforming lives from wandering to settling, to owning land with enforced boundaries. The rise of the tiny gadget directs consciousness inward and creates realities catered to individual biases. You exist in this wave of change. But it's not a wave that travels forward. It's an eddy. An eddy that exploits your hardwired preference for confirmation into a spiraling undertow that narrows your attention to a sliver of reality. You do not know that you do not know. Let me be clear: if you get most of your information from your smart phone: *You* are missing information. Not just *other people*.

The eddy communicates and affirms: you are right they are wrong, and this has effects. There is data that sorts out the cause and effect of the social media experience.

## Sorting Out Cause from Effect

When Ann typed "planting tulips" into a search engine, then checked her social media, she may have been served different article and advertisement choices than Abby, who typed identical key strokes to begin. Will their opinions on whether improved perennial Dutch bulbs are worth the price be affected by the different information they receive? It is a question of cause and effect. How does one sort out cause from effect here? After all, the computer algorithms spit out tailored information based on Ann and Abby's past clicks and reads.

There is complexity in determining whether algorithms actually cause a change: if Ann decides the new bulbs are too expensive, it could be because this is what she believed anyway. It is reasonable to consider the possibility that she received the article on affordable generic bulbs because she was frugal to begin. Abby was provided an article about curb appeal and financial returns: but perhaps that is because she searches for high end décor often. The articles selected for them by the omnipresent algorithms may not be causing any attitude shifting—or are they? How can one tell? Cue praise for the scientific method: Data has been carefully collected to answer this question, it's been analyzed, and the results are publicly available to enlighten us.

Jaeho Cho and colleagues began by logging in to computers using newly created user profiles with accompanying tabula rasa search history. Next, they searched differently (based on real world search terms actually obtained from liberal and conservative users) and then clicked on the liberal versus conservative sites which the search terms generated. This was all carefully planned, and designed to simulate actual searching (some liberal or pro-Democrat searches and clicks; others conservative or pro-GOP viewing). After seventy politically slanted searches, the newly made search histories were ready to be investigated. Now the newly made user profiles logged off, and when they next logged on to youtube.com, the first five political videos served up to the users were noted and recorded. These five represented "biased search results" from YouTube recommender algorithms. For purposes of comparison, an all-new user profile was once again created and the generic search query "2016 presidential election" was entered, and the first five YouTube videos generated for this newly created and unknown new "person" were noted. This was used for comparison, representing the unbiased control videos.

To recap: The researchers generated YouTube algorithm search results based on different political leanings. The researchers also checked what the search results for a new user (with no previous search history for the algorithms to work on) would be. Now they are set to check for the elusive cause and effect. You know what is coming: they randomly assigned people to watch the biased algorithm YouTube results, using the method that can determine cause and effect.

They used a kind of advanced statistics called "partial correlations" to allow a careful isolation of the changes due specifically to the videos watched, as opposed to pre-existing political beliefs or anything like that. Remember the causal question being considered: What is the *effect* of viewing your personalized algorithm served content? And, how is it different from viewing non-algorithm content on the same subject? The outcome measure in their research was a straightforward one: How does Hillary Clinton/Donald Trump make them *feel*. This was measured by straightforwardly asking them to rank their emotional responses before and after the viewings. Hope? Sadness? Joy? Anger? Fear? Was there any effect beyond their pre-existing attitudes caused by watching the biased content?

Drumroll. . . . There was a change. There was an effect detected, found to be caused by viewing the recommended algorithm-generated content. The change was in anger. It was a big effect. These results show something that matters to society. Carefully, and meticulously, with prudent use of statistics, the following was documented: First, if a person searched based on their natural user preferences and then watched some content, the recommender algorithms would start to change their viewing options. This was shown by Cho and colleagues when they asked their participants to list common search terms, and then employed these terms to trigger the algorithm (their publication, in the references at the back of the book, goes into detail about *exactly* how they did this). Second, these new search results, which were the cause they wanted to study, themselves caused politically polarized anger.

If you think back to your introductory social science courses, you learned correlation does not imply causation. To be sure, people who search for political content on the issue du jour have strong polarized feelings on issue du jour: but that is correlation, and doesn't establish cause. What research method can investigate cause? Experiments with randomly assigned control groups that isolate the cause of interest. Cho, Hilberthaidt, and Ahmed randomly assigned people to receive selected search results and thus were able to demonstrate the cause and effect of the video selections beyond any pre-existing disposition.

Watching the algorithm recommended results, as opposed to general results on the topic of interest, increased anger for Clinton if you were conservative to begin, and increased anger for Trump if you were liberal to begin. This is important to grasp so allow me to labor the point. Remember those partial correlations mentioned above? This statistical technique allows the removal of the pre-viewing valance. Scientific data is helpful: the experimental design, measures from before and after the videos, combined with the appropriate statistics, allowed this research to answer the question of interest. Not much of an effect on hopefulness one way or the other, not much effect for sadness. But anger? Bingo. It made people madder.[1] People who leaned left felt angrier about Donald Trump; and people who leaned right felt angrier about Hillary Clinton.

## Problem Detected

What does this mean for society? It isn't good. Persons paying attention have been hand wringing for some time. Social Psychologist Jonathon Haidt, in his December 2019 interview with PBS, cogently discussed the negative role of social media in the new divisiveness. The apprehension that historical reflections affords is stunning. James Madison knew that political division ruined democracies, but he felt the largeness of the land in the then-new United States would be a shield. And Haidt then specifically refers to the dangers of instant-spread anger.

> [James] Madison is musing the fact that factions have destroyed almost all previous democracies: somebody will inflame passions and then they don't care about the common good. They just want to fight the enemy. But he says, in a very big country such as ours, the thirteen colonies with vast distance, someone could start a fire in one place, but the country is so big, so big that it couldn't spread to all the other states. By the time news got there, passions would have cooled. Well, fine, but what if we get this new technology that allows passion to spread instantly?

---

1  Cho, Hilbert, and Ahmed (2020) had an additional third condition for secondary comparison that represented a possible algorithm recommendations for a person who did more social searches. For simplicity in conveying the gist of the results, this third condition was left out of the above summary.

The concern about hot-headed instant-spread passion with the potential to destroy democracies is echoed by today's free-thinking, instant-spread masters, the social media influencers themselves. The number one podcaster in United States, Joe Rogan, laments that social media supplies viewers with viewpoints and content that makes them mad and get excited. "They engage and that's what they will click on" and this increases the advertisement revenue. "It's a bad advertising model . . . (that) inadvertently supports outrage," (Joe Rogan Experience episode 1295). He continued, "It's a crazy thing that has happened, that we gravitate towards the outrageous. . . . When you cultivate feeds so that people get pissed off, you are making America a shittier place."

Ironically, Rogan's cool-headed, open-minded interviews with people of all manner of opinions sometimes puts him in hot water. But more mainstream influencers see the same. Bari Weiss, former *New York Times* journalist and now host of the influential podcast, *Honestly*, states, "The thing we call social media is deeply anti-social, the thing that promised to unite us has done precisely the opposite." Moreover, the founders of social media themselves have been sounding the alarm. Sean Parker, the first official president of Facebook, has gone on record as worrying about the effects on our brains and admits that the original goal was to, "consume as much of your time-conscious attention as possible," and that the "exploitation of a vulnerability in human psychology" was a conscious decision on the inventors' part."

Consider the quotes above carefully. They indicate that anyone paying attention to social media will agree we have a problem with the way it is working. Us versus Them, and lightning fast to boot. Sorry, Mr. Madison. All of us, the users of smart phones and social media, are being actively corralled. The buffering of time and distance that gave James Madison some hope against the tendency to factionalize has evaporated, and indeed we can and do effectively shut ourselves within confined subsections of our own personalized mobs. We don't want opposing information. It all makes us angry. We feel good about our righteous anger. The seldom helpful human foil of confirmation bias has been fed uber-steroids that make small differences grow.

## Take Any Variable

Consider any given item that can be measured. If you measure enough of any naturally occurring thing that varies, there will be that classic bell curve distribution. Let's use broccoli sentiments as an example. There will be some health food devotees who cherish its antioxidant nature, love the taste, and eat some daily. There will be a few who eat mostly junk food, hate broccoli so much they would throw away a whole dish if even one floret were in it. Most people are in the middle somewhere.

What algorithms and social media do is detect that a mild dislike may exist, and then present testimony of how broccoli is overrated with pictures of unappetizing broccoli dishes, negative information about people who love broccoli, and invitations to join groups where people talk about how much they hate broccoli. Meanwhile, the people who more or less like broccoli, are sent information about the level of antioxidants found in broccoli and associated anti-cancer benefits. Testimonials of healthy, happy people who eat cruciferous vegetables. Pictures and recipes of gorgeous tantalizing broccoli soups and well-plated broccoli side dishes. They are presented information on how many people are obese, and how many teens don't eat enough vegetables, the cost of obesity to health care system. Invitations to groups that cook and eat healthy. In six months, what was a bell curve distribution is two distinct curves.

The pro-broccoli group feels animosity and resentment about obese people who think only about their short-term pleasure. The anti-broccoli group begins to perceive the sense of superiority of those people, and to resent them.

Although this feels great in the short term and is an understandable effect, an effect predictable based on neurochemistry, what is the consequence when one steps out to the level of greater society? As in the greater good referred to in why we have free speech, as articulated above with the opinion in *Red Lion v. FCC*: The right of the viewers and listeners to receive fair and accurate information had been formally judged by the Court to be fundamentally above the right of the broadcasters' free speech.

The decision, written by Justice Byron White, elaborated that the overarching reason and legal principal for the FCC's opinions in this area, the "ratio decidendi" was established back in 1949 with the FCC's Report on Editorializing. As the late Senator John Pastore was quoted within the Supreme Court decision, the importance of receiving opposing views on issues, congressional intent was to "be a continuing reminder and *admonition to the Federal Communications Commission and to the broadcasters alike, that we were not abandoning the philosophy that gave birth to section 315*, in giving the people the right to have a full and complete disclosure of conflicting views on news of interest to the people of the country." This seems to indicate there was a patriotic philosophy that the Fairness Doctrine represented, but did not contain. The philosophy was core, transcending the FCC's whims, it could not be abandoned, was permanent and immutable. Providing opposing information was recognized as fundamental to a democracy where different opinions are present. That we have a problem with personalized information eddies is an understatement.

Do not underestimate Lies of Omission; they are lies. A lie of omission means withholding needed information to correct a false belief. It even has a legal definition: in court, it means to intentionally fail to tell the truth in a situation requiring a fuller disclosure to avoid deceit. The key treatise of this book is that social media algorithms function as lies of omission against every single consumer, every single day. Once a person clicks on information they are interested in, ones and zeros get flipped and the consumer is then served an agreeable piece of information next time they check in. Beware: you live in a world where your favorite device functions ingeniously to turn you into an extremist.

CHAPTER FIVE

# Critical Thinking and How to Read this Book

This book truly is not about changing your mind on issues you care about, and the book won't do that. As Anderson's research shows (see chapter 2), that is not going to happen anyway. It is best to accept that we cannot change others' views. The goal is to gain insight into what has happened to you, your neighbor, your relatives, your friends. Hopefully, it might make you consider that even though you naturally think you are right (by definition of having an opinion), and you are dopaminergically aware via those likes that lots of people *do* agree with you, there is still a non-zero chance you are wrong about something. I hope you will step back, look at the stars a few minutes, think about your society and humans, and really consider what your smart portal is doing. Take a very deep breath, and take a step away from the 2020s confirm-my-view zeitgeist back towards the need to know opposing information, an agreed upon bedrock principle of our democracy for two hundred years. As a psychologist, I am going for empathy and insight, not political influence.

The pros and cons that follow are not asserted to represent the best arguments, are not exhaustive, and are not intended to represent a consensus view of the reasons people come to a similar conclusion. I have endeavored not to include information stated as fact that I know is not factual. For example, people say that Kyle Rittenhouse carried an illegally bought gun across state lines, but this is clearly not true. Therefore, I would not include that (he took the gun across state lines) as a reason to think he was guilty, even if many people do. It seems to do otherwise would make the book inane.

People are polarized not because they *really* hate the person with the opposing view but because they can no longer imagine how people could reasonably have such an opinion. There is no common information, and the portal will never provide it. Get out of the portal and into a hard copy book whose permanence can't later be edited after the fact, and can't be changed depending on who is reading it. These essays are meant only to show how it is *possible* that someone intelligent and caring does not agree with you. Read the views you agree with, and read the views you disagree with, not to be persuaded, but to avoid demonizing those who hold those views. These essays are written to address the divide that has grown, that has caused riots and destruction and may be bringing the USA to civil unrest, perhaps the fall of a great democracy.

## Dear Reader

I am writing based on what I see as a scientist, as an educator seeing the changes over time, and as a mother of four, concerned about the future. Before the reading of the opposing views chapters that follow, it may help to clarify a few ground rules.

## Readers' Notes on Critical Thinking

When reading opposing viewpoints, a *conclusion should be understood as distinct from a statement of fact*. For example, "On page 103 of the document, Smith admits that the sign was green." That is a fact. It isn't a fact *the sign was green*; it is fact that on page 103 it is written that Smith said so. The fact is that the words exist on the page. If a reader can look on page 103 of the document to verify: it's a fact it is on the page. The distinction matters.

Second, if something is presented by one side as a fact, and both sides of an issue have acceded it as accurate, it should be assumed as factual. For example, if two invested and opposing sides agree that something sworn under oath is true, we can do no better. If the defense has a witness that says Joe was at the bakery one hour before the murder, *and the prosecution agrees* this is true, we will accordingly accept that as part of the facts of the case.

*A fact is not undone by a person merely saying it isn't so.* A factual statement of reality does not become undone because Aunt Bess says it isn't true, or even if President Joe Biden says it is isn't, or even if a fact-checker say it isn't. A real example, Kyle Rittenhouse testified where the gun was at various times, and that the gun was not transported across the state boundary. He testified to this under oath, there were witnesses to support it, no evidence against it, and in the end, it was not disputed by the other side. A news anchor tweeting he took the gun across state lines does not magically undo the confirmed locations of the weapon.

*A fact is not a fact because a fact checker or authority says it is.* It would still require convincing evidence. This point is worth beleaguering because it seems to be a point of increasing misunderstanding. First, appeal to authority is considered a logical fallacy when an argument relies on an authority's testimony over facts and evidence. A conclusion or opinion by an authority may be well supported by facts and logic, but it might not be. Assertions of fact (no matter who it is from) is not proof. Someone saying something does not have the power to make it true.

Consider the following:

a. Fact Checker Smith wrote that the V in COVID-19 stands for video.
b. The Centers for Disease Control, the World Health Organization, and Dr. Do, Chief of the Food and Drug Administration, along with twenty peer reviewed journal articles state the V stands for the word virus.
c. According to Dr. Re, as stated in his podcast that is freely available to view, he himself coined the term with his colleagues.
d. There are multiple videos of an event where the name COVID-19 was publicly used. No earlier use of the term has been uncovered. It was in a presentation by Drs. Do, Re, and Mi. They all stated the V stands for virus.
e. Smith is wrong.

A, B, C, and D are all statements of fact. But E is a conclusion. B and C and D facts provide strong support for concluding that Smith's opinion is incorrect. Facts can (and should) support conclusions. That is, we should want our conclusions to be supported by facts, not just testimonials. That a person said something, can indeed be a fact. But this is different from the content of what he or she said being taken as fact. That may seem trivial, but in the current times, the distinction has probably never mattered more. I will not treat an appeal to authority as a sole basis for establishing an opinion as fact.

*When does citing an authority count?* It always counts, but there are times it counts more than others. Citing an authority who agrees with you, while leaving out opposing views, should be minimally persuasive. It *is* persuasive if you cite authorities who are known to disagree with your preferred conclusion, on a point of fact that supports your conclusion. This is because some might not realize what is, and is not, in dispute. Noting that both sides of an issue agree on something will help move the points of *actual* contention forward.

For example, Anna is contending that hospitalization counts for Covid cases are straining hospitals, and a well-respected advocate for taking Covid very seriously (such as National Institute of Allergy and Infectious Diseases [NIAID] director Dr. Anthony Fauci or someone equally respected) is on record as saying some people counted as hospitalized for Covid are not hospitalized because of Covid, but just have it while in the hospital for other reasons. This matters more than if Florida Governor Ron DeSantis says the same thing. Why? Because DeSantis is often thought of as downplaying the pandemic, at least compared to Dr. Fauci's approach. Downplaying Covid's effect is not something Fauci is ever accused of. Therefore, Fauci making the statement matters more: we can reason that if Fauci states it, this point should probably be conceded. This would not be true in the same way of DeSantis.

Note that this logic is *not* based on any assumption that Fauci's word is above all others, but because his known position on the matter in this case helps focus the actual points of dispute. Apparently, at least some portion of the number of hospitalized Covid cases are not taking up a bed because of Covid illness. The question has focused: how many does this apply to (is it 1 percent or closer to 20 percent?).

## Readers' Notes: Value of Knowing Opposing Views

The opinion positions that follow are written for one purpose: to illustrate "how it is possible" for reasonable people to have different views. To glimpse at what the portal might be omitting. Unlike in years past, effort spent trying to be informed on a topic of interest won't work in terms of broadening the mind: indeed it will tend to narrow it. We cannot be informed of opposing views with the current media functioning as it does.

The almost famous parable of red and black ants that has been attributed to David Attenborough goes something like this: If someone catches 100 large red fire ants as well as 100 big black ants, and puts them in a jar, at first, nothing will happen. They are together without incident. However, if the jar is violently shaken and the ants then are all dumped back on the ground, now the ants will fight until they finally kill each other. The thing is, the red ants feel like the black ants are the enemy and vice versa, when in reality, the only enemy is the person who shook the jar. You are mad at the Republicans or you are mad at the Democrats. Or at the unvaccinated. Or at store owners requiring a mask. Or at the broccoli eaters. But your contempt is more properly directed at the algorithms that have told you things that make you mad, make you believe that your fellow Americans with different views are idiots, are your enemy.

But they are not the enemy. They are fellow Americans and fellow humans. Complex humans whose experiences and inclinations result in differing views are too often imagined in black and white stick drawings. A caricature sketched by information feeds that drain the humanity out, like removing the color from an oil painting. The enemy is the omissions. There aren't snowflake libtards and there aren't racist MAGAts. There are Blue ants and Red ants. Someone is shaking the jar.

I have sometimes considered the essence of opinions. I define an opinion as an individual level judgement about something, an outlook one believes to be valid and true, by definition. From thinking about my own opinions over the years, and conversing with others about their thoughts, I have guessed the odds that I am wrong about at least one item I currently believe to be truth, to be astronomically high, more than 99 percent. I ponder this. Does keeping this in mind make it easier to accept and even to be curious about what others around me believe? I think it does. In the end, I have reflected that wisdom grows not from learning more and more data that support current views, but from trying to find out which current views might need revision. From talking to others and observing those who seem humble and those who seem to be overconfident in that Dunning-Kruger sort of way (see chapter 13). I have come to this odd realization: A clear signal that someone's views are worth listening to is the person's ability to list three things they have been wrong about in the past year. An acknowledged known record of being wrong correlates with knowledge.

## Science Recap

We can recap the scientific research and put it together. First, science tells us it is indeed possible to randomly feed people to accept bogus information. They will absorb it and stick to their belief. A key step may be to have them profess their belief (savor the easiness of social media comment fields). Essentially nothing changes opinions once they are adopted and professed. That synopsis comes from confirmation bias research, especially the early seminal work of Craig Anderson using the firefighter and risk-taking connections.

Second, starting about ten years ago computer algorithms began to recommend information or opinions that were pleasing to the user. Manifestly, this is done to increase reads, tailor advertisements, and maximize readership of the advertisements. But the side effect has been to present users of social media with nearly opposite information and opinions.

Third, the effect of viewing political information that is selected for you based on automatized algorithms has been studied using experimental research methodology. It has been found to result in increased anger for persons who have opposing views. Cho and colleagues demonstrated this be checking emotional reactions after viewing algorithm generated versus control political content.

Fourth, likes and finding others agree with you is naturally reinforcing. Social media comments that affirm your stated opinion can be presumed to release dopamine in the ventral tegmental area and nucleus accumbens. It's at least mildly addicting for most people.

We have a perfect little storm here. Thinking about 1–4 above, consider the parallel: A magic gadget portal is provided that you can take with you literally everywhere, it is always on, and you can even sleep next to it. This gadget will automatically detect any slight opinion you have and feed enjoyable information to you that makes your opinion more and more extreme as the weeks go by. After a few weeks, the information makes you feel angry. This gadget makes it trivially easy to publicly profess your beliefs via those short, pithy comments. If others agree with your outrage, you are informed, and as your brain evolved to enjoy approval and affirmation—you find this pleasurable. Dopamine is released and building on this evolved module, the magic gadget inevitably makes you want the fortification, seek more dopamine dollops, check the Twitter feed.

* * *

The essays are written as a snapshot one might put together based on selected bits of evidence and carefully chosen statistics. Each chapter begins with a reminder of the fundamental reason people diverge so sharply: users receive divergent information via algorithms. For each issue chapter, this reminder is followed by few sentences on the general topic before presenting the divergent information. I believe the opposing views content is based on correct facts, but should you doubt it, the highest compliment would be for a reader to look up a fact or source independently. I have done my best to represent views I do not have, and it is possible that even with my best effort, I could have something a bit wrong.

Please keep in mind the goal is to show readers what is missing, to use paper and ink to reset the gadgets' Lies of Omission.

# PART TWO

# CHAPTER SIX

# Critical Race Theory

*If you are angry when you imagine the other side's views, try considering the default mode today is to be fed a false narrative about the other side. A side effect from the natural preference for dopamine release that agreement gives, and that the wicked pocket portal obliges.*

Polls from June 2021 show less than one third of citizens in the USA support teaching "Critical Race Theory" in schools, whatever that means. Critical Race Theory (often abbreviated as CRT) actually refers to a movement within upper levels of academia to consider racial identity and power dynamics as central to understanding law, society, and social justice. Especially in recent years, the term is also used to refer to the downstream results of adopting the tenets of the CRT movement. The term can apply to a broader conceptualization of emphasizing the study of racial inequality as central to society.

Today, Critical Race Theory is sometimes understood to encompass attempts to teach associated ideas and associated curriculum within society more broadly, including within elementary and secondary schools (e.g., The 1619 Project might be considered as CRT). The term itself has become politicized and divisive, without a commonly understood definition. This is the first fact to appreciate: the term means different things to different people. As historian Jeremy Stern states, "The right has adopted the term as a convenient bugbear—presumably because it can easily be made to sound like 'being critical of people for their race,' and because it suggests a single, organized 'movement' that can be neatly targeted for purgation." Stern goes on to assert that the "media has been lazily credulous in adopting the term" (Stern, 2021).

To the left, the term refers to something studied in upper level academia. To the right, the term includes questionable methods in public school that emphasize race above other human characteristics and culture. To see and understand what the algorithms have done more clearly, it is best to set this term aside in place of words that mean what the user intends. Other than within the headings, confusing and recently polarizing terminology is not used.

## How Can He Support Critical Race Theory?

At least in part because of the kind of information that algorithms and social media serve him.

Many people today are blissfully unaware of even the fundamental historical facts that underlie racial conflict and oppression, much less the way all the pieces fit together. The reasons for this are complex, and likely partly relate to the advantages that ignorance endows to groups wishing to avoid change. When persons in a society know that hard work and talent is what leads to good grades, good educations, good jobs and success, then poverty is not systemically caused. Instead, it is due to lack of ability and lack of hard work. When a high school dropout battling addiction violates parole and ends up in prison, we are sad, but of course it is obvious he could have made different choices. Simple. Reassuring. There is no need to change anything. Whether or not a) his city's high crime, b) the fact that his father was in prison, or, c) his elementary school had forty-three kids per class with a rotating series of substitute teachers and a mold problem played a role, is not addressed. A belief that hard work and talent are the deciders could be mostly true, could be true sometimes, or it could be mostly fiction for a typical child with poor schools, parents with addictions, and lead paint dust settling in their bedroom.

Some experts who look at the problems closely see the explanation of white persons having more wealth and better jobs as not very much due to ability and hard work, and much more due to societal advantages, built right into the society. It appears to these observers that the maintenance of all the ways the weaker segments of the population are kept weak is built into society, and needs to be changed top to bottom, Small changes won't, can't, undo the ingrained inequality that exists everywhere. One area is the failure to even acknowledge the decisive role that power and racism have played in how society has been structured.

## Ignorance of Race History

In any event, there is definitely ignorance of the United States' racial past. In 2018, a poll commissioned by the Southern Poverty Law Center showed only 8 percent of high school seniors identified slavery as the cause of the Civil War, and less than half recognized Frederick Douglass, "Box" Brown, and Harriet Jacobs as persons who had been slaves. Only about half of history teachers include any information on how past slavery connects to life today. Fordham University conducts a careful analysis of History and Civics standards among schools in the United States. In the 2011 report, as written by historian Jeremy Stern and colleagues, a majority of states received an inadequate rating.

Texas was a state with a 3/10 score, as described in the online report, "Texas's heavily politicized 2010 revisions to its social studies curriculum have attracted massive national attention. Indeed, both in public hearings and press interviews, the leaders of the State Board of Education made no secret of their evangelical Christian right agenda, promising to inculcate biblical principles, patriotic values, and American exceptionalism" (p. 141). Essentially, teachers in Texas were not formally expected to teach the history related to America Indians, nor segregation. Specific examples were noted, "Native peoples are missing until brief references to nineteenth-century events. . . . Sectionalism and states' rights are listed before slavery as causes of the Civil War . . . there is no mention of the Black Codes, the Ku Klux Klan, or sharecropping; the term 'Jim Crow' never appears. Incredibly, racial segregation is only mentioned in a passing reference to the 1948 integration of the armed forces," (p. 142).

In the 2021 report by Fordham, some improvements were noted, but still twenty states were considered inadequate in both subjects. To foster understanding of the complex ways that history affects current reality, it is urgent that schools teach history more fully and accurately. Three examples that grew out of slavery, whose connections to today have not been well taught and are generally not understood, include housing discrimination, government sanctioned theft, and violent attacks on Black wealth.

## Tulsa and Greenwood District

The Tulsa Race Massacre is an event that happened in United States history more than a half century after the 13th Amendment (abolishing slavery) was adopted. The massacre is an example of how Blacks were still not free to accumulate wealth; how the wealth of Blacks was, in fact, destroyed by white society. The Greenwood District of Tulsa, Oklahoma had become a prosperous area of Black-owned wealth, often referred to as Black Wall Street. Many Black families were prospering, with upscale homes and wealth beyond that of typical whites in the South. On June 1, 1921, 1,256 Black-owned houses were burned to the ground, and hundreds of others looted. The Greenwood attack reportedly included low flying planes shooting at fleeing civilians, certainly including children.

The entire district was essentially destroyed: newspapers, the library, a hospital, a school, and too many churches and small businesses to count. People went missing, never seen again, bodies never found. To this day, it is unknown how many Black persons were killed. Estimates have ranged from the absurdly low, original undercount of twenty-six confirmed bodies, to modern historians' estimations of three hundred based on the missing persons who were never recovered. In any case, over eight hundred were seriously injured, documented by records of admission to hospitals for their serious injuries. Moreover, six thousand supposedly free Black Americans were detained in harrowing conditions in internment camps for several days. In the end, at least ten thousand formerly successful, prosperous persons were suddenly homeless and penniless, children orphaned, and no one without relatives dead or injured. The scale of the families affected boggles the mind.

Consider there were women who were teachers, and husbands who were mechanics, people who had been born shortly after the Civil War, whose parents would have been slaves. Perhaps the new generation found the threat of lynching and segregation within their home states sufficiently fearful that they took the initiative to look for freedom and opportunity elsewhere. Perhaps they found similar hard-working persons and formed a community. They opened theaters, bakeries, and hotels. Perhaps they found success and started families.

The above sentences describe real people who lived. Couples like John and Loula Williams, who are known to have fled the violence of Tennessee to become business owners of the Greenwood district. Loula was a teacher, and John worked on steam engines when they met and decided to move West. Their business savvy is documented; they ultimately owned and ran a successful bakery, a garage, a 750-seat theater, and a boarding house. For the times, they were a forward-thinking, egalitarian couple, known to share decisions, and Loula's business sense was mentioned in newspapers that survive today. As such, they became one of the wealthiest families in the district and were the first family in the Greenwood District to own a car. There is a historical picture of them as a young, happy family with their son John, in this car.

Photo by Greenwood Cultural Center/Getty Images.

There was a film in progress at the Williams' Dreamland Theater when the massacre began. It was burned down. They, like hundreds of their friends and colleagues, lost everything, and never fully recovered. Loula physically survived, but seemed to never recover from the events. The formerly happy, successful business woman declined in the months after the massacre. Four years later she was in a sanitarium and was declared incompetent in 1927, the year she died. There is no doubt among historians that the massacre was downplayed in US history and that the events as they occurred were concealed: *The Tulsa Tribune* physically removed the newspaper stories from its record (the bound volume), and decades later historians realized official documents like police records were missing as well.

## Sanctioned Destruction Was Not Isolated

Two years before the Tulsa tragedy, on July 27, 1919, a thousand Black family homes were burned by white rioters in Chicago. Two years after the Tulsa massacre, the Rosewood massacre in Florida occurred. When it ended, every home and business in the Black community of Rosewood, Florida had been burned down, and surviving Black residents were driven out, never to return. The sum of these events, and others like them, systematically kept Blacks from accumulating wealth, and kept wealth in the control of whites. This is the history of the United States.

We can consider what it would have been like to have lived through the day to see your home and business as ashes, family wealth demolished, and yet absolutely no recourse. The Florida crime was executed with the cooperation of the city's government. In the Tulsa massacre, city officials "deputized" scores of white men, gave them guns, and sent them into the district with torches. One thing these events have in common besides the lopsided destruction of Black-owned property, was the lack of arrests. The violence was largely sanctioned by authorities.

People of color, seeking to avoid the violence of racism, and Jim Crow laws began to settle along the sparsely-populated coasts in the early part of the twentieth century, which brings another way that hard-won Black wealth was attacked. In the 1920s, these beach areas began to be sought-after locations, and then Black owners were harassed and sometimes, if they refused to leave, the government confiscated property.

The injustice of the Bruce Family travesty is instructive, and the details have recently emerged. This particular case now has the unusual distinction of having been chronicled in the courts. The California coastal property was purchased in 1912 by Mrs. Willa Bruce, whose husband worked for the railroad, and had prudently saved enough money to start a business. After a couple of years, they ran a successful Oceanside resort where people of color were welcomed and were the main guests. At first the location was considered too rural and of little interest for typical white people. However, as the coastal area began to develop, the property became desirable. Harassment began and accelerated. The harassment included arson, car vandalism, and overt pressure to leave, including by at least one city official. But the Bruces valued their lifestyle and the ability to offer a pleasant vacation experience for other Black families. They refused to be intimidated, literally standing their ground, and would not sell nor leave. After twelve years of successful business and incredible moxie (in the vernacular of the time), the city powers took the shocking step of formally condemning the land, and the Bruces were finally forced to vacate, against their wishes, for $14,000. Today, the property's value is almost incalculable, but is definitely in the millions.

The 1920s are only four generations back. There are surviving direct descendants of these families, some of whom would presumably be wealthy today, owning homes in prosperous areas, had their family's land not been confiscated. Studying these events fosters acknowledgement that surviving persons may deserve compensation. History connects the dots as to how injustices of the past link to current realities.

## Redlining Mattered

The actual history and extent of redlining is not widely acknowledged, but must be known to understand the ramifications. For housing patterns, the critical history traces back to the Federal Housing Administration (FHA) being created in 1934. During the Great Depression, the government was actively trying to facilitate home ownership among middle- and working-class families. It did so by guaranteeing that any banks that gave loans to such families would be paid back (insuring the loans). Surviving records document that minorities were not only discriminated against, but actively prevented from participation in this government program. Printed manuals at the time stated that lenders were to avoid any areas with "inharmonious racial groups." Questionable areas (areas where minorities were permitted to buy) were circled in red ink on maps.

During the 1940s and 1950s, 98 percent of these FHA loans went to non-Blacks. The National Board of Real Estate published a Code of Ethics during this time, it stated the importance of not allowing, "members of any race" to buy in an existing neighborhood if their "presence will be detrimental to property values." Real estate agents would, under no circumstances, for any amount of money, allow non-whites to buy in white neighborhoods. In the late 1960s, in Texas, the newly hired, Hispanic vice president of a local college was told by a real estate agent he could not buy a house that was for sale in a white neighborhood. When the man explained he was the newly hired vice president of the local college, would be working nearby, and easily had the money to buy, the real estate agent looked him in the eye and said, "I don't care if you are president of the United States, you can't buy a house in this neighborhood," (personal communication, family history of author). History like this should not be lost. It matters still today.

## Connections to Today

The effect of the (Food and Drug Administration (FDA) housing practices was to concentrate areas of low property value in the places banks would not (were not allowed to) insure loans, meaning the places minorities were allowed to live (but not own unless they could buy without a loan). In sum: The ghetto was born. The next effect was some neighborhood schools (being property tax supported) existing as underfunded. The next effect was run-down schools with plumbing problems and leaking roofs, without playgrounds, or modern textbooks, or lab equipment. Next came overwhelmed teachers and overcrowded classrooms, then revolving substitute teachers instead of permanently assigned teachers became common (see Kozol's accounting of extreme public-school differences). The next effect was predictable: sky high dropout rates that diverged by race, and too many children not learning to read. Then comes a generation with very low rates of college. The next effect was crime looking more attractive. The next effect was racial differences in crime and incarceration rates. An unusually gifted and ambitious child could overcome: when this happens, it is wonderful (and well touted as "See, it can be done!"). But most won't, and this would be true of any race where the average circumstances are so monstrously disparate. They will be kept down, as it is the nature of the world for the powerful to try to hold on to their power.

The full connections and ramification may not be apparent until one further considers that for most people in the United States, the family home is the largest financial asset; it has been the literal foundation of wealth building for most middle-class families. People of color were legally locked out of this at least until the 1970s. The disparity of wealth distribution needs to be connected not to laziness or moral character or personal choices, but to systematic and systemic locking out of the "American dream" based on skin color. Today, in 2021, a typical white household has not double, not triple, but ten times the amount of wealth as the typical Black family. Yes, individuals' choices matter. Yes, individuals can sometimes overcome, but this does not change that the greater pattern and big picture discrepancy of wealth and power stemming from systemic racism and past violence against Blacks and other minorities when they did accumulate wealth. The victims of racism should not be blamed. Unfamiliarity with the historical roots of the current inequality fosters opposition to affirmative action and other programs to increase minority access to higher education. Resentment of targeted mortgage assistance, prison reform, efforts rehabilitate more than punish, and public assistance programs exists because the extent of racism's reach is not widely understood.

Just as the ghetto, poor schools, and crime are predictable outcomes of systematically denying one group the ability to own property. Single parent homes are the predictable outcome of sky-high incarceration rates of Black men. Moreover, court records and analyzing sentences for matched crimes and circumstances show the racial disparity appears specific to men of color versus white men (see for example Steffensmeier and Demuth, 2006). Incredibly, in modern times—on top of the historical reasons—Black men who have identical histories and commit identical crimes as whites are still given significantly longer prison sentences. Racism in the past, racism in the present, all connected. It needs to end. Most people who look at the problems carefully feel that it cannot end if not understood and acknowledged.

Obscuring this history supports stereotypes that people of color make poor choices, and are responsible for the poor schools minority children disproportionately attend, the high crime in minority neighborhoods, and the lack of wealth within many minority communities. The impoverished schools are a direct result of low tax bases, which is a direct result of housing discrimination. Acknowledging history gives proper perspective.

## Why Are People Opposed to Critical Race Theory?

This question requires knowledge and consideration of the information the opposers are receiving.

First, the objection is not related to the inclusion of troubling historical events in history classes. The overwhelming majority of people today want and expect the facts of slavery in the USA (and world) to be taught: 79 percent to be specific. Moreover, the 2021 Reuter's poll on the topic found that among self-identified Republicans, only 16 percent were either strongly or somewhat opposed to teaching high school students about slavery *and it's impacts*. The inclusion of impacts was part of the question, this is not the objection. Teaching United States history can include things like the Tulsa Race Massacre, the beatings of Emmett Till and Rodney King, the Trail of Tears, internment of Japanese Americans, and more. Reasons for objection center on the mechanics of implementation, factual accuracy, and over zealousness. There is definite opposition to lessons that appear to teach children, who are too young to grasp complexity, to either feel guilt (if white) or anger (if non-white) or deep confusion (if both). The overall effect is to divide people. Portions of these lessons are seen as worsening race relations.

## Questions of Content

Children in many states are reporting to parents that lessons in Art, Health, English, and Math are all, simultaneously, heavily emphasizing the themes of racism, and there are credible reports of teachers telling children that if they are white, they are guilty. Biracial, white, and Black families might all reasonably object to this, and still support an account of racial violence to be part of history lessons. There are recordings of impassioned Black voices available on social media asking their school boards to make it possible for their children to attend school without being taught their white neighbors and family members oppress them, and not to have them learn to judge others based on skin color (e.g., Moms for Liberty Quisha King, Newsweek Watch Black Blast CRT). People who are watching these videos can be moved by the display, and when hearing real world testimony of how racial theory is being implemented, perceive that it may in fact overemphasize skin color as a primary defining feature. But only some people see such evidence.

## Math Curriculum

There are real-world excesses in the classroom. They can seem absurd and harmful. One example is the State of California Department of Education. On their website, the CDE makes public their requirements for math instruction (CDE, 2021). Indeed, they formally require that math instruction, at all grade levels, specifically include ample content to ensure equity and inclusion, and "provide examples to support professional learning in topics for universal access in mathematics and include content for administrator- and teacher-led facilitation." What does this mean?

Source: California Department of Education.

As shown in the figure above, California's Department of Education website links to the Dismantling Racism in Mathematics document that provides specific guidance on implementation. Within the Dismantling Racism curricular guide, math teachers are asked to "Recognize and name the mathematical strengths of students of color," and to "identify and challenge the ways that math is used to uphold capitalist, imperialist, and racist views." As if there is a consistent and important difference by race, teachers are urged to "recognize the ways that communities of color engage in mathematics and problem solving in their everyday lives."

On page 10, teachers of math in the public-school system are blatantly urged to foster activism against a hypothetical arrangement to keep minorities out of certain jobs, "Encourage them to disrupt the disproportionate push-out of people of color in those fields." Teachers are asked to bring these ideas into math classes, and to get students to act against racism. Teachers are asked to consider, and even write out, each month how they have personally kept Black students oppressed when they teach math: "Reflect on your current classroom practices to identify the ways in which they perpetuate white supremacy culture," (p. 11). An additional example is "Expose students to examples of people who have used math as resistance," (p. 9). If this is surprising, it is simple to go to the equitablemath.org website and do a search for these phrases (as of February 2022). What is taught within math class has radically changed, at least in some schools.

Besides the concerns about the inclusion of this curricula in math, there are also questions about what is being lost. Teachers are expected to agree that white supremacy culture pervades math instruction and that emphasizing the "right answer" in math instruction, sequential teaching of skills, and requiring students to show their work in a standard way stem from, and continue, white supremacy culture. What does this mean in terms of what can be taught regarding math in a typical forty-minute math class? Math does have right answers. Wrong answers make bridges fall, and engines not work.

The United States needs architects, computer experts, and engineers, all of which require real expertise in math. The education system in the USA is falling behind, students are less often learning the basic content for a successful society. China comes in first in math abilities, the USA comes in at number thirty-seven, behind most of Europe, behind Australia and New Zealand, behind Russia, behind Korea. Under such conditions, students need to be taught how to do math correctly and well (see the article by Professor of Math Percy Deift and colleagues for further discussion).

The effect of overzealous diversity training impinging on the content of math classes can be expected to compete with learning key math content, like how trigonometry functions are used in electrical engineering, or in global positioning, or architecture. Such changes are a concern to mathematics scholars such as Percy Deift, member of the American Mathematical Society and Guggenheim Fellow. These changes are not benign and can be expected to meaningfully disrupt the development of our science and technology work force for the upcoming generation (Deift, 2021). Individual students, of any race, who are precocious and are ready and eager to learn trigonometry, the would-be engineers, will miss the chance to learn essential content and foster their attraction to higher math.

Persons who start clicking and sharing criticisms of current trends in math instruction, start finding more information, and find that a proposed California mathematics framework asserted that mathematics education in the United States has been structured to prepare privileged, young, white men for entrance into elite colleges. The belief that rigorous math classes can foster systemic racism leads to pushing aside how-to math lessons, in favor of lessons on how math is racist ("identify and challenge the ways that math is used to uphold capitalist, imperialist, and racist views").

Parents who believe quality education, including correct answers and sequentially taught math skills (algebra and geometry before calculus), are unhappy with this approach. Moreover, some teachers are not going to agree that algebra classes should or can be centered on antiracism, and may reasonably believe that using class time to help their minority students to be able to do the math content is more imperative. This does not make them racists. The curriculum divides people and causes resentment among people who would otherwise work to end disadvantages associated with race and poverty.

### 1619 Questions of Accuracy and Trust

Today's teaching of race centric history has taken liberties with the historical record. Indeed, some presumably well-meaning scholars, in an effort to clarify the importance of America's racism, seem to have tried to rewrite history by inserting inaccurate information. The 1619 Project has been held up as the pinnacle of Correct History by proponents, but it contains factually incorrect claims, and shifting declarations. As originally published in August as a series of articles by (then) *New York Times* columnist Nikole Hannah-Jones, the 1619 Project sought to establish 1619 (the date the first slave ship landed) as the true founding year of the United States of America. Relatedly, the Project asserted that the Revolutionary War was subsequently fought to preserve slavery. That is the Revolutionary War against Britain of 1775, not the Civil War of the 1860s. Such assertions are indefensible from the historical record, indeed are disproven by the historical record. Yet somehow, the Project remains as a foundation for school curriculum. To many parents and citizens (the ones who are aware of the extent of the mistakes), this is disturbing.

Hannah-Jones, primary author of the 1619 Project, had July 4, 1776 struck through, and August 20, 1619 as the replacement text, as her literal banner (Twitter background banner). If this was not clear, she tweeted "I argue that 1619 is our true founding." Screen shots of her (since deleted) tweet are abundant. Yet later, after the *New York Times* edited the original wording of the story, she tweeted, "The 1619 project does not argue that 1619 is our true founding." This gives some people a deep sense of uneasiness and mistrust. Historical claims being rewritten in real time. Nonetheless, thousands of classrooms in the USA have used the materials. The *New York Times* wrote, "educators around the country (are) teaching the 1619 Project." The Pulitzer Center has developed and released lesson plans for the Project.

At any rate, the edits around key claims gets directly at something that ought to be beyond dispute for something used in classrooms: the veracity of what the Project teaches about US history.

## But Slavery Is Not the United States' Raison d'etre

Here are the words of Jake Silverstein, managing editor of the *New York Times*: "In one instance of digital display copy, we referred to 1619 as our 'true founding.' It is this use of this last phrase, and its subsequent deletion, that was the subject of significant criticism." The phrasing was used. It was deleted. It was deleted because facts, evidence, and records show this statement to be indefensible. Unless facts do not matter at all, it must be clear that originally the Project asserted that 1.) 1619 is the year of the true founding of the United States, 2.) criticisms and facts resulted in a back pedal of this assertion. And importantly, 3.) historical facts do not support that assertion (since both the original publisher and the original author have distanced themselves from the claim).

A misstatement or overreach born from a passionate desire to improve things could be forgiven. But forgiveness of a mistake comes with an expectation it does not keep happening. As of February 23, 2022: the curriculum for schools available via the Pulitzer Center website has a cover page for the 1619 Project that begins, "The 1619 Project, inaugurated with a special issue of *The New York Times Magazine*, challenges us to reframe US history by marking the year when the first enslaved Africans arrived on Virginia soil as our nation's foundational date." Persons who care about history will reasonably object to the continued assertion, and mistrust of the project's curriculum is perpetuated on this example alone. But there are others.

## The Words of Historians and the Factual Record

Concerns about statements of facts began quickly and within three months, there were dozens of top historians sounding alarms. Note, the historians were not objecting to emphasizing the importance of slavery in the history of the USA, but there were concerns. As the Pulitzer Prize–winning author of the book *The Radicalism of the American Revolution*, Gordon Wood is often considered to be *the* leading historian of the American Revolution. Professor Wood wrote in December of 2019, "I have no quarrel with the idea behind the project. Demonstrating the importance of slavery in the history of our country is essential and commendable. But that necessary and worthy goal will be seriously harmed if the facts in the project turn out to be wrong and the interpretations of events are deemed to be perverse and distorted. In the long run the Project will lose its credibility, standing, and persuasiveness with the nation as a whole. I fear that it will eventually hurt the cause rather than help it." It is clear in his letter (2019) to *New York Times* editor-in-chief, that Wood worried that faults in the Project would lead to problems achieving the stated goals, that the nation as a whole would not accept it. The warning was not heeded.

There is historical documentation on the War of Independence. Regarding the assertion that "one of the primary reasons the colonists decided to declare their independence from Britain was because they wanted to protect the institution of slavery," Woods noted there was no evidence to support this, and plenty of evidence to the contrary. Indeed, there is simply nothing in the historical record to pin this on: no colonists are known to have said or written they wanted independence in order to preserve their slaves. Similarity, there is no record of colonists expressing fear about Britain's abolishment of slavery. There is ample evidence in the writings and documents from the time that the Stamp Act of 1765 was the impetus for seeking independence (see Wood, 2019).

In March of 2021, Professor Leslie Harris, a woman of color with a PhD in history from Stanford wrote an article published in Politico. "On August 19 of last year, I listened in stunned silence as Nikole Hannah-Jones, a reporter for the *New York Times*, repeated an idea that I had vigorously argued against with her fact-checker: that the patriots fought the American Revolution in large part to preserve slavery in North America." Within her article, which is available via a quick internet search (if it does not automatically appear in one's feed, Harris noted that her opinion was sought by the *Times*, "Because I'm an historian of African American life and slavery, in New York, specifically, and the pre-Civil War era more generally, she wanted me to verify some statements for the project." She asserts she disputed any claim that the colonists Declaration of Independence and Revolutionary War of 1775 was to protect slavery. She provided evidence and references and explained, but, "Despite my advice, the *Times* published the incorrect statement about the American Revolution anyway."

Ignoring historians has a price, and the 1619 Project enrollment in the Culture Wars was ~~predictable~~ predicted if this maintained. [special text strikethrough word]

*How did Wall Street get its name?* The assertion that the capitalist icon Wall Street was so named because slaves were paraded on a wall when they were sold there is a . . . well . . . a fabrication created, if not a lie. The record of use of the term is clear, there is no actual dispute the name of this location, and later street, came from the Dutch of then–New Amsterdam building a wall to keep Native Americans out, long before any slaves were sold there. Wall Street did not get its name from the slave trade, it was named after a wall that was built as a shield against the original inhabitants, Native Americans. Usurping the actual history that documents the poor treatment of one race, with fictionalized information related to (actual) mistreatment of another oppressed race is bad karma, besides being nearly Orwellian. It is ironic: this is done under the banner of setting the racial record straight.

*Was New Orleans the banking capital?* The 1619 Project asserted that New Orleans, as a slave trade center, was the biggest banking capital in the Americas (due to slavery) at the outbreak of the Civil War. In reality, it was far behind New York City in terms of number of banks, banking capital, or any other reasonable measure. New Orleans was not the banking capital.

*Is there history of whites fighting against racism?* Lessons prompted by this approach often seem to emphasize that Black Americans have fought against racism and against whites. But it has not been Blacks alone who have fought against race-based oppression and slavery, and this too is history that needs to be taught. To many people, it seems evil to think whites have seldom if ever opposed racism, and even worse to teach such a thing. John Adams tolerated slavery in his younger years, but grew to vehemently oppose it. An opponent of Adams, Henry Wise, described Adams as, "the acutest, the astutest, the archest enemy of Southern slavery that ever existed."

John Jay and Alexander Hamilton were members of a society that worked towards the end of slavery, especially any slaves of African heritage in New York. Founding Father Rufus King made this quote on the floor of the Senate, "I hold that all laws or compacts imposing any such condition as slavery upon any human being are absolutely void because they are contrary to the law of nature, which is the law of God." Would the Underground Railroad have been possible without white Quakers risking their lives for the freedom of their fellow humans? Did Benjamin Franklin not free all his slaves and become president of Pennsylvania Abolitionist Society? Was John Adams not clear when he said Southern power depended on human bondage, a practice of "colossal evil"?

In more modern times, Gale Cincotta worked tirelessly against redlining and housing discrimination. The Freedom Riders included white people who risked their privilege and their lives to help end segregation. Jonathon Daniels was a peaceful, white activist who gave his life in 1965 to shield Black teenager Ruby Sales from a gunshot aimed at her during a civil rights protest. There are countless examples, and this too is history. It can be pointed out that even in the Confederacy, about 75 percent of families did not own slaves, and destitute whites were not uncommon. Not all whites have ancestral histories of some similar privilege, especially in comparison to persons of any racial background born into security, wealth, and power.

## Formal Scholarship and Its Terminology

Scholars of race relations who emphasize the ongoing effects of long-term structural inequality, are articulate, persuasive, and show every appearance of wanting to improve the world. Yet this does not make it beyond criticism. The basic tenet may be captured in the words of Bree Picower, whereby racism is seen as foundational and so fundamentally woven into fabric of United States' society that it must be understood as "the major condition that must be analyzed" to understand inequality today (p. 198). This may be true, or it might be partly true, or it might be not true at all. Accepting the tenets in the writings of this approach, means other sub-tenets become assumed.

There is discussion of how white people use tools to avoid accepting the reality of society. This practice may be helpful in the academic discussions, but labeling disagreement by conceptualizing it with words like "tools of whiteness" or "resistance" (see Picower, 2009) does not make it true that racism is the major condition of society above all else. Many parents do not want their children taught that founding fathers were racist, that counting the day a slave ship landed as the founding of the United States makes sense, or that the USA even might have been founded to foster slavery.

Terminology might be important when thinking about the math curriculum. "Students' negative reactions to multicultural education are typically referred to as resistance in the literature on White teachers and multicultural education" (Picower, p. 205). This branch of scholarship teaches that people may respond to attempts to change their views on race will involve "relying on a set of 'tools of Whiteness' designed to protect and maintain dominant and stereotypical understandings of race—tools that were emotional, ideological, and performative. This phenomenon is typically referred to as resistance," (p. 197).

The complexity of the most common concerns might be distilled into this: Even if racism is still a problem, even if slavery needs to be better taught, it simply does not follow history can be changed, nor that any of this should be part of math class. Further, to assume that concerns are a tool used by the dominant group to maintain power is a problem. It means criticisms are just part of the bigger problem of maintaining oppression. Voila: objecting that Wall Street was named for the selling of African slaves is a tool to protect whiteness. If a legitimate concern exists, conceptualizing the concern this way would be condescending and divisive.

## Begging the Question

Dismissing criticism of centering lessons on racism as ignorance and part of racism, is to start by assuming the world view that race is critical to everything is correct. It might not be, or some aspects of implementation might be doing more harm than good. Most critics feel it would be possible, and desirable, to teach about racism. Real discussions about the lingering effects of racism could be had if real dialogue could be had with respect for all. Are objections really only about protecting racism? Maybe, but to start by assuming so is to start debate by assuming your position is correct (begging the question). Maybe it is. But maybe it's not.

The poll by Reuters documented that among Republicans, a nearly identical number supported teaching students about racism and its impacts, as agree that "critical race theory" is being used as a tool to erase and change the history of white people (and it is a strong majority, approaching 60 percent for both). This is evidence that the concern is *not* with the teaching of history or the effects of racism. It is something else. As Professor Gordon Wood feared when he reviewed the 1619 Project, it has become a confusing wedge issue, rather than helping race relations.

# CHAPTER SEVEN

# Covid-19 Mandates

*Disgust for persons who have a view different than yours interferes with peaceful coexistence. Try considering you might have received a false narrative about what others believe. Humans tend to consume information that affirms their beliefs, and today's social media makes this trivially easy.*

If you happened to have watched the Joe Rogan interview with Dr. Robert Malone regarding side effects and censorship, then you know the content presented, if not—then you don't know, and imagination fills it in. If you watched Dr. Paul Offit on C-Span explaining how well the vaccines work and the important data documenting the life-saving protection they provide, you know that content. If not—then you do not know that information, and you may assume incorrectly. This all *seems* obvious, but the divergence has enormous ramifications. The omissions of needed knowledge run deep and have palpable effects. Otherwise nice humans are literally wishing other humans dead. Indeed, I have heard the comments with my own ears from the mouths of people I know to be basically nice, empathic human beings. "Well, if she's not vaccinated, and she dies, that is what she deserves." What happened?

It seems like long ago, but in the early weeks of the pandemic, a large majority of the public supported staying home, closing schools and restaurants to flatten the curve and lessen the strain on hospitals. As weeks turned into months, and months turned to years, the unity waned, then broke. Overall, more people have become skeptical of public health officials and the CDC, as reflected in Pew Research Centers' ongoing polling on this topic. It can be assumed that some people have a breaking point; freezing detention centers for anyone who tries to refuse a daily injection that causes an hour-long migraine would probably be too much for virtually everyone. Others may cross the line at very low level of hassle: "I am not covering my face unless it can be proven the risk of death is almost certain without it." It is somewhere between these extremes for probably everyone. Perhaps seeing the painful death of loved ones has been a deciding factor in tolerance of long-term mask wearing and continued closures, or conversely perhaps getting Covid and giving it to one's parent after being triple vaccinated caused someone to throw in the towel.

Where this line exists may be *partly* due to individual differences in how much risk they want to tolerate, and may be *influenced* by individual experiences, but ultimately it is a function of one's judgement of Covid risk compared to the benefits of the intervention (school closures, mask wearing, vaccination). And this is primarily a function of information received.

## How Can a Person Be against Wearing Masks or Refuse Covid Vaccination?

People are receiving markedly different sets of information, especially about the individualized risks and benefits of interventions.

To put risk from pathogens in some perspective, per CDC data, in a bad flu season (like H1N1 virus that started in 2009 through June of 2010) there were about 350 child deaths attributed to the flu in the USA (CDC, 2010). According to the CDC (2022), at the end of April 2022, there have been about 1200 total Covid-related deaths for all persons under eighteen: this is approximately 500 per year. The age distributions differ. Independent researchers have also collected relevant information which is available to the public, material that some people are receiving from their selected information streams.

### Covid Is Low Risk for Healthy Children

Dr. Nia Williams from King's hospital in London and her colleagues combed through more than a thousand research articles and then focused on twenty-eight studies from across the world that reported descriptions of children with severe Covid disease and death. The data tell us, in the words of the publishing scientists, "there are two fascinating features of SARS-CoV-2 as pertaining to disease in children; the risk of acquiring the infection appears to be lower than in adults (1% v 3.5%), and once infected, the risk of severe disease is almost 25 times lower than in adults. . . . The immune mechanisms underlying the dual phenomena of enhanced resistance to infection and enhanced resistance to severe disease are yet to be elucidated; however, the magnitude of this effect appears sufficient to protect most children. . . ." (Williams and colleagues, page 694).

Covid *is* a danger, but the risk varies across age groups and demographics. Children (ages five to fourteen) in the USA are more likely to die from accidents (top cause of death), cancer, homicide, or heart disease. Moreover, as reported by the CDC within their data visualization website, tweens and teens (10 and over), death from despair in the form of suicide is a bigger risk: in 2020, for children aged ten through fourteen, in the USA there were 581 suicides (CDC, 2021). For comparison, again according to the CDC, as published by CDC scientists Farida Ahmad and colleagues in the CDC's Morbidity and Mortality Weekly Report, for children aged five years to fourteen years, there were sixty-seven deaths that included Covid-19 as a contributing factor in 2020.

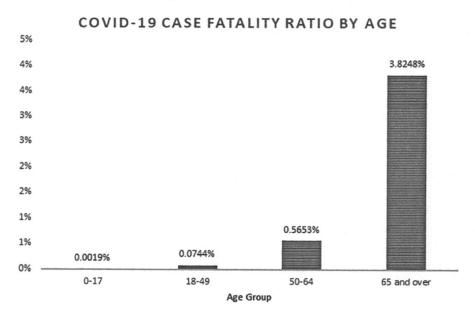

COVID-19 CASE FATALITY RATIO BY AGE

On the other hand, as shown above, a person over age sixty-five with a Covid diagnosis has a disturbingly high 4 percent chance of dying. But this is two-thousand times more than the risk among ten-year-old children who test positive for Covid (see CDC, 2021 for the data). These numbers are called Case Fatality Ratios (not to be confused with the lower *Infection* Fatality Ratios, which estimate chance of dying if a person catches a disease, not just those diagnosed via doctor visit).

## The Dangers of Overestimating Risk

The last chapter in this book features a lengthy discussion of this primary divide in today's culture, and details a study in which students in the USA were asked to estimate risk. As a preview, somewhat shockingly, 80 percent of college students made guesses that were at least ten times over the actual estimated risk according to experts. Using CDC data, as was done by health experts Avik Roy and Chris Conover writing for *Forbes* magazine, if one million kids (age zero through nineteen) were infected, about thirty would die, the large majority with another known preexisting health condition sharing blame for the death.

Some people may be comparing risk from Covid to risk of serious outcome to that of cancer, accident, or suicide risk, and judge the risk from Covid is low enough that it does not justify the disruption of closing school, or even requiring masks. It seems that if the risk of death from depression and suicide is higher than from Covid, an intervention that might reduce Covid exposure, but increases depression would be contra-indicated. Social isolation is a major risk factor for worsening depression. Some parents may believe drastic measures (cancelling their child's senior year, sports season, and important rites of passage like prom) are not justifiable by the data on the risks from Covid, and become resentful and skeptical of Covid mandates in general.

Consider a single mother of three in a small, urban apartment (with no yard). She may reasonably experience a year-long shut down of public school for her three healthy young children as a truly appalling, unjustified, long-term disruption to their lives. It does not seem like a benefit for her children, but the stress and harm are visible to her every day. The children are restless, angry, and they fight more. The parks are closed, and they get further and further behind the pre-pandemic grade level learning standards. Interventions have harms, and the justification is questionable.

## Facts Are Not Facts

After a year, some people noticed the discrepancy in so-called factual information, and began to mistrust standard edicts from authorities for a variety of legitimate reasons. Fact checkers are not always the unbiased reviewers of scientific data. In the fall of 2020, assertions that Covid-19 could have originated as a man-made virus created in the lab were fact checked as false. Facebook affixed misinformation warnings. However, this was never settled science, and as time went on, the lab leak theory was seen as more credible. Whether the virus was helped along by humans in the lab is not the point here: the point is debate by experts should be off-limits from the censorships of fact checkers. Fact checkers should never play any role in shaping legitimate scientific discourse by inserting their judgment on unsettled questions. The lab leak question is only one example of shoddy fact checking, but it is a red flag.

*PolitiFact*, which published under the Poynter Institute, ruled that an article that was circulating on Instagram that purported the survival rate for Covid infection to be over 99 percent was false (2021). *Not nuanced, not gray, but False.* The fact checker was challenged by multiple people. Here are the details of one such exchange (with this book's author). But it speaks to a problem and is worth considering at length.

After agreeing that the wording used in the fact-checked article did indeed refer to surviving the infection, which is the infection fatality ratio (IFR), the fact checker continued the email exchange with a scientist (the author, CD), noting the case fatality ratio (CFR) had been estimated to be 1.6 percent by Johns Hopkins University, which is not less than 1 percent. The fact checker asserted that the exact number for the IFR was not known. Therefore, it was deemed okay to say the number for the IFR given by the fact-checked article was wrong (yes, that is odd logic). Even so, according to all known experts and authorities at the time of the writing: it was quite correct to put it above 99 percent. The fact checker went on to give reasons, that individual risk must be considered, and it varies a lot, and that for at least *some* groups, it was not 99 percent. And yet, not acknowledging the simple basic fact that the overall survival for persons who contract Covid is/was above 99 percent, even in the face of expert published data establishing this as true. Concluding that to be false, is itself false. It takes some effort, but it is important to be very clear because it epitomizes a problem that has divided the country (appendix B has the full exchange). Here is an excerpt from information provided to the fact checker. It clearly supports survivability above 99 percent:

> Thanks so much for responding back . . . Levin and Colleagues (From Dartmouth, Harvard and the Center for Economic Policy Research-UK) determined age-specific infection fatality rates for COVID-19. Their exhaustive

meta-analysis included 113 studies, (and 34 geographical locations). Age-specific IFRs were computed using the prevalence data—and importantly as you referred to in your fact check—they reported fatalities four weeks after the midpoint date of the study (to address any delay in fatalities and reporting). The estimated age-specific IFR was 0.002% at age 10; and 0.01% at age 25. The IFR increases progressively to 0.4% at age 55, 1.4% at age 65, 4.6% at age 75, and 15% at age 85. Take a look at their pub: [full ref provided] . . . point estimate of overall IFR was 0.68% (CI 0.53%-0.82%). I am sure you follow, but this is less than 1% and thus actually 99% surviving [full ref given].

The fact checker, who turned out to have been an undergraduate senior on a paid summer internship at the time, was shown additional supporting statistics that were published, in the scientific literature, by respected expert scientists, that supported more than 99 percent surviving, by more than one actual scientist. But the young fact checker did not/was not allowed to correct, nor even revise his ruling as questionable nor as in dispute. Stood as labeled Fact-checked and False. This is not isolated, and the bigger problem is not the fault of this individual fact checker, but it is a problem. It represents a root cause of why reasonable people do not have an agreed upon set of "facts" to even begin a discussion.[2]

## A Fact-checker's Judgment :

## Available Science at the Time: *It Was True.*

Our Ruling:

An Instagram post claimed that the COVID-19 survival rate is over 99% for most groups.

We rate this claim as FALSE.

Levin and Colleagues (From Dartmouth, Harvard and the Center for Economic Policy Research-UK) determined age-specific infection fatality rates for COVID-19.
✓ The estimated age-specific IFR was 0.002% at age 10;
✓ and 0.01% at age 25.
The IFR increases progressively to
✓ 0.4% at age 55,
✓ 1.4% at age 65,
✓ 4.6% at age 75, and
✓ 15% at age 85.
They go into detail about the importance of not listing a single number since it is so varied by age. Levin et al., (2020). Assessing the age specificity of infection fatality rates for COVID-19: systematic review, meta-analysis, and public policy implications. *European journal of epidemiology.*
Meyerowitz & Katz, 2020. "A systematic review and meta-analysis of published research data on COVID-19 infection fatality rates") found 24 published estimates of the Covid-19's infection fatality ratio included in the first meta-analysis published between February and June 2020. They gave an overall estimate (across ages, which is problematic, but it does address the headline of the fact check most clearly)
✓ They point estimate of overall IFR was 0.68% (CI 0.53%-0.82%). I am sure you follow, but this is less than 1% and thus actually 99% surviving.

"Courtesy of Catherine DeSoto, PhD, in reference to the misleading "False" rating from Politifact.com."

---

2 For clarity and to avoid any confusion, the full, unedited, exchange is in Appendix 1.

Just like that, skepticism of "fact" by reputable sources becomes reasonable.

## Treatments to Lower Risk

Moreover, once people start to click on videos and articles skeptical of the mandates and restrictions, they receive further data and information from experts on how one can further lower risk. After about a year, there was some good information emerging, after two years, there was more. Some newsfeeds are highlighting this information.

### An Example: Quercetin

If one opens PubMed (the scientific index of record for biomedical research) and enters the search terms "Quercetin Covid," one finds this is a pigment in some foods that has long been believed to boost immunity, and that myriad scientists and medical doctors have detailed quercetin's mechanisms of action relevant to Covid-19, as well as published clinical trials. For example, a person can find that Di Pierro and colleagues (2021) conducted a controlled clinical trial (forty-two Covid patients were randomly assigned to be given quercetin, versus those receiving standard care alone). After just seven days, *sixteen patients* in the quercetin group were negative for Covid and twelve patients had all their symptoms resolved. Whereas in the control group, *only two* patients tested negative and only four patients had their symptoms partially improved. These results were mirrored when measuring C-reactive protein in the blood, which reflects inflammation and cytokine levels: the quercetin group had 55 percent lower levels compared to the control group.

Some evidence is not the same as being definitively proven via a large clinical trial. There has not been a large clinical trial regarding quercetin by the CDC . . . *but why not?* This is seen as a reasonable question without a reasonable answer. Covid-relevant mechanisms of action have been elucidated, and small clinical trials show efficacy. It has been two years. There have been large government-sponsored clinical trials for some treatments. Thus, a reason for skepticism of government recommendations is knowledge of information the government is not emphasizing, nor investigating.

## Why Not Vitamin D?

The medical literature contains evidence that adequate vitamin D levels are protective. There are several exhaustive reviews. One with 215 references was published in August 2021 by Shah Alum and colleagues, and a more formal "meta-analysis" (a method of combining statistics from several studies on a similar topic) the month prior (Pal et al, 2021). It is widely known that many people in the USA are low in vitamin D, especially in winter months. Most people would benefit from vitamin D supplementation even without Covid; it isn't dangerous.

One example of a small clinical trial featured fifty patients seeking hospital care for Covid who were randomly selected to be given vitamin D; their outcomes were compared to twenty-six similar patients who did not receive vitamin D. (All received the Spanish hospitals' standard of care—which included the infamous hydroxychloroquine, by the way.) In the control group: half required ICU care, and two died. Of the fifty persons who had vitamin D added to their care upon hospital admission, only one ultimately required admission to the ICU, and none died (Entrenas-Castillo et al., 2020).

The data suggest vitamin D could be a highly effective treatment. The fact that CDC does not promote the use of vitamin D, an inexpensive and safe supplement, strikes some people as suspicious. Suspicious in terms of promoting one medical option over any others, which are then not even investigated. As of December 1, 2021, the CDC still summarizes the data on vitamin D by referring their readers to two clinical trials that showed no benefit for high dose vitamin D supplementation—(wait for it. . . .) among critically ill patients, *none of whom had Covid-19*!

## Reasons to Question Authority

Here is an interesting quote,

> . . . they don't give the key data that tells us which kids are dying of Covid. If we had that data, we could target our strategy. It turns out that there's probably only been one child in the United States who has ever died of Covid, who was healthy, that is didn't have a comorbid condition. . . . And number two, the hospitalization rate was lower for Covid than it was of influenza. The CDC sits on a lot of data.

That was a quote that was made on television in June of 2021, subsequently printed in Newsweek.com as well as other locations, and widely circulated among some social media feeds. The quote is from one of the most influential and respected doctors in medicine, Dr. Marty Makary of John Hopkins and editor-in-chief of Medpage Today. There are a lot of quotes like this and—in spite of what some media conveys to some users—there is no actual consensus on pandemic response. Uber vaccine promoter Dr. Paul Offit does not think everyone should have a Covid booster vaccine. Dr. Vinay Prassad and Dr. Monica Gandhi think natural immunity should count and that most adolescents might benefit from one, but not two, doses of the vaccine. Dr. Robert Malone thinks the risks of the vaccine are not being openly discussed.[3] Dr. Peter McCullough thinks effective treatments are being suppressed. The Director of the Food and Drug Administration's Office of Vaccines Research & Review does not think boosters for all are necessary, even with the omicron variant. The USA's leading vaccine experts, FDA's Vaccine Advisory Panel, voted overwhelmingly *not* to authorize the Covid vaccine boosters outside of elderly people or persons otherwise at heightened risk of severe disease. Who knows this information? And who does not?

Concerns that science is not being followed, but being dictated, has plagued both recent administrations. Indeed, the Director of the FDA's Office of Vaccines Research and Review, Marion Gruber as well as the Deputy Director Philip Krause apparently felt strongly enough about the science that both resigned when the CDC continued to recommend booster shots for everyone (see for example Griffith, 2021 for coverage from a conservative leaning source). These resignations and the reasoning of experts who dissent from CDC's one-size-fits all approach have been heavily covered in conservative sources and feeds, but were virtually absent from many media feeds. Some coverage has seeped into various news sources here and there.

A *Politico* article (Owermohle, August 31, 2021) began with this sentence and went on from there, "The Biden administration's decisions over when to administer coronavirus vaccine boosters are triggering turmoil within the Food and Drug Administration, frustrating regulators and sparking fear that political pressures will once again override the agency's expertise." But overall, in some news circles the resignations were big news, heavily covered, and validating, while some feeds barely mentioned it. Many readers were either inundated with this story and commentary, or they may have missed

---

3 The above was written before the Joe Rogan podcast controversy. One can see that, among various things Dr. Malone may be right and wrong about, his assertion that dissenting views are suppressed certainly appears valid.

it, even while monitoring their news feeds for important information on booster recommendations.

## Views on Covid Vaccine Risks

It is possible to be aware of the range of side effects without being influenced by false information. Indeed, this is the definition of informed consent. Blood clots and Guillain-Barré type paralysis illnesses are a rare risk for all, but myocarditis is a serious risk focused heavily on young men and teens that is not very rare. Myocarditis is inflammation and damage to the heart, recovery even without death, takes weeks or months. Moreover, a degree of disability is sometimes permanent. For young healthy men, the risk of myocarditis after the *second* dose of an mRNA vaccine is a significant risk to consider.

Research entitled, "Safety of the BioNTech mRNA Vaccine" (2021, by Noam Barda and colleagues) featured analysis and outcomes for the largest health organization in Israel. Each person who had been vaccinated was matched with a similar person (e.g., same age, gender, health) who had not been vaccinated, and both groups were monitored for any adverse health events. Myocarditis was noted in twenty-one persons who received the Covid vaccine and six in the control group. When considered in sum, it might not seem like a large risk: twelve more cases out of almost a million people. However, there were many requests for the authors to publish additional information based on age and sex, which was then subsequently published the following month in a supplementary appendix. This is the data many will care about when making individual health decisions. The data shows the risk of the treatment (vaccination) is heightened based on age and sex. Moreover, the potential risk from Covid lowers based on age and overall health. The risk versus benefit is not one-size-fits-all.

*Following the science* is not a slogan, it means to let scientific data guide decisions. Here, there was no increase in myocarditis cases for young women. There was no increase in risk for men older than forty. The risk was for males aged sixteen to twenty-nine. The numbers are within the supplementary appendix of the publication (see the references and it is publicly available to check). Sometimes pictures are much clearer than words, these figures below were created to illustrate the data. There is a risk for young men and teens to receive the second dose, a risk not observed in other groups.

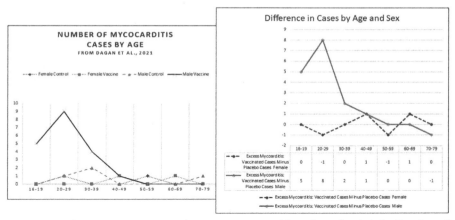

"Courtesy of Catherine DeSoto, PhD. Figure created based on the data by Barda and colleagues, 2021."

For ages sixteen to nineteen: there were 94,000 boys (and 88,000 girls) in the data set. No girls experienced myocarditis. No boys who did not get vaccinated experienced myocarditis, but *five* in the vaccinated group had this effect. Among the twenty-year-olds who were men, there were *nine* cases in the vaccinated group versus one in the unvaccinated group. Look at the other age groups: all the risk is concentrated. If one is a twenty-year-old man, *this is data that matters.* This research out of Israel was published in August of 2021.

In January of 2022, additional Israeli data was published analyzing five million fully vaccinated persons. In sum, the risk of myocarditis is clearly an actual risk, "This association was highest in young male recipients within the first week after the second dose. In our study, definite or probable cases of myocarditis among persons between the ages of sixteen and nineteen years within twenty-one days after the second vaccine dose occurred in approximately 1 of 6637 male recipients and in 1 of 99,853 female recipients," (Mevorach and others, p. 2147, *New England Journal of Medicine*). It is a risk for males, after the second dose.

Israel is not the only population that shows this risk. The US Military has excellent records that have been analyzed and made public by Dr. Jay Montgomery and colleagues (2021). Twenty-three cases of myocarditis occurred. As stated in the research article, all were men, fit by military standards, without any known heart concerns. Symptoms began between twelve hours to four days after the vaccination, almost all after the second shot. In another analysis by yet another group of scientists, records of

153,438 persons from Kaiser Permanente health care system were analyzed regarding risk of myocarditis. Dr. Katie Sharff and colleagues found that a relevant health code for myocarditis had been overlooked in prior research, in essence causing cases to be missed and underestimating risk level. Adding these additional cases resulted in the risk being similar to the Israeli data above. There is convergent data for boys in their upper teens or men in their twenties: There is somewhere around a one in seven thousand chance of myocarditis after the second dose of an mRNA vaccine, probably higher or lower depending on the exact age. That is following the science.

## Benefits and Risks

There are about 75 million persons under eighteen in the USA. One might try to judge risk from Covid this way: about four hundred persons under eighteen per year have died since the pandemic began, which makes the overall chance of death *somewhere* around one in two hundred thousand per year for teens, as an educated guess. The benefit from vaccination is that it protects against this risk. The protection from vaccination is not really from getting infected, as originally advertised, but offers protection from serious hospitalization or death.

If the risk of one serious side effect (myocarditis) is about one in seven thousand for young men, this is not an obviously favorable risk to benefit profile. It is true that most cases of myocarditis are not fatal, but they typically require days of hospitalization and often long-term recovery, which might not be complete. Further, the risk of serious Covid can be further predicted based on Body Mass Index and the presence or absence of other serious health conditions. Myocarditis, unlike serious Covid, seems to strike the otherwise fit and healthy.

And, it should be emphasized, the risk is for the *second* dose. The benefit of the standard two-dose vaccination for *all* persons is objectively questionable. Labeling someone who realizes this as "unscientific" may be perceived as unreasonably dismissive, perhaps even as censoring valid debate. It does not engender adherents.

### Science Says: Immunity from Prior Infection Counts

The discounting of natural immunity is another concern, and the two-dose vaccination mandates make no adjustment for having immunity after having the infection. A study from Israel followed sixteen thousand patients who had documented Covid infection with no vaccination, who were compared to another sixteen thousand who had only received the two-dose vaccination. They found that people who had been infected with Covid and recovered were at much less risk of later catching Covid than those who had been vaccinated. "This study demonstrated that natural immunity confers longer lasting and stronger protection against infection, symptomatic disease and hospitalization caused by the Delta variant of SARS-CoV-2, compared to the BNT162b2 two-dose vaccine-induced immunity," (Dr. Gazit and colleagues, p. 1).

There were 257 cases of breakthrough Covid infection in the vaccinated group, compared with only nineteen reinfections in the recovered group without vaccination (p. 12). There may be some small benefit of a single dose a few months after natural infection in terms of immunity studies (Gazit and colleagues) but the second dose appears especially unjustified. Germany is an example of a country that expects vaccination, but counts recovery from prior infection as immune. CDCs own data shows that "among unvaccinated persons with a previous COVID-19 diagnosis," hospitalization rates were fifty-five times lower than unvaccinated persons without prior infection (p. 5). It is important to realize this: some people have sincerely followed the data on natural immunity, know that some countries count recovery as the same as vaccination, and know the data supports such a policy. If they have had Covid and recovered, they do not want the risk of side effects.

## Reasonable Resistance

If one really wants to understand how ordinary people can feel strongly against universal mandates, a thought experiment on an individual's choice on this might be helpful, which is loosely based on an actual person. Consider the current recommendations from the perspective of a registered nurse or "an essential worker" who put their health at risk helping others, and caught Covid in early 2020 before the vaccine was available. That is, they caught it working overtime, during the first surge, lost their smell for six months, and were sick in bed for a week, and recovered. Now, they do not want the vaccine based on their knowledge of natural immunity from corona viruses in general, as well as having treated a few cases of non-trivial side effects after the Covid vaccine. Under pressure, they accepted the first dose, and got a fever of 102 and missed a day of work. Even without any life-threatening side effects, the "non-serious" side effects might feel serious enough to be some deterrent.

For persons in their late fifties and sixties, over 30 percent have a fever after the second dose, and over 20 percent (one in five) have enough pain to disrupt normal activities. The nurse, with a symptomatic natural infection and one dose, is already highly immune. But she will be fired if she does not get the second dose, because the hospital is following CDC guidelines. Eventually, she takes the second dose which is not scientifically justified, and she harbors resentment. This contributes to a generalized doubt about the reasonableness of the CDC position. As this chapter was being written, while some medical professionals with natural immunity had been fired, hospitals were allowing nurses with symptomatic infection and a positive Covid test to work as long as their symptoms were "mild," (WPRI.com 2022). Overall, this can turn some, who were originally pro-vaccine, to gently hesitant, to militantly skeptical.

### Some Cases of Serious Side Effects

According to the Washington State Department of Health, Jessica Berg Wilson, a mother in her mid-thirties, died of blood clots shortly after receiving the Covid vaccine. Jessica did not want the vaccine but was coerced by her desire to volunteer at her children's school, which required vaccination for everyone, even persons who have recovered from Covid. People who found and clicked on stories about this case via their smart phones probably also learned that Twitter took down her obituary that her husband posted, and therefore feel her case and others like it are censored.

Another click, and the testimony of Kyle Warner will be offered. Warner is twenty-nine, a professional bike racer and three-time champion. Unlike Ms. Wilson, he was not hesitant about the vaccine, he was eager because he wanted to help stop Covid from spreading. He developed inflammation of the heart lining and severe reactive arthritis. He has been bedridden, unable to work, and wholly unable to exercise. For months. His career is likely over. He is not asking for an end to vaccination, but is asking for investigation and tangible help for those that do get injured. His talks, which are delivered to some people and not others, show a sympathetic man, who seems incredibly genuine, asking for things to work better.

The original clinical trials for the vaccine included a twelve-year-old, Maddie de Garay, who is now disabled, presumably permanently. There seems to be no dispute that she was a healthy developing girl before her family signed her up for the clinical trial: they were glad to do their part and help to end the pandemic. She developed severe chest pain, and erratic blood pressure and heart rate. She lost the ability to walk. The mother talks about her support for the trials, states that she understood there was some risk to enrolling her daughter in the clinical trial. The emotion in her voice is palpable when she states the surprise was less about the adverse effect, than about the lack of support and follow up they encountered. According to her, the manufacturer of the vaccine used in the clinical trial has not contacted her, nor has there been investigation and support.

Brianne Dressen also signed up for a vaccine trial, hoping to help stop the spread. She testifies she suffered life threatening reactions that persisted for months, and that she still has not fully recovered. Her testimony is compelling, *if you see it*. She says at first, she did not want to go public, thinking it was rare and not wanting to discourage others from the vaccine, but she has since realized that there was not going to be any investigation of her case as part of the trial, and realizing others are having similar reactions, she has begun to speak.

### Pharmaceutical Safety Record

If the goal is to explain how it is possible people could oppose mandates without being anti-science troglodytes, it must be noted that pharmaceutical companies are recognized as for-profit entities, required to try to maximize profits. Pharmaceutical companies may well develop and deliver life-saving products, but pharmaceutical companies do not have a record of pure benevolence and goodness. Trust in their data has not been earned.

For example, Pfizer (a.k.a. Wyeth) agreed to pay $491 million over the illegal marketing of Rapamune, with almost half of the sum being for criminal fines. If one asks social media to provide information on pharmaceutical lawsuits, and begins clicking on some of the offerings, one can find out there is an active lawsuit about funding terrorism that invokes Pfizer and AstraZeneca, that payments to victims have been made for a drug tested on children in Nigeria, and more. There is concern that government agencies who monitor the trials and pharmaceutical companies have not remained independent, and pharmaceutical companies have the money to buy influence and media favors.

As written by Chris Isidore of CNN Business, "Pfizer reported that earnings and sales more than doubled in the past quarter, and it raised its outlook for results the full year, thanks greatly to its Covid-19 vaccine. The company reported adjusted earnings of $7.7 billion. . . . The vaccine business alone was responsible for more than 60% of the company's sales," (CNN. com, November 2, 2021). Corporations are expected to make good business decisions, decisions that will not hurt profit.

There is a lot to interfere with trust. It is the totality. The two-doses-for-all, the discounting of recovery from the illness, the harm of school closures, the history of pharmaceutical companies, not to mention that masks, school closures, and vaccines are not as effective as once touted: this is why some people oppose mandates.

## How Can He Support Mandatory Vaccination?

Because the information algorithms and social media serve him provide good evidence for this position.

### The Case of John Eyers

It seems to many beyond discouraging that people at high risk for Covid continue to die alone and in pain from a disease they could be vaccinated against, at no cost to themselves. John Eyers was an avid rock climber and body builder before he died in August of 2021. After a few days battling Covid, he went to the hospital, then intensive care. Eventually he required a ventilator, and finally succumbed to the disease after four weeks in the hospital at the age of forty-two.

His friends and family report John had become highly resentful of Covid related restrictions. Not being able to go out to exercise led to depression and then anger and mistrust of the government. He expressed an exaggerated fear of vaccination side effects and an ultimately fatal underestimation of the risk of Covid. According to his twin sister as reported by Sirin Kale in the *Guardian* newspaper, "John started saying really crazy things that didn't make sense and about how people were only getting the vaccine for free McDonald's, and there was formaldehyde in it." She said John thought fearing a minor disease like Covid was not rational, that if you are young and fit, "you would be fine."

As reported by the *Guardian*, and in keeping with CDC estimates, if 1,500 forty-year-old persons contract Covid, data suggest that only one will die, and even this risk is concentrated for persons with "co-morbidities," being overweight, having heart problems, or diabetes for example. Mr. Eyers's views were partially correct in that if one only considered the forty-year-old with zero underlying health problems, the risk of dying from Covid in a given year was very low: perhaps about one in 28,500. But that is still a significant risk, and a risk he had the power to change.

Yes, obesity and diabetes affect risk, but the risk is vastly different based on vaccination status too. The risk versus benefit calculation was probably not understood by Mr. Eyers, and based on what his sister has stated in news sources, probably would have been discounted if presented to him via a government source. According to USA CDC data, for this time period and Mr. Eyers's age group: there were just over thirty-three Covid deaths per one million persons, among persons without vaccination. Among vaccinated persons, there was one per million. It seems irrational to eschew a treatment that triples your odds of surviving a contagious illness that is actively spreading in your community.

## Clinical Trial for Pfizer

Let's consider the risk and benefit using the clinical trial for the Pfizer vaccine overseen by Dr. Fernando Polack and twenty-nine of his colleagues. The study featured about nineteen thousand persons receiving the vaccine and about nineteen thousand persons receiving a placebo injection, followed for at least one month via electronic diary for side effects and outcomes. Because the participants were randomly assigned, differences in pre-existing health, risk, or fear about Covid and any associated differences in behavior are not able to account for the effects. With some variation for which dose (first or second in the two-dose series) and the age group, 66 percent to 83 percent of vaccine recipients had pain, swelling, or fever after injection; compared to 8 percent to 14 percent in the placebo group. Among other things, this establishes the ability of the methods to detect and measure side effects. Injection pain and temporary fevers are not the side effects of concern however.

During the trial's observation period, there were indeed six deaths: four in the placebo and two in the vaccine group. There was no evidence any deaths were due to the vaccine. There were four adverse events of a serious nature, though none were life threatening, acknowledged as conceivably related to the vaccine. There was one case each of: a lymph node problem, a heart problem, a shoulder injury, and leg sensations suggesting nerve damage. By comparison, there were twenty times more cases of Covid in the placebo group. Nine cases in the placebo group were severe. Presumably, some of these placebo cases infected others.

Each case affects not only the individual, but potentially others around him or her. If John Eyers had received the vaccine, odds are that he would be alive and healthy today. But that is not the only thing that matters. His four weeks in the hospital prior to dying would also probably not have happened. Resources matter, especially when hospitals space is in short supply. The nurses' and doctors' and custodians' time, and the medical equipment could have been saved. When people refuse the vaccine, they waste time, resources, and are more likely to catch and spread the virus. It is not that it is impossible to die from Covid if vaccinated, it is not that vaccinated persons cannot spread it, but the odds are greatly lessened. It benefits the individual, but also society to become vaccinated against a contagious disease.

## Israeli Data

Monitoring 38,000 people (as explained above) for a few months in a controlled clinical trial is in many ways the gold standard, but clinical trials are not the only data. Clinical trials have limitations of their own. As clearly stated by the authors of the original Pfizer vaccine clinical trial published in the *Journal of the American Medical Association*, the trial was not designed to find effects that occurred in less than one in 10,000 doses (p. 11, Polack and colleagues). However, Israel has since monitored and published data from its largest health care organization.

Each of approximately 900,000 persons who *had been vaccinated* was matched with a similar person (e.g., same age, gender, health) who had *not* been vaccinated and both groups were monitored to find even rare adverse health events. Indeed, there were some serious adverse effects that were more common among the vaccinated group. Heart infection (myocarditis) was three times more likely compared to people who were not vaccinated. To be specific, there were twenty-one cases compared to three in the non-vaccinated group. Out of a total of 939,000. That translates to two or three extra cases of serious (but non-fatal) per 100,000 persons. To put this is real world context, we can pause a moment and refer briefly back to the sad case of Mr. Eyers.

Recall Mr. Eyers believed himself to be at low risk of dying from Covid. Statistically, he was correct about that. Yet, even at the very low risk associated with considering only super healthy persons, Mr. Eyers's risk of death from Covid infection was around one in twenty-eight thousand (as explained above). The cold hard data show the benefits of the vaccine preventing death for his age group outweighed the risk of myocarditis. The data show that serious side effects from vaccination can occur, but it is important to clearly understand the numerical level of rarity, and to realize that "low risk" can still be significantly higher than very rare side effects.

There is a lot of data here. The scientific method is a wonderful thing, and it really can provide interested persons with data we can use to select which opinions we should retain versus revise. Making the data understandable can be a challenge, and the added confusion of some media feeds highlighting information about risks, and others highlighting benefits complicates it further. Most people want to judge the risks *and* the benefits. The large Israeli data set analyzed by researchers led by Dr. Noam Barda includes a key comparison of interest if people receive it: a tally of serious adverse effects associated with Covid infection compared to Covid vaccination itself. Death is (of course) not the only outcome of interest, and the vaccine, as well as Covid infection, both might result in dangerous (yet ultimately non-lethal) outcomes, such as myocarditis.

Let's step back here, and reconnect with the point of this book. Information feeds are dividing people, making people confident in their opinions, and yet not providing a fair discussion of opposing viewpoints. As discussed in chapter 2, this is the antithesis of what, until fifty years ago, was universally accepted as the role and responsibility of broadcasters in a functioning democracy. Myocarditis, heart inflammation, is an acknowledged risk factor of the Covid vaccine, but for any single person to make an informed choice, they must have accurate information on both the precise risks and benefits for themselves. Here is what some feeds emphasize: 1. It is a very rare side effect (but need data on exactly how rare?); 2. Most people recover (but how many do not?); 3. Myocarditis can be caused by Covid too (but how often does this actually happen?). To make this meaningful and use the scientific data available—it is the questions in parentheses that need to be brought into focus. All of it. The data is available, but the gist of number one is well featured in some feeds, while the gist of two is more overtly presented to some people's feeds, to the detriment of all involved

Here is some data of interest. Indeed, myocarditis was increased not only *by the Covid vaccine*, but also with having *experienced Covid disease*. Within the clinical trial data published by Dr. Barda and colleagues, this is explained and also pictorially represented in a clear summary figure, found on page 1087. Which one was riskier? Truthfully, in statistical language the "confidence intervals overlapped" for myocarditis. This means scientists can't say for sure, put practically speaking the percent difference in risk (the "relative risk") was larger for the Covid infection versus non-infection, than for the vaccine versus the control. This means that overall, even for the most serious side effect of the vaccine, the data suggest getting the disease is at least as risky as the vaccine, probably riskier based on the observed outcomes.

Bottom line, even for myocarditis, having the vaccine is likely overall "safer" than having Covid. Moreover, pulmonary embolisms, heart attacks, brain hemorrhage were all substantial and life disrupting risks associated with Covid infection, even when the disease was ultimately survived. This is the data that people care about. This is the data that everyone needs to make educated health decisions, but not everyone is getting it. As Dr. Barda and the team summarized the results for monitoring illness and outcomes of two million people, "SARS-CoV-2 infection was also estimated to substantially increase the risk of several adverse events for which vaccination was not found to increase the risk." This included "acute kidney injury (125.4 events), pulmonary embolism (61.7 events), deep-vein thrombosis (43.0 events), myocardial infarction (25.1 events), pericarditis (10.9 events), and intracranial hemorrhage (7.6 events)," (p.1087).[4]

This gets to the heart of the question. The risk of non-lethal outcomes associated with infection is significant; observation and documentation of the outcome from millions of people documents it. The data is publicly available and really beyond reasonable dispute: The risk associated with infection is higher for experiencing the illness than the risk seen with vaccination. It should be noted this data was published by Dr. Noam Barda and colleagues, many months after the Pfizer sponsored the original vaccine trial, and they did not receive funding from any vaccine manufacturers for the work. People who do not have this information cannot incorporate it into their health care decisions. If they (correctly) know that vaccination poses risks to healthy people, they are still harmed by the Lies of Omission regarding a lack of knowledge about data regarding the well-quantified risks of the disease.

The disease is not equal in its mortality: it hits older persons, overweight persons, and chronically ill persons harder. Vulnerable people. Many people consider that each person who gets the vaccine is at least lessening the likelihood of spreading it, as well as being less likely to require a hospital bed if an elderly or vulnerable person needs it. Some people may have doubts about the vaccine's ability to prevent hospitalization, especially if their news feeds do not make the data readily available. The United Kingdom publishes clear data on ongoing efficacy for mortality (UK Health Security Agency); even after about six months, efficacy remains around 60 percent, even for the

---

4  The numbers in the quote are expressed in terms of risk per 100,000 persons.

newer Omicron (p. 10, Week 16 UK Report). In fact, there are many hospitals and research groups who have independently published their data.

## Additional Data

Even if one is skeptical and mostly discounts data that is sponsored by, or connected to, the major vaccine manufacturers who performed the original trials, there is still plenty of data that documents the vaccine's effectiveness. One example of additional independent investigation, using yet a different kind of research design was published in August of 2021 by Dr. Jamie Lopez Bernal and colleagues. The data was comprised of all persons over age sixteen who a) had symptoms of Covid, and b) had received a test for Covid. Next, persons were divided by vaccination status to see if being vaccinated resulted in people being less likely to have Covid. The key outcome was the ratio of positive Covid tests for persons who were vaccinated to those not vaccinated. Some people find this method compelling because it controls for health seeking behavior (all the people sought out medical attention for their symptoms, and were then tested).

For people who were unvaccinated, the odds of having the Covid test come back positive were 7.6 percent. For persons who *were* two-dose vaccinated, only about one percent came back positive. The exact numbers and estimated efficacies are in the publication—along with a lot of details on the sample. It is worth noting that the data set used was the complete health data set in the United Kingdom with vaccination status verified by the National Immunization Management System. The research was signed by nineteen researchers, and none had ties to any pharmaceutical companies.

## Final Words on Vaccine Risk and Benefit

Research like this, along with the clinical trials, continues to document that vaccination reduces infection, hospitalization, and especially mortality. It is not true that all the data on efficacy comes from the makers of the vaccine. Instead there is converging evidence from across the world, with various kinds of study designs that come together to resolve: the vaccines are preventing Covid deaths and illness.

By comparison, available data on the risks associated with the vaccine show it is tiny in comparison with Covid-19 risk. The virus is sure to continue to spread (especially with people still refusing the vaccine this is all but guaranteed). There will be peaks and lows for the foreseeable future. It can probably be assumed that everyone will eventually be exposed. Maybe not this year, maybe not next, but at some point. Overall odds of dying (when infected) are one in two hundred. Does anyone really think anywhere near one in two hundred are dying or having serious side effects from any of the vaccinations?

Most people should be able to look around and count persons who have died from Covid, and compare that to persons who have died or been disabled from the vaccine. With 70 percent of the population fully two-dose vaccinated, most with booster shots, if the vaccine were anywhere near as dangerous as the disease—everyone would know people who had died from the vaccine. It is not assumed that there are no adverse reactions, nor is it assumed that no one will have serious or even lethal reaction to the vaccine. Nonetheless, the risk versus benefit could not be clearer.

Why do people deny the data on this? They aren't denying it: they aren't getting it. People like John Eyers, who received some correct information, but it was partial, it was incomplete, it was lying by omission. May he rest in peace. There are high risk people, obese people, people over seventy who will not consider taking the vaccine. Their risk of dying *when* they catch it is high, not to mention possible weeks of miserable painful illness and serious complications that linger. They have more than a 5 percent chance of not recovering, and dying a lonely and painful death from it. Five percent means that one in twenty will die (see for example Conover's article, 2021). Yet people eschew precaution available to them.

## Data on Masks—*Theodore Roosevelt*

Another precaution that likely prevents spread of Covid is wearing a face mask when in public. Yet social media is full of people self-righteously refusing to wear a mask when using public transportation, shopping, or walking through a crowded restaurant. This seems inexplicable to persons who are looking at data and understand that while at first the benefits were less clear, as data has been collected and disseminated, the benefits are clear. If someone sneezes near people the day before her symptoms appear, a mask matters.

There was an outbreak of Covid on an aircraft carrier, the *USS Theodore Roosevelt*. People who reported they wore a mask were found to have been less likely to have become infected. Using a more careful case control method, Duong-Ngern and colleagues studied persons who contracted Covid and compared them case by case to people similarly exposed who did not. Among an approximately 1,100 people who had high risk exposure to an active Covid case, wearing face masks during the exposure was protective and not wearing a mask was associated with risk of infection. It is understood that surgical and cloth masks allow virus-sized particles to pass through the mask material, but the amount when talking, coughing, sneezing is greatly lessened. This lowers the transmission. Seventy-four hospital units in Vietnam (where mask use was normally inconsistent) were randomly assigned to consistently wear surgical masks (all workers supplied with two disposable masks per day), cloth masks (which they were responsible for washing), or control group wards without increase in mask use. There was a significant benefit to consistent surgical mask usage in that influenza-like illnesses were higher in the control group compared to the hospital units where all health-care workers wore disposable surgical masks.[5]

## Data on Masks—Transmission in the Home

Researchers in China carefully studied 124 families who had one or more symptomatic cases of Covid and monitored transmission to the family members, studying which factors were associated with chance of the virus spreading. Face mask use by the family was associated with a significant decrease in transmission risk. As the scientists explained in the report, universal use of a face mask is ultimately a low-risk intervention with likely public health benefits.

Wearing masks before symptom onset was most important, "Almost a quarter of family members became infected, and the findings suggest that the risk was highest either before symptom onset or early in the clinical illness, as most primary cases were hospitalized after diagnosis, and interventions were not effective if applied after symptom onset. (Analyses showed that) wearing a mask after illness onset was (helpful but) wearing it before symptom onset (appeared most) effective. Viral load is highest in the two days before symptom onset and on the first day of symptoms," (Wang p. 6). Given the information that covering the nose and mouth have been found to lower the spread of illness, the refusal to wear a mask when in close-contact public places during a pandemic strikes some as selfish or ignorant.

CDC scientists Drs. John Brooks and Jay Butler begin their review of mask wearing research in February of 2021 with a clear synopsis, worth repeating in its entirety.

---

5 Cloth mask use did not reduce illness, and instead increased it. Subsequent research by the authors showed that proper washing within the hospital resulted in increased effectiveness of the cloth.

Prior to the coronavirus disease 2019 (COVID-19) pandemic, the efficacy of community mask wearing to reduce the spread of respiratory infections was controversial because there were no solid relevant data to support their use. During the pandemic, the scientific evidence has increased. Compelling data now demonstrate that community mask wearing is an effective nonpharmacologic intervention to reduce the spread of this infection, especially as source control to prevent spread from infected persons, but also as protection to reduce wearers' exposure to infection. . . . Community mask wearing substantially reduces transmission of severe acute respiratory syndrome coronavirus 2 (SARS-CoV-2) in two ways. First, masks prevent infected persons from exposing others to SARS-CoV-2 by blocking exhalation of virus-containing droplets into the air (termed source control). This aspect of mask wearing is especially important because it is estimated that at least 50% or more of transmissions are from persons who never develop symptoms or those who are in the pre-symptomatic phase of COVID-19 illness. In recent laboratory experiments, multilayer cloth masks were more effective than single-layer masks, blocking as much as 50% to 70% of exhaled small droplets and particles. In some cases, cloth masks have performed similar to surgical or procedure masks for source control. Second, masks protect uninfected wearers. Masks form a barrier to large respiratory droplets that could land on exposed mucous membranes of the eye, nose, and mouth. (page 998).

## Team Politics Trumping Data

Very strong opposition to businesses that require patrons to wear a mask or to be fully vaccinated can appear to be politically motivated, rather than based on understanding data. There is evidence for this contention. In late 2020, researchers queried 1,700 respondents about their politics, knowledge of Covid, behavior related to prevention (mask wearing, social distancing), as well as intentions to become vaccinated against Covid disease. Trump approval predicted vaccine intent and even more strongly predicted lack of engaging in preventive behaviors like wearing a mask in public.

Testing availability as well as individual choices in deciding to seek a test, will impact case counts, but deaths from Covid per population are a reliable indicator of impact. The effect of politicization is heartbreaking. Persons who support former president Donald Trump, and dislike current president Joe Biden may be letting their animosity get in the way of rational health decisions, and this frustrating evidence is served to people who find it engaging. As written by David Leonhardt of the *New York Times* unlike earlier in the pandemic, by the end of 2021, "Twenty-five out of every hundred thousand residents of heavily Trump counties died from Covid, more than three times higher than the rate in heavily Biden counties (7.8 per hundred thousand). October was the fifth consecutive month that the percentage gap between the death rates in Trump counties and Biden counties widened," (Leonhardt, 2021).

The gap in mortality was not there, in 2020 (so it's not likely due to regional differences in health or health care availability). It has, in fact, grown bigger over the months, and the death rate change matches not only with the county level vaccination rates, but with voting choice.

*  *  *

This is the kind of information that exists and that some segments of the population are seeing on a daily basis. These are the reasons that it seems to many that the fears and behaviors of some are not based in reality, but are affected by adherence to a conspiratorial political ideology that not only interferes with cool analysis of reality, but causes real world harm.

What does this all mean for society? Fractured information streams are harming us (is there still an "us"?). The above is information that some segments of the population passively receive as they scroll through YouTube, or check what their friends are sharing on Facebook. Obviously, being aware that Covid deaths are higher and growing in areas of the country that voted for Mr. Trump, while receiving a steady stream of information that vaccination remains effective will affect a person. Moreover, exposure to stories of relatable human beings, with family and hobbies (think of John Eyers), dying from Covid while avoiding a vaccine is going to make people frustrated. This is—or should be—understandable. But it isn't. Not to some people.

Support for universal mandates is not understandable at all to people who are instead encountering pictures and interviews with real people with real families whose lives have been fundamentally harmed and changed by vaccination (think of Breann Dressen). Is it really so far-fetched that a rational human could become frustrated over mandates? Think of a young nurse who had Covid and does not want the second dose of a vaccine that made her sick for two days, and is now faced with losing her job? Or the doctor who fights Covid all day in full mask, but is not willing to wear a cloth mask when running alone on a windy beach, but is taunted for it? Really, this frustration too should at least be understandable. But it isn't.

The idea that opposing information is not dangerous, but is valuable, is far too passé to even be considered quaint. No, to even hint that both views can be reasonable is itself sometimes linked to being a sheep, selfish, ignorant, and treacherous. What is happening? The spread of information that "makes it make sense" (it being Other View) will begin to disappear from the moment affirming information is clicked upon. The life raft of explanation that can maintain the link to your former friend's information begins to disappear from your horizon. The portal will begin to hide it deeper and deeper away.

But then . . . (the algorithm whispers) what does it matter if the rare vaccine injury stories are hidden, suppressed? Does it do any good to tell people about the rare side effects? Perhaps it is all harm and no benefit to share information, that even if technically accurate (Brianne Dressen did appear to have a devastating reaction to the vaccine. See Joanna Broder's *Newsweek* story from May of 2022). Is bringing attention to it still, as a whole, not misrepresenting the net reality that vaccines are on average safe and effective? We are on a tough and slippery slope. Can we not think of how this could be harmful? Really harmful? Harmful in terms of the goal of getting everyone who can be saved from Covid vaccinated? No possible way that telling parents side effects are unimportant or not real, when they are seeing cases of myocarditis in their media feeds? Could it work against trust in institutions and promote skepticism? Could this itself have played any role in John Eyers's extreme distrust of health information?

No one knows. But people who are paying attention are aware that there is a wide chasm on virtually all issues that people care about, and that The States are not united anymore.

# CHAPTER EIGHT

# Kyle and the Second Amendment

*When the opposing side seems so unimaginable, it suggests the other side may not be understood. It is possible that the other side readily encounters information, some of which you haven't encountered. This is how the information world works in modern times.*

During a Black Lives Matter protest on August 25, 2020, seventeen-year-old Kyle Rittenhouse shot three men, killing two. Media portrayals have polarized the situation, so that essential facts are unclear. Media sources assume, or even overtly state, media from the other side is to blame for confusion and polarization. Few take responsibility for any false information they have assumed and then circulated to the public, who takes it as truth.

Historica Wiki does not claim to be accurate, and grew from the originally based alternate reality war games website. Nonetheless, the narrative is close to what has become assumed reality. Historica Wiki Fandom begins the Kyle Rittenhouse page thusly, "an American right-wing vigilante who shot and killed two Black Lives Matter protests (sic) amid chaotic protests in Kenosha, Wisconsin. Rittenhouse was hailed as a hero and patriot by leading conservatives (including Donald Trump. . .). . . ." And there you go. Next, this page states that leading progressives say he is a white supremacist and terrorist. This Black and white view of the Kenosha events may be supposed to be kind of a metaphor of reality, but the tail may have wagged the dog. This simplified version, with the information about who supports him and who does not, has the teams all lined up.

## Why Do People Think Kyle Rittenhouse Is a Vigilante
## Who Killed Vital Protesters?

Because they have different current and different background information. Moreover, once an opinion is adopted and then publicly professed, people seldom change their opinions (see chapter 2). Here are some reasons that might seem important for a person with this view. This case intersects with multiple themes.

### The Nature and Need for Protests

First, the protests where Rittenhouse killed two men were being held to stop police violence against Black people. The violence against minorities by police is seen as beyond intolerable. Trying to stop, or in any way work against, these protests is viewed as efforts to continue the problem of police brutality against minorities. The shooting of Jacob Blake by police, which triggered the protests, appears to be a result of unreasonable fear and reaction by the police against a man who was, fundamentally, a father trying to drive away with his children in tow. But it is crucial to realize the protests were about a larger and ongoing problem: police who aggress against minorities without good reason.

Jacob Blake and George Floyd shootings each sparked extensive protests, as did the shooting of Michael Brown a few years ago. It is unclear why some cases result in massive protests and others do not, but the problem is real and ongoing. These protests are needed. Needed to bring attention to the cases, and needed to provide pressure to change. Too many cases have not been met with enough outcry. Jacob Blake and George Floyd are not isolated incidents. This is the bigger context to the events of the August 2020 Kenosha riots. It is one thread in a tapestry.

### Steven DeMarco Taylor, April 18, 2020

Taylor was a father who undoubtedly was experiencing the stress of the lockdowns, like most people in April of 2020. There were, at one time, multiple video recordings of his death with full audio circulating on social media. Some people probably saw the recordings, and others probably did not. For unknown reasons (perhaps at the family's request, it is unknown to the author), as of February, 2022, the videos are difficult, if not impossible, to find (author's efforts), and only the officer bodycam footage is available, with missing audio. Those whose feeds showed the videos, probably saw the videos as shocking. Mr. Taylor did not appear to be a threat in the bystander videos, and he did not appear to be trying to steal the bat. His behavior gave the impression of waiting and practicing one's swing. That is, his stance did not look threatening, and the bat was swung in a similar way a few times, like a slow-motion batter, then like a twirling baton, without audible threat or eye contact at any one in particular. Moreover, people nearby were going about their business, purchasing and bagging their items, and did not appear alarmed.

Police arrive and begin by ordering him to stop and put down the bat or weapon, (without the original video and audio, memory may somewhat fail). He does (clearly) refuse, and appears to resent the order. When police approach, he puts the bat back and over his head, and could appear threatening, or it could be seen as an attempt to keep the bat away from the reaching police officer. He did not appear to be in imminent attack mode when tased. When the Taser was deployed, the bat was not raised. Taylor was backing up and was told to drop it, which he does not do. After being tased (again?), he stumbles, appears quite affected, and takes halting steps towards the officers, hunched over, falling, but still clutching the beloved bat, which is held pointed down, near the ground. He is then shot (fatally) in the chest, visibly bleeding onto the floor as he stumbles away, and tased again as he falls.

Media stories at the time quoted police, and perhaps unsurprisingly the quotes gave the impression that Taylor was brandishing a weapon (the bat), that police felt threatened, that there was a credible fear he would hurt customers or the officers with the bat, and was thus justifiably shot by a "veteran police officer." The early stories often did not include quotes from the family, or witnesses of the event. If this is all one heard about the case, that's all one would think: a man was shot while trying to steal a bat, trying to hit at police officers who were just doing their job. Moreover, how many people know the actual follow up?

Months later, some facts have emerged, even without the bystander videos available, based on the court record, because charges were filed. Officer Jason Fletcher arrived alone and radioed other police officers. He said it was not a robbery, nor a brandishing weapon situation. In effect, no danger, no rush. After attempting to get the bat from Taylor, and another officer arriving, a Taser was drawn, and fired. Taylor was pointing the bat down towards the ground and slowly stumbling when the fatal shot was fired to his chest. After having been shot with a Taser as well as having been fatally shot, the officer handcuffs the unconscious dead or dying Black man.

From the time the officer entered the store, it was only forty seconds until Taylor was lethally shot in the chest. Apparently, as more facts emerged, Taylor had been accused of trying to steal, denied it, and had said he would wait for police, which is what he was doing when the officer ordered him to drop the bat, then reached for it.

The officer since has been charged with manslaughter, with motion to dismiss denied. Referring to an independent report that found fault with police behavior, District Attorney Timothy Wagstaffe stated, "The mistaken belief here is that at the moment lethal force was used, it was reasonable. Based upon the evidence, it was not," (as reported by Gartrell in the *Mercury News*). The original stories in the media, which quoted officers and described Jason Fletcher as a veteran officer, or an officer with twenty plus years' experience, did not note that twice before federal lawsuits had been filed against him, once for shooting a dog, and once for beating a man during an arrest, as later reported by the *Grio*.

BLM protests are essential.

### Elijah McClain, August 30, 2019

Police officers confronted a young and slightly built twenty-three-year-old massage therapist with no criminal, drug, or violent history. Indeed, he was a vegetarian known for his gentle disposition. But Elijah McClain was Black, and wearing a sketchy ski mask walking home ("Sketchy" was the words of the officers to explain why they stopped him). The body cameras of the officers inexplicably malfunctioned that night, but one still recorded as audio only. McClain was forcibly held to the ground with his hands cuffed behind his back. He was also given the drug ketamine supposedly to sedate him: a handcuffed 130-pound man was too much for the three police officers. McClain had a heart attack, and was pronounced brain dead three days later.

Aurora police officers had met with the coroner, and police investigators were also present during the autopsy, which was originally "inconclusive" regarding the cause of death. Nearly a year later, on June 24, 2020, after a social media outcry and protests, a new investigation from outside the county began (June 24, 2020). Results of the protests and getting outside the county were almost immediate.

Within five days, photos from October 2019, taken at the site where Elijah McClain was detained, drugged, and experienced the fatal heart attack, surfaced. Specifically, photos showed three officers smiling and illustrating the neck restraint used on McClain, were "discovered." One officer who was present and involved in the death, received a copy of the picture via text, to which he typed back, "Ha Ha." One officer immediately resigned and three were quickly fired over the pictures alone. (Yes, get these cases out of the county they occur in.) A few months later, in September 2021, the three police officers (Nathan Woodyard, Jason Rosenblatt and Randy Roedema) and two paramedics (Jeremy Cooper and Peter Cichuniec) were charged through a Colorado grand jury with manslaughter and other lesser charges for the death of Elijah McClain.

But visualize if the protests had not happened, or had not worked, and the case never gotten outside the county? This is why the protests must continue. How many times has this happened? Does this happen? The final words of Elijah McClain, recorded by the malfunctioning body cam that still captured audio, are worth printing. Listen to his words. The world wants change.

I can't breathe. I have my ID right here. My name is Elijah McClain. That's my house. I was just going home. I'm an introvert. I'm just different. That's all. I'm so sorry. I have no gun. I don't do that stuff. I don't do any fighting. Why are you attacking me? I don't even kill flies! I don't eat meat! But I don't judge people, I don't judge people who do eat meat. Forgive me. All I was trying to do was become better. I will do it. I will do anything. Sacrifice my identity, I'll do it. You all are phenomenal. You are beautiful and I love you. Try to forgive me. I'm a mood Gemini. I'm sorry. I'm so sorry. Ow, that really hurt! You are all very strong. Teamwork makes the dream work. Oh, I'm sorry, I wasn't trying to do that. I just can't breathe correctly. —Elijah McClain.

This is why people protesting against such evil must be encouraged.

## Sandra Annette Bland, July 15, 2015

Ms. Bland, who had a college degree and was about to start a new job, had recently been posting videos about police mistreatment of African Americans. She had a minor criminal record, the most serious was driving while intoxicated and shoplifting. She had no outstanding warrant. On the other hand, according to sources, Officer Brian Encinia who pulled her car over had reportedly issued many hundreds of minor tickets in the past year, "using the pretext of little-enforced minor infractions to then perform random searches," (see Wikipedia article, Sandra Bland).

She was pulled over for failing to signal a lane change, which happened after Officer Encinia accelerated rapidly on her, and she switched lanes to let him pass. The recording by a bystander and Bland's phone establish she was not being threatening, that the officer was escalating the situation. He loudly and aggressively ordered her out of the car, opened her door, pointed a gun or Taser at her. Recording shows she was not threatening. Her tone of voice was incredulous, but not loud, "All this for a traffic violation?" Eventually, being forcibly pulled from the car, she noted she could sue. She was then roughly forced to the ground and arrested. The officer's recording had missing segments due to "technical difficulties," but other recordings establish the facts. The arrest appears completely without reason. After three days, Sandra Bland is discovered dead in her jail cell, which was ruled a suicide.

This causes some to feel deep rage, and to want Black Lives Matter protests to continue.

### Bad Cops, Bad Evidence, and Bad Judgement

The shooting of ninety-two-year-old Kathryn Johnston in her home is notable not because she was a law-abiding citizen killed by police who broke into a private home without identifying themselves (as were Amir Locke, Breona Taylor, Eurie Stamps, and others), but because officers were convicted of planting drugs in her home after the fact. To be fair, this happens to other races as well (Dennis Tuttle and Rhogena Nicholas for example), but it shows that police do this sometimes, and we can probably assume they do not always get caught. The legal ability to suddenly enter a person's home with guns drawn is a tool of great power that can too easily be misused.

Police brutality arises not only because of malicious abuse of power, but also because society simply gives too much unchecked power, and because the power is therefore used cavalierly. There are cases that suggest shockingly poor training coupled with too high of a fear response, perhaps coupled with low fear of any serious sanction. Timothy Russell and Malissa Williams were a recently acquainted minority couple, driving in his car when they were pulled over for a minor violation, not ticketed, and released. Then, from the police report, the car backfired which police thought was a shot. This resulted in sixty police cars chasing them for twenty-three miles.

It is possible the two were afraid, not knowing why they were being chased at high speed after having been pulled over by police and then released, only to be chased a moment later. In the end, they pulled into a middle school parking lot where any questions about whether a fear of stopping for the inexplicably aggressive, high-speed chase was paranoid or reasonable were put to rest. They were—in fact—summarily shot to death while in the car. The officers state that when one officer fired, other officers thought they were being fired upon. At least 137 bullets were fired, killing them many times over. They were unarmed (and drug free, in case that matters to any readers).

There had already been a formal investigation by the US Department of Justice Civil rights Division (2014). It had already found that the Cleveland Police department, where the above case occurred, "Fails to adequately investigate civilian complaints of officer misconduct," (p. 38 of the investigative report) and in general, "engages in a pattern or practice of unreasonable amounts of force in violation of the Constitution." (p. 58).

Absurdly violent beatings like those of Rodney King and Emmett Till in decades past, and war veteran Walter Harvin, and school teacher Robert Davis more recently, must end. This will take public pressure. These cases must end: Tamir Rice. Sean Bell. Oscar Grant. Amadou Diablo. Aiyana Jones. But the recent protests have mattered. Look at the case of George Floyd, or Elijah McClain, or Stephen Taylor. The fraternity is beginning to be broken through the effect of the protests. Honest police are speaking out and overzealous bad cops have been prosecuted. There is so much more to do. It is important for the country as a whole that the energy continues.

## United States Gun Culture

Second, the ease of acquisition and lax regulation of firearms is a topic many US citizens view as contributing to high police fear of criminals and as generally increasing deadly violence. Criminals' and vigilantes' easily acquired lethal ability is like carrying a torch near a gas leak. Kyle Rittenhouse's behavior appears to epitomize the foolishness of bringing guns everywhere. Many find it bothersome that a white person would want to open carry an assault style rifle at a BLM protest. For some, it is nearly impossible to imagine he was not looking for trouble with his assault rifle in tow.

It is important to realize how much of an outlier the USA is regarding the protection of gun culture. The United States has more than one gun for every person, including children and babies. First, compared to other industrialized countries, the murder rate is about seven times higher than other nations, and the gun-related murder rate is approximately twenty times higher. Almost all the murders where a woman or a child is a victim involve the use of a firearm. The ease of purchasing objects that can so quickly and so easily kill so many is stunning. In 2019, Conner Betts' weapon, which was legally acquired and owned, killed nine human beings in Dayton, Ohio in less than one minute; and fifty-eight people were killed (and over eight hundred wounded) in less than ten minutes at a Las Vegas concert. In 2021, ten people were shot to death in a Colorado grocery store. Less than two months later, in the same state, seven people died when an angry person with a gun starting shooting at a birthday party. The love of guns and the ease of obtaining them escalates situations, making lethality easy.

When other countries have experienced mass shootings, they have passed laws to restrict the ability to quickly and easily buy guns in an effort to end these kinds of mass crimes. It has worked. A mass shooting at a school in Scotland in 1996, the Dunblane Massacre, killed sixteen children and a teacher, injuring more. The shock of the tragedy resulted in publicly supported gun legislation. The government introduced gun control legislation and there has been only two mass shootings since. In April of 2021, Australia celebrated twenty-five years of effective gun control legislation and mourned the Tasmanian mass shooting that killed thirty-five with a semi-automatic weapon and wounded an additional twenty-three. Such a man-made disaster has not been repeated. Such weapons make it too easy to murder: once a person has a loaded gun, just a quick pull of a trigger ends lives in a split second of emotion.

In the USA, one can buy an assault rifle without a background check quickly and easily by going to a traveling firearm market, referred to as a "Gun Show." Buyers do not perform the check; the onus is on the seller, and many don't do it. Skeptics may wish to specifically ask YouTube to reveal Virginia Congressman Dan Helmer doing just this. He covertly filmed the transaction, which was very clear. In the film he bought an assault rifle in just minutes, with no background check, sealed with a handshake.

No other industrialized nation allows and encourages citizens to buy multiple rapid-fire high-powered rifles, much less open carry them when out and about in public. It is not unreasonable to consider that the high availability of guns, the lax and unenforced gun laws, and overall laissez-faire attitude about obtaining weapons have been a direct cause of the mass shootings that so frequently occur in the USA. It is reasonable to assume that if Nicolas Cruz could not have gotten his hands on a semi-automatic rifle, some of the seventeen blameless students shot in Parkland, Florida would not have been shot, and would be alive today.

Sanity and reason must begin to prevail in regarding gun laws in the USA. Even with differences of opinion on many gun related issues, there are a few points of near universal agreement. According to Gallup's annual poll on gun attitudes, over ninety percent of citizens (including gun owners) favor requiring background checks for every gun sale, and nearly 70 percent support laws that require purchasers to be twenty-one years old. Yet, even these measures, that nearly everyone supports, cannot get passed. The gun laws, gun lobby, and gun culture in the USA seem hopelessly broken. Perhaps no case epitomizes this as clearly as the case of a teenaged Kyle Rittenhouse and the three men who died by his gun.

## Only in USA: Teen Openly Brings a Rifle to a Riot

It was in dispute whether Kyle Rittenhouse was or was not legally carrying the gun used to kill two persons in Kenosha, Wisconsin. This alone is astounding. Civilized societies do not condone or allow teenagers to bring assault rifles into a riot. Yet somehow this itself may have been a legal act. A teenager toting an assault rifle during a riot has an outcome that is easy to predict. The teenager brought a gun because he knew well he might get a chance to use it. An aspiring police officer who supported Blue Lives Matter, he detested the looting that had been shown on television.

The young Rittenhouse had even stated he would shoot looters if he had the chance. Gun Culture. His statement was on video, but was inexplicably found not admissible by the presiding judge during the trial. The Assistant District Attorney wanted the statements as evidence in the trial because it spoke to intent. The motion addressed a video widely available to any who searched for it, although *some would have it delivered* right to their hand held via the algorithms. In any event, the footage taken from inside a car shows what appears to be shoplifters leaving a CVS store. The incriminating words heard are, "Bruh, I wish I had my fucking AR, I'd start shooting rounds at them."

As District Attorney Blinger's motion read, "The defendant was watching the situation from a vehicle parked across the street and had no actual interaction with anyone involved in the incident. Quite simply, the defendant saw something, jumped to a conclusion based on exactly zero facts, and then threatened to kill someone based on his baseless assumption and wrongful interpretation." The motion was denied and the jury never heard it. It is hard to understand how evidence of intent was not deemed relevant during the trial: the defense was that he was only shooting in self-defense. Bottom line: if Kyle Rittenhouse had not had a gun, if he had not brought the gun, if guns were not so ubiquitous and glorified, Joseph Rosenbaum and Anthony Huber would still be alive today, and Gaige Grosskreutz would have full use of his arm.

As sometimes happens with protests, there was indeed some unfortunate vandalism, but there were no deaths other than those caused by Kyle

Rittenhouse's gun. It is not so much that it is shocking that the deaths occurred, but that from top to bottom, including a judge and jury, the message is that the shooting was legal, that the deaths that unsurprisingly occurred at the protest were justified. At the protest seeking to end the shooting of Black men.

Was Kyle Rittenhouse acting as a teenaged vigilante during a Black Lives Matter protest? Absolutely. Vigilante has a definition, he met it. The word means a person who tries in an unofficial way to prevent crime, or to catch and punish criminals, usually because they do not think official organizations (such as police) are controlling crime effectively. Merriam-Webster defines the word as "a member of a volunteer committee organized to suppress and punish crime summarily (as when the processes of law are viewed as inadequate)." This seems like what Kyle Rittenhouse did.

Joseph Rosenbaum was not a threat. He was unarmed, a bit smaller than Rittenhouse, and did not have superhuman strength; in fact, he had just gotten out of the hospital. A healthy seventeen-year-old male can defend himself from a shorter unarmed man, of approximately the same weight. The gun escalated an inherently volatile situation to the loss of human life. Without the guns, it might have been a fist fight. Even Kyle would have been better off—a few bruises would have been far less disruptive to his life than the past year. It is entirely possible that without the confidence that carrying a rifle provided, Kyle would have acted differently, and nothing would have happened. We will never know, because he shot Joseph Rosenbaum, an unarmed homeless man, just released from the hospital. Rosenbaum was not the only one shot, before the night ended another man was shot and wounded, and another man killed.

The gun turned the problem lethal. The USA needs restraint and reason in its gun laws. And the protests against killing Blacks by police must keep happening. The case of Kyle Rittenhouse is emotionally explosive because it so clearly affronts the intersection of these two problems in society.

## How Can People Think Kyle Rittenhouse Did Nothing Wrong?

Fundamentally, it is because they have received an entirely different set of reports about the case, and see gun laws differently. They have a different focus, and do not receive the same information.

Kyle Rittenhouse lived about twenty minutes away from Kenosha, Wisconsin with his mother. He worked in Kenosha where his father and various other members of his family lived. He had stayed the night in the small city, the day city garbage trucks and a community trolley were burned, along with at least a hundred other vehicles and an armored SWAT vehicle. News outlets in Kenosha were reporting that the protests, which were peaceful in the day, escalated and became destructive during the night. The Department of Corrections had been burned. There was aerial video of the destruction. Owners of a Kenosha furniture store were reported to sob as they looked at the rubble that had been their family business for forty years.

The local news (madison.com) published a story of a police officer hit with a brick and falling to the ground, with other police coming to his aid, along with a graphic video. The newspaper also published that police scanners had recorded an officer saying the police did not have the resources available to handle the situations, and were abandoning some locations. One quote from photographer Gideon Verdin-Williams covering the aftermath for TMY4 news on August 25, 2021 was as follows: "You never quite know the pain of watching your neighborhood burned down until you have experienced it yourself. It's a feeling of hopelessness you cannot explain. Many residents were crying as they watched cleanup efforts. The whole experience in Kenosha during this terrible time is one I will always remember," (see Groh, 2020).

During his trial, Kyle's (undisputed) testimony was that he had worked in Kenosha and then stayed the night at a friend's in Kenosha. The following day (August 25), when talking about the damage with his friend, he testified they consumed the news of the damage, and wanted to do something to protect the city from further damage. It was testified that an owner of a car lot, which had suffered extensive damage the night prior, was seeking help guarding his other business location. Kyle and his friend decided to participate.

There is a photo of Kyle with a member of the car dealership family (Sahil Khindri). Although Sahil said no one asked Kyle to guard or watch over the dealerships, in addition to the photo, another member of the dealership family had given Kyle his personal phone number a few hours prior, and there were phone records of the calls. In sum, testimony was conflicting, with Kyle and his friend saying they were explicitly asked to help and offered money to do so, with Sahil denying money was offered. Importantly, it does seem a key to the car lot was handed over to the group of volunteer guards. There is video of police handing an armed Kyle Rittenhouse a water bottle. The exact truth may not be known, but to many who know the totality of these facts, it seems at least reasonable for the young Kyle Rittenhouse to have sincerely believed his help was desired.

Most Second Amendment advocates do not think a seventeen-year-old should have gone to the riots with a semi-automatic weapon, but they do think given the lack of armed protection for businesses and lack of arrests for looters and rioters, the decision was at least understandable. If he was going to go, it was wise to carry a gun. Mostly they believe his desire was to help, and that he would have been killed or maimed by a mentally unstable felon had his gun not been with him and loaded.

People with conservative algorithm feeds are probably clear on the following facts that emerged during the trial, while to others some of this may be sketchy, unclear, or unknown. Joseph Rosenbaum had definitely set multiple fires during the riots. He was a felon convicted of sex crimes against young boys. He was suicidal and had been released from the hospital that day after a failed attempt to end his own life. He had spent a decade as a white man in a penitentiary, and had no history of supporting BLM. Witnesses testified Rosenbaum used the N-word to taunt people at the protest, and this testimony was accepted by both prosecution and defense. His girlfriend, Kariann Swart, was quoted in an Associated Press Story of November 19, 2020. "The couple lived in a tent for seven months before moving into a motel. In July, Rosenbaum was arrested for domestic violence and ordered to stay away from Swart. But days later, he contacted her, then overdosed and was in a hospital's intensive care unit for five days, Swart said." After some time in the local jail, and another hospital stay, he had been released that day. According to the AP story, "he then went to talk to Swart, who would not let him stay with her." He had nowhere to go. He was not there to support Black Lives Matter.

Rosenbaum was at one point seen pushing a burning wagon towards a crowded area, and the fire was put out with a fire extinguisher by a person with a gun wearing a shirt color the same color and style as Kyle's. The idea that this gives some people is that Rosenbaum was unstable, had a death wish, and may have mistakenly thought Kyle had been the one to put out a fire he had set, which angered Rosenbaum. Video and testimony suggest Rosenbaum was carrying a heavy chain as a weapon shortly before the shots were fired.

## Some Media Coverage Confused Basic Facts

Early news reports portrayed the events as peaceful Black BLM protesters hunted in cold blood by an out of state predator and white supremacist.

It is disheartening to know the facts, and reflect on these media reports. November 5, 2020, the *Chicago Tribune* wrote, Rittenhouse "crossed state lines" to go to Kenosha (not true) and that the rifle was "illegally purchased" (it wasn't). Truth did not get closer, but farther away as time went on. A year later almost to the day, Representative Karen Bass (California) said (November 4, 2021, CNN interview), "You have a 17-year-old boy who was driven by his mother across state lines with an automatic weapon — frankly, she should have been detained for child endangerment." That did not happen: the mother did not drive him, he drove himself to Kenosha the day prior for work. The gun was never in Illinois and never crossed state lines.

## Much of Media Got It Wrong

The prosecution's own witness, a former Marine, Jason Lackowski, revealed in court that white man Joseph Rosenbaum had used the N-word at the BLM protesters, referring to them as the N-word, causing actual protesters to react negatively to Rosenbaum. What a juxtaposition for the media to portray him as a peaceful BLM protestor. Exaggerated or incomplete media reports matter; they make people angry over things that did not happen and distort reality. We will never know if public opinion would have been different if the media had gotten the story correct from day one, because that did not happen.

Media outlets seemed so intent on telling a narrative about a white man killing Black protesters that objective reality could not get in the way of the preferred story. Even after the trial, after the basic facts of the night had been methodically established via hours of testimony and videos from every angle in a court of law, media were not dependable. On November 19, 2021, the *Independent* newspaper in the United Kingdom reported Kyle Rittenhouse was acquitted after having shot three Black protesters. Within a National Geographic book published at the close of 2021, while discussing the state of patriarchy today, it is stated that Rittenhouse "killed *two black men* in Kenosha" and while "waging a glorious race war." All persons shot were white. This is the danger of news bubbles and why fairness in reporting to the public matters: facts begin to be irrelevant.

## Gun Was Used in Self Defense

Some facts are beyond dispute: Joseph Rosenbaum had threatened to kill Kyle Rittenhouse earlier that night. In the end, Joseph Rosenbaum was crouched behind cars and came out and started to chase Kyle. Kyle attempts to leave, and shouts, "Friendly!" His escape is blocked by cars, Joseph himself, and another man that had been setting fires with Joseph earlier. There are witnesses. It is on video. Multiple videos. Joseph moves closer toward Kyle. The other man then shoots his own gun directly behind Kyle. It was at this point, that Joseph runs toward Kyle and grabs for Kyle's rifle, putting his hand on it and pulling. Kyle pulls the trigger, hitting and killing Joseph. Media tells some: a peaceful Black protester was gunned down. It was near textbook self-defense. The altercation was caught on video and the earlier threats not disputed by either side during the trial.

Media stories suggest the idea that Kyle was asking for trouble by showing up with a gun, yet do not say Joseph was asking for trouble by setting fires, saying, "Shoot me N-----," and running at a cornered boy obviously armed with a rifle. It is hard for some to bridge the discrepancy. A mob formed, saying things like "Get him, shooter!" and "That's the shooter!" Overhead footage and phone videos clearly show Kyle remaining at the shooting scene, talking to a person giving first aid. He left only after the mob began. Yet some interested persons who were seeking information the days after it happened were not privy to that context, they were told only Kyle "fled." Lies of Omission.

He was heading towards the police line with his hands up, he eventually approached police, who sent him away, apparently not understanding he was the shooter. This is testified and corroborated by clear video. He said he told police he had shot someone, but was not heard in the confusion and was sprayed with tear gas and ordered to leave.

The crowd was chasing him, and threw things that hit his head: he fell. This also is on video in addition to the court testimony. Kyle was then jump kicked in the head. A mob was forming. The photos and video of the kick are quite violent. Next, he was hit with a skateboard by Anthony Huber. Not a tap, a full force swing with impact to the head and neck while Kyle was down on the ground. This was the second person shot by Kyle Rittenhouse. The skateboard attack by Huber was fundamentally from a person not involved in the original shooting and who had not seen what had happened, but presumably believed he was trying to help stop an active shooter.

The facts around the Gaige Grosskreutz shooting seem unknown to too many people. Gaige thought Kyle was a bad guy, and his goal was to neutralize him. From Gaige's own testimony, "I thought the defendant was an active shooter," and he was motivated to act from a desire to prevent Kyle from causing harm. Gaige, unlike Joseph Rosenbaum, was indeed a strong supporter of BLM. He was there to protest police brutality, and like Kyle, had a history of paramedic training, and wanted to aid protesters who might get hurt. Moreover, and also like Kyle, he brought a gun to the protest. In another remarkable similarity to Kyle, he exaggerated (or may have misrepresented) his medical background. Gaige said he was a licensed paramedic—but his license had expired years ago. (Kyle had said he was an EMT, but he was only a lifeguard with first-aid and CPR certification, and enrolled in some nursing classes).

Gaige approached Kyle, who was still on the ground after falling. In the end it was undisputed that Kyle did not shoot until Gaige pointed his own loaded gun at Kyle's head. Kyle shot the arm that held the loaded gun pointed at his head. Ironically, it was not Kyle's gun that was illegally carried. Gaige's use of a concealed firearm was indisputably illegal because he did not have a current license to conceal and carry. Kyle's open carry, due to an odd technicality in Wisconsin state law, was actually *not* breaking any laws. Only because this was so often repeated, for the record: Gaige Grosskreutz carried his weapon concealed under his clothing, in violation of Wisconsin law. He brought it to the protest because he "believed in the second Amendment," per his testimony, his words. Is this a double standard by the Kyle haters? No, it isn't. Because of the omissions in the stories. Most people who think Kyle was a terrorist for bringing a gun do not have the information about Gaige supporting the second amendment, bringing an illegal gun to the riot, and pointing it loaded at someone, who then shot his gun arm.

How do people support Kyle Rittenhouse? In sum, the first victim that night was Rosenbaum, a sad man and clearly mentally ill, but also a violent criminal, and possibly a racist by the manner in which he used the N-word. Grosskreutz and Huber were legitimate protesters, trying to support BLM. But they did become part of mob that was forming to chase and attack Rittenhouse. They approached a man with a gun with intent to harm him (Huber did harm him with a bruising skateboard to the head, and Grosskreutz pointed a loaded gun at him). Mobs are dangerous and protests attract unstable troublemakers as well as peaceful protesters, and everything in between. Most people who support the acquittal think Kyle had to act fast, and the shootings happened because Kyle reasonably believed he was about to be badly hurt or killed.

His desire to "do something to help" also seems sincere to many. Although some media chose wording to downplay the help he did provide (was "*said* to have decided to clean graffiti" or was seen "removing BLM graffiti"). Kyle was indeed scrubbing profanities spray painted on a school. And he was videoed providing first-aid to people at the protest earlier in the night, before the shootings. The level of destruction, that some news feeds stopped providing after the shootings, was happening in a town Rittenhouse considered a home. As the photographer from the local news station put it, *"You never quite know the pain of watching your neighborhood burned down until you have experienced it yourself."* This destruction apparently prompted Rittenhouse to try and do something to help. He likely understood there was some danger, but still wanted to help prevent further destruction.

It will be discounted by people whose minds were set by the initial coverage, never to be changed. Yet when asked by Tucker Carlson how he felt about BLM rioters, Kyle likely surprised Mr. Carlson. He said he was a supporter of the Black Lives Matter cause. His words won't matter, facts won't matter. Separate narratives for increasingly separated peoples. Some media will forever recite that he was a terrorist and white supremacist who shot and killed peaceful Black protesters in cold blood, with a gun he snuck across state lines.

# CHAPTER NINE

# Transgender and Being a Good Sport

*If you are unable to imagine the other side's views, try considering the effect of fundamentally disparate information. The pocket portal is designed to display whatever you want to see.*

Humans are presumed to be able to identify as male or female based on their internal feeling of gender, and polite society in 2022 tries to respect this. People have opinions about how much acceptance for the individual is warranted based on their judgement of the proper balance of respect for the individual and what will work for society. Individual opinions are based on information that individuals have. Emotions can run high, and the goal has to be to bridge some of the information gap.

Individuals who support universal participation often think about the harm to people who are denied the experience of sport competition, while those opposed may consider biological differences as paramount. There is certainly a wide gulf in attitudes. The gulf of the divide cannot be surprising if we appreciate that daily Lies of Omission widen any existing small differences with separate information feeds. With every click about how a trans woman athlete is a real woman, a user is ferried further away from some of the relevant information on differences in cardiac function as detailed below.

Pause and seek acceptance of the undeniable fact that human beings cannot agree on everything. If we realize that social feeds are feeding dichotomizing information, if we then seek and find opposing information and look at it with curiosity instead of a priori contempt, we can facilitate understanding. This is possible without changing our deeply held beliefs.

## Why Do Some People Think Transgender Athletes Should Be Allowed to Compete?

Because some combination of life experiences and information they have received lead them to recognize advantages of doing so, and to perceive the harm in not so doing.

Individuals who are transgender have many obstacles to overcome. They typically experience a confusing, difficult, and hard life, especially during adolescence and young adulthood. Besides the prejudice and misunderstanding of society, the stress of feeling like one's body does not match ones' sense of self is itself stressful. The extent of the problems may not be fully appreciated.

## Trauma

The first objective collection of data on the difficulties associated with growing up gender variant was probably by Lorraine Trenchard and Hugh Warren in the 1980s. About four of every ten gender variant people were found to have been the victim of violence or overt, ongoing harassment, and half of these had attempted suicide because of the difficulties. Gender identity, which refers to subjective sense of being feminine, masculine, or androgynous, is not binary, and can be fluid. The prefix trans refers to beyond or bridging, and a common definition for transgender is a person who exists beyond or across binary gender. Specifically, they do not identify as their biological sex and/or the sex assigned at birth.

Clear information is somewhat lacking, but one in thirty thousand people assigned male at birth have sought gender reassignment (via surgery) at some point in their lives. Best available evidence puts suicide risk at an alarmingly high rate for transgender people. Some estimates put the rate at eight hundred per one hundred thousand, about seventy times higher than the general population, and about one in four transgender persons report a suicide attempt, with attempts highest in young adults and youth.

Even a typical adolescence is conflict laden and confusing, with concerns about fitting in, friendships, and romance—but for a transgender person, it is compounded by identity confusion and society conveying they are wrong, or maybe even sick. The stories these humans tell of the harassment and pain they have endured are the stuff of nightmares and include vandalism, ostracism, beatings, with lack of support from school and police. In the *Riddle of Gender*, by Deborah Rudacille, we read the cases of Alyn, Gwen, and Dylan, all were harassed and bullied to despair. Gwen, who dropped out of school unable to cope with the harassment, was murdered at the age of seventeen. Alyn was beaten up by a group of eight. Dylan was constantly bullied and once was held down by a group to have make-up applied roughly to his face; this led to time in a mental hospital.

Clear expressions of acceptance by peers and family have been shown to work against suicide risk. Acceptance on sports teams has not been specifically investigated as mitigating risk, but it is reasonable to extrapolate this would be protective. Is it too much to allow transgender people who love sports to keep playing if they come out publicly to live as authentic? Do they not need the benefits of engaging in one of the most healthy and protective activities known: organized sports.

Participating in sports has benefit beyond physical health. It fosters social functioning, is associated with better cognitive functioning, and better performance in school. Especially for a person who has enjoyed sports, forfeiting participation in one's sport of choice would be understandably traumatic. Imagine having to choose to live as a male when everything in you feels feminine. Finding the courage to express yourself, and then having to give up the one thing that has been a constant joy in your life: sports. It is beyond unfair.

## The Exaggerated Threat to Women's Sports

The arguments against allowing transgender athletes to compete often crystallize into concerns that it will ruin women's sports. It is important to realize real world data offers no support for this hypothetical problem. People were hysterical that transsexuals would takeover women's sports two generations ago when Renee Richards played tennis. Renee Richards, who underwent sex reassignment surgery and was legally a woman, played professional tennis as a woman in her forties, from the years 1977 through 1981.

Most writings, even then, were neutral if not supportive, but there were worriers. A satirical editorial from 1976 appearing in the *Oakland Tribune* (by Gerald Machman, appearing on page 22), reflected the concerns of the times that letting Richards play, "has led to a serious lowering of standards and has encouraged transsexuals to play both sides of the net." The journalist sarcastically fretted what would "happen to the spirit of international competition?" The concern (of others) was plainly expressed, "If we let Dr. Richards and her kind casually wonder in and out of women's tournaments—where do we draw the line?"

In an article by Associated Press writer Frank Brown, regarding the effort to limit women's tennis to persons with XX chromosomes, then executive director Jerry Diamond of the women's tennis association, was quoted on August 12, 1976, "Women's tennis is for women. If she is genetically a woman, then she can play tennis," and otherwise not. Diamond was wrong; she did play. Director Diamond had to admit as much a few days later, rather irked. In a letter sent to all members of the Women's Tennis Association, he penned, "to the best of our knowledge, a biological male has been admitted to the women's tournament." In a phone interview with *New York Times*, Diamond noted women players could choose not to play, and some did (see *New York Times* Archives for August 14 and 20, 1976).

As it turned out, Renee Richards played professional tennis for four years. It did not result in a flood of men changing their sex willy-nilly and beating all the women in professional tennis. Indeed, although the sport has remained open to other trans women, it was thirty years before another trans women entered the professional arena.

Transgender athlete Sarah Gronert went professional in 2008. There was hand-wringing and accusations that it was unfair. A coach of another women's tennis player at the time, stated "There is no girl who can hit serves like that. . . . If she begins to play continuously, within six months she will be within the top fifty," (see Brassfield, 2009). From 2008 to 2012 Gronert won some and lost some, never won any national titles, and her peak rank was 164. The fear mongers were, in fact, wrong. The fear was overblown.

Sarah Gronert was designated at birth as a "hermaphrodite," with male and female characteristics (we do not know an actual medical diagnosis). Based on her birth certificate and her self-proclaimed gender: she identifies as, and is, woman. She showed talent in tennis from a young age, and played often and well. Perhaps this was a high point of her life, perhaps her childhood and adolescence were a bit more confusing than most. Perhaps having her gender publicly questioned by the tennis insiders, "That's not a woman, that's a man," was painful to a person who was finding success at something she liked. She has said she was absolutely overwhelmed by the hostility, and considered giving up tennis. Is this what we want for transgender people? Since the first transgender athlete in 1976 the haters have been wrong. No one has cheated and won unfairly. Tennis has not been ruined.

Each year, two hundred thousand women compete in NCAA events. NCAA rules allow trans woman to compete. Should they not do so because of the controversy and fear? And really—how common is it? Consider the following: If just one in thirty thousand people are transgender women (based on 2011 report of persons who seek surgery), which is probably a gross underestimate of transgender persons, by chance alone—there should be around seven transgender competitors a year in the NCAA competitions.

In the ten years that NCAA has allowed trans women to compete, there has been one NCAA champion that is a trans woman. There may be another this year with swimmer Lea Thomas. At some point, there is bound to be. The women who are competing are people who grew up with the sport, for whom it is an important part of their personhood. For these people, it is a violation of their rights to live a full life to require them to stop their sport. It may be conceivable that mass quantities of men will declare themselves to be women and compete as women—but so far cisgender men have not en masse eschewed their masculinity to live as women for a few years so they can dominate the sports world as a female. Moreover, the trans women who have competed have, as a group, not dominated their sports.

Laurel Hubbard participated as a transgender Olympian, but her weight-lifting ability was bested by cisgender women: she did not medal. Trans woman Cece Tefler won the national championship 400-meter race, but she does not always win. Cortney Nelson, a cisgender competitor, beat Ms. Tefler in the 100 meters. Caster Semanya won the gold medal for the 800-meter 2016 Olympics, and also took first place the following year in the 2017 World Championships, but she came in third in the 400-meter. The athletes are not unbeatable. This fear that has ebbed and peaked over the decades is thus, objectively, not based in reality. On the other hand, making policy that denies participation based on fear is certain to cause real, non-theoretical, tangible harm to human beings born into vulnerable, confusing bodies.

## Cheating is Cheating

Does the possibility of someone exploiting the rule in a selfish and unfair way exist? It does. But it would be like any other kind of cheating. It is deplorable. But what is most important here? Ensuring that only the fully gendered, those whose gender characteristics all line up neatly in the same row, are the ones who play sports—or keeping sports open to all? Including persons who likely have had an extra hard childhood and adolescence?

What is *most* important? It was important to Dr. Richards, who had always been athletic and had a killer left-handed serve. She competed, she often won, but she did not always win. She retired. And women's tennis went on.

Most people who advocate for letting people define their gender, and letting competition be based on that gender, are fully mindful that there are people who through no fault of their own *do not* fit neatly into one gender category. Typically, they are not blind to the possibility of abuse and are able to see that false gender conversion would be possible and that this would be cheating.

Cheating is possible as has been the case in all sports at all times. Cheating is, and would be bad. But let's not pretend the possibility of cheating is somehow unique to transgender athletes. Sometimes it is caught, sometimes it is not. A scandal where professional soccer teams colluded with referees to win matches was uncovered in 2006, resulting in sanctions for several teams and a prior title being stripped from the Juventus Club and then being downgraded to last place along with an entire board of directors for the team resigning.

In terms of unfair hormonal advantages, cheating via taking peptide hormones like human growth hormone, or androgen enhancers, is apparently ubiquitous. Such doping was caught in the sport of bicycling where entire teams were disqualified for doping, winner after winner of the Tour de France has had their title revoked for cheating. Famous athletes have accused other famous athletes of doping, and then they themselves caught doing the same, having their own championship titles subsequently revoked as well (Floyd Landis and Lance Armstrong). Track has the Ben Johnson and Marion Jones cases. Alex Rodriguez and Ryan Braun in major league baseball. It is unclear why one manner of possible, theoretical cheating should be so emphasized. It would be neither more nor less abhorrent than other sorts of cheating. Do we have a distinct, set-aside abhorrence for transgender people?

Here, cheating would be a man who does not *really* feel like woman, and who has not experienced the confusion of being inherently transgender nor the bravery of making the public transition. Pretending so that he can win against women. It is not that this is thought to be impossible, indeed it is obviously something that could happen. What is believed: it is *exceedingly* unlikely that this will be a major problem. Accepting transgender athletes will not make this start happening. As evidence, it has not happened in the fifty years openly transgender athletes have been possible.

If women's basketball, track, swimming, volleyball, and soccer start to become uncompetitive for ciswomen in race after race, sport after sport; if sports-loving cisgender women do begin to sit on the bench in high schools and colleges and cease qualifying for the Olympics, then, and only then, will we have a problem that justifies banning people from sports participation. If the Venus Williams or Martina Navratilovas keep getting beat by newly interested-in-tennis young trans women year after year at Wimbledon—the defenders of Title IX promise to re-evaluate. History shows this is not likely to happen. In the meantime, let humans be humans.

## Why Do Some People Insist There Are Only Two Biological Sexes?

Because their education and information received have provided them evidence for this view and they cannot deny the information. Once clicks and shares of social media begin, the information streams divide and too often never meet again.

Evolutionary biologists are clear on what determines if an animal is a male animal or a female animal. Males produce sperm, females have eggs. If an animal has both, they are both sexes. It is also important to clearly state that for an overwhelming majority of humans and other animals, the egg versus sperm distinction matches with having XX versus XY chromosomes, predictable estrogen and testosterone ratios, and external genitalia (having a vagina versus a penis). Often, but certainly not always, this also predicts sexual behavior, preferences, and some aspects of behavior (interested readers may see Geary, 2021 for an authoritative overview).

Preferences and senses of maleness and femaleness are often considered to be the question of gender. Biologists are not ignorant of exceptions to the normal state of affairs, cases where all of these do not match, which could include congenital adrenal hyperplasia (1 in 10,000 births) or androgen insensitivity syndrome (1 in 20,000 births), or the very rare 5-alpha reductase deficiency. Some people have neither XX or XY chromosomes, women with Turner's syndrome have XXX (about 1 in 2000 births), a man with Klinefelter's may have XXY (about 1 in 1000 births). Sometimes a clear reason is not discernable.

## Bimodality

Exceptions to the norm, or gender variations, do not make the bimodality of biological sex a social construct. The topic is political, polarized, and information is channeled to persons based on their beliefs. Some people may believe that evolutionary biologists question whether a human can subjectively and strongly feel like a member of the sex that is not the one his or her genitals and society assign. In fact, evolutionary biologists would not dispute this, although there might be some dispute about how often this arises naturally. It is beyond dispute this happens.

In the 1970s, John Money published a case he oversaw where a boy child had his penis accidently destroyed as a baby, and believing that the feeling of male and female was socially constructed, the parents were instructed (by Dr. Money) to raise the child as a girl. The child rejected this. Consistently throughout childhood she behaved as a boy and indicated she wanted to be a boy. Upon becoming a teen, without knowing his history, David insisted he was male. The case is fascinating, and if a reader has not heard of it, the case of David Reimer is of great interest. David was given hormone therapy, told he was a girl from the time of infancy, given typical toys for girls, and required to dress like a girl. The doctor in charge falsely reported for years the gender assignment was going well. Psychology textbooks from the 1970s to 1990s taught that the part of gender that exists between the ears was socially assigned based on this case. A typical passage from a standard textbook read as follows,

> . . . Environmental influences determine an individual sex role identification and subsequent sexual behavior. In a now classic study, Money (1965) found that hermaphrodites could develop the normal identity and behavior expected of either sex, depending on how they were raised by their parents. This research strongly supports the notion that the environment, not genetics or hormones, is the determinant of sexual identity. . . . (Rimm & Somervill, 1976, p. 345).

It was not until 1997, when David Reimer told his story to Dr. Milton Diamond, that the truth became known. Clearly, it is *possible* for the brain to have a strong sense of its maleness or femaleness, and this can be independent of what society attempts to construct. Where does this come from? Although there are some commonly observed neural differences in male and female brains (corpus callosum, the sexually dimorphic nucleus within the hypothalamus) science lacks definitive answers. Yet, it plainly happens.

There are well-documented cases in which this happens without any botched circumcisions, yet in pretty much the same way: a child from early on steadfastly and subjectively *feels* like "a boy," even though they are in a girl's body and society says, "you are a girl." Or conversely, a child from early on steadfastly and subjectively feels like a girl even though they are in a boy's body and society says, "you are a boy."

A case that reads a bit like the experience of David Reimer is that of neurobiologist Dr. Ben Barres, born a female, as described by Deborah Rudacille in her classic book, *The Riddle of Gender*. As a child, Ben (born Barbara) never felt like a girl, and as an adult transitioned to a man through surgery and testosterone. Zero regrets about reassignment, he was nonetheless unequivocal that gender is bimodal, that there is something innate about feeling male versus female. "Otherwise why do they (transgender children) feel so strongly from the time they are born that there's something wrong? Why can't they just get used to the way they are? That doesn't come from the way society treated me, it comes from deep within," (Ben Barres, p. 29).

## The Nature of Hormones and Behavior

Hormones are chemicals that the body builds and then sends out into the bloodstream as a signal to another part of the body. During prenatal development, the relative amount of androgens begins to diverge as function of having (usually) the Y chromosome (but as above it doesn't always work, like with congenital adrenal hyperplasia). Prenatally is when males and females start to diverge. Level of testosterone can be assayed from a sample of urine, and there is a correlation between early testosterone levels (first six months of life) and play behavior at fourteen months. It is just as you might guess, for girls more testosterone predicted more play time with trains (compared to the old standby: dolls).

Scientists using animal research have gone so far as to randomly assign newborn rats to have extra masculinizing hormones or to be castrated (blocking the testosterone surge). Not only does this have a subtle influence on adeptness at later maze learning—but it actually impacts what the rats pay attention to once they grow up and explore the maze. Normally developing male rats and female rats given extra hormones like to look outside the maze, considering the distant edges and corners of the external room. Female rats—as well as males who are castrated at birth and who therefore never get that extra testosterone surge—were far more interested in a bolt that was within the maze itself. They did not seem to consider the external geometry of the room around them. How was this shown? By simply hiding the external room and observing what happened.

Males and extra-hormone females were lost, like they never had been in the maze before—while the typical females and the males who were castrated it was business as usual—as long as the bolt was there—they were fine. Same old maze. But if the external cues were obscured, the male rats (and the females who had masculinizing extra hormones given) were a mess; they didn't know where things were if they could not see the room around them. This is strong evidence that it is early hormones that shape the way brains think about space and navigating in their environment.

Biologists, based on all data and observation, know there is something *in the mind* that is sexually differentiated, and they respect it. A person's genitals, chromosomes, or sex cells sometimes conflict with their sense of gender: this can and does happen. Most knowledgeable people today think this is to be respected as a human right—to the extent that is reasonable and does not harm others. The extent of reasonableness is where any question lies.

## The Extent of Accommodations

There can be empathy, understanding, and respect for persons like the late men written about above (David Reimer died of suicide in 2004, and Ben Barres of pancreatic cancer in 2017), who lived the pain of growing up in bodies that did not match their internal identity. To many, this only underscores the reality of two basic sexes. To echo Dr. Barres, only if it comes from within can it stand up to a contra-message from parents, teachers, society, and one's own genitals.

I have never heard an evolutionary biologist nor a psychologist disagree: transsexuality is real and it is best to simply respect a person's feelings on this. But that would not suggest to a biologist that data documenting physical differences between men and woman should be discounted. The reality of people whose experience with gender transcends the usual dichotomy of sex doesn't require discounting biology when such issues matter. Use the bathroom you look like, present with, and prefer. Live with and marry who you want. But these are not the only issues: when it comes to sports competition, or things like where to go to prison, others' rights and safety may conflict with desire to accommodate.

To many evolutionary biologists, majority of the public, and a fair number of transsexuals, allowing persons born male, who experience the testosterone surge during adolescence and associated physical effects, to compete against persons for whom the male puberty changes did not occur is not reasonable. It undoes Title IX to the core, and represents an accommodation that impinges on others' rights.

A May 2021 Gallup survey shows that 62 percent of US citizens support transsexual persons competing on sports teams based on their biological sex versus playing on teams matching gender identity (34 percent). Senator Patsy Mink, the major sponsor of the bill that became Title IX, saw it become law in 1972. The legislation outlawed sex-based discrimination in sports. In 1994, Senator Carole Mosely Braun sponsored the requirement that colleges must disclose their progress on having more women participate in sports, as the goal of Title IX was to increase girls' and women's participation in sports. It has worked well. Participation of women in sports at all levels has improved and the number of elite women athletes in the Olympics has steadily increased since Title IX.

Schools, by federal law, are required to try and maintain nearly equal number of men and women participating in athletics. Why not just open football, basketball, and baseball to women and be done with it? Would that work? It's worth considering: Why do we have "Women's Sports" and why is Title IX important? It is odd that an advanced society includes educated persons that avoid acknowledging the biological fact that testosterone and the cascade of effects a Y chromosome results in that eventually makes the male body bigger, more muscular, with higher cardiac stroke volume, and stronger bones. Because basic information about biology seems so often left out of some arguments, there is a lot of misunderstanding. It suddenly seems like science is unknown.

## Physical Sex Differences

A reasoned discussion of how to define men and women's sports is tantamount to appreciating physiological differences. There is a great deal of data that speak to the question. There are thousands of research articles and hundreds of text books representing data collected in many labs, over many decades. For parsimony, the focus is limited to an overview of differences in heart function and one example of muscle development.

### Cardiac

Sex differences in cardiovascular function occur at rest, and during moderate, vigorous, and peak exercise. The gap between the sexes is not identical at the different levels of exertion. This has been directly measured. Many times. Women have less blood output from the heart compared to males, this is not only due to body size: the difference remains when body surface area is corrected. Women have lower systolic blood pressure and reduced artery pressure to the pumps. Vascular resistance (resistance to heart pump ejection of blood) is not different at rest, but when blood needs to get pumping (during hard exercise), men's arteries provide less resistance.

The fact that this difference is not always present, but emerges when exercise becomes vigorous, implies a sex differentiated interplay of blood pressure and cardiac output (the male response to exercise is different). Such information is not theoretical: it is empirical. Scientists and physiologists have done, and continue to do, things like insert venous catheter to measure arterial blood pressure, while measuring blood oxygen, sugar, catecholamines (adrenal gland hormones), and carbon dioxide. When measuring and trying to understand things like cardiac output resistance and actual output, differences in body size and many other variables are considered, and size is not the explanation. Nor is history of exercise. Nor is effort and percentage of peak watts.

Cardiac research has its own medical nomenclature. I am not an expert, so let me share a quote from actual experts when discussing their research on max oxygen uptake (max $VO_2$) and cardiac output (parentheses are insertions in place of jargon to help translate):

> We also made comparisons after correcting for differences in (exercise intensity) to determine if this was driving the differences observed. We found that the differences remained between males and females except that they were in the opposite direction, such that for a given (intensity level) females were demanding more, having a greater (cardiac output) and its components (stroke volume and heart rate), for a given (intensity) when compared to male participants. This elevated Q (cardiac output, heart rate and stroke volume) highlights a greater cardiac work needed to meet the same physical work demands. In an attempt to compensate for the specific reduced cardiac performance, these women (the 33 women who came into the lab for the research and were measured) increased (oxygen taking from the body) as evidenced by the higher (difference in the oxygen content of the blood between blood coming from versus going to the heart) when corrected for wattage." (see Wheatley and colleagues, p. 9).

Conclusions are generally that a physiologically based sex difference in stroke volume is a fundamental cause of sex differences in cardiac output during exercise.

The genes of biological men and women are obviously different: this includes transcription of genes for lungs, muscles, and heart. Some (not the majority) of the genes that relate to the parts of heart function that are expressed in a sexually divergent manner are found on the X or Y chromosome (in other words, are formally "sex-linked"). Male hearts are larger (even after controlling for body size, and this difference begins at puberty). Peak VO2 has different norms for men and women. It is unequivocally not a side effects of differences in body size. If this were the case, the norm tables would not be separated for men and women, but instead would be normed for different body sizes (see Inanloo, 2017 for recent genetic data or an overview of the overall data on cardiovascular sex differences).

A twenty-year-old man in excellent health will have a VO2 of sixty-two or greater, a level that would be off the charts for women. Per standard norms, a *forty-year-old man* in excellent health would have a VO2 max greater than fifty-one, which is the level of a woman in excellent health *at age twenty*. The difference in peak VO2 is relatively small during childhood and early teens; the gap really begins in adolescence, when male and female bodies diverge.

## Muscles

The protein that forms the basis for muscle fibers to contract is called myosin. Myosin features two heavy chain heads connected to a neck region and tail and plays the key role in muscle contractions of skeletal muscles. About forty genes direct the shaping of such myosin. Eleven of these genes code more specifically for the amino sequences that result in slight differences in heavy chains of myosin, and each muscle fiber can be classified based on the exact amino acids.

In humans, four genes are predominant in establishing the coding of skeletal muscles' heavy chain building—which are then further classified. Type I refers to smaller fibers with more oxidative capacity. Type II, which comes in subtypes, are larger with more enzymes for rapid glucose usage. At birth, Type I tends to be larger and there are no or few sex differences in muscle fibers. This changes at puberty, and after puberty, the fibers types tend to become larger in males, and muscle biopsies have quantified the differences for decades. For example, in 1989 Doctors Jean Simoneae and Claude Bouchard biopsied 418 thigh muscles of men and women, some physically active and some not. Both men and women showed a lot of variation across individuals, but there were very clear sex differences.

The average cross-sectional areas of both Type I and Type II muscle fibers were significantly larger for men, with the biggest difference in the Type II: the average cross section area of Type IIB fibers was 2800 $\mu^2$ in women and 4400 $\mu^2$ in men. Men had significantly more Type II fibers, and women had significantly greater proportion of Type I fibers. This leads to observable differences in performances. Recovery is quicker in women after strong exercise, but men have greater force generation. The force generation difference is due to the predominance of larger Type II fiber types.

Myriad testosterone and estrogen effects, with consideration of estrogen receptor subtypes and aromatization of testosterone, have been studied in humans and other mammals. Although beyond the scope of this chapter, it must be stated that hormonal changes of puberty, ultimately guided by the genetic code, are the root causes of these sex differences. This is biological reality.

## Sports Must Be Separated

This is of course why there are men's and women's basketball teams: so that both men and women can enjoy the sport and gain the benefits of participating. It is why no matter how much a little girl loves hockey and how great she is and how many hours she spends playing after about age fifteen, the girls will no longer be able compete with boys who practice less and who have less innate talent. Men can slap the puck harder, hit harder, and skate faster and longer: look at the peak VO2 charts (the volume of oxygen a body can consume in a minute is an index of fitness and endurance).

Ask the top men and women gold medalists to race across the ice at full speed then to slap shot a puck from across the ice: the cardiac output, rapid use of glucose, lung capacity, and upper body strength muscle fibers are not negated by willpower or talent. This is why, so far, no women have played in the National Hockey League. We have come close. Kendall Schofield, Olympics gold medalist, competed in the 2019 fastest skater event in the NHL. Someday it may happen. But it hasn't happened yet, and I assert that it is *not* because no girls love hockey, or that they lack talent. Instead, the best women athletes lack the long femurs, the upper body strength, and the cardiac output of the best men hockey players.

It is not all unfair: women have less risk for early heart disease for most of their lives, and their immune system is better. She will be more likely to survive cancer or the flu, but he is bigger and can increase heart and lung output and skate faster. It is probably insulting to imply women aren't in the

NHL, not because of these differences, but because they don't practice as much and aren't as competitive. Denying physical differences is what is not fair and sexist. To explain the difference in performance without admitting differences in athleticism requires insinuation she isn't trying hard enough. Gross. In spite of all the data that exists documenting physical sex differences, besides observations and experience.

Men's high school basketball is faster, with higher jumps than women's. People who state that a person has no inherent advantage based on their biological sex, or by having a body that experienced puberty as a male, are not only denying data, it could be dangerous if taken too seriously. A couple of talented, competitive, post-puberty male bodies inhabited by transgender women would dominate a women's hockey team, and be a danger to cis-women athletes on the ice.

## Sticks and Stones

Even professional athletes, who presumably know competitive sports—even those who have relentlessly championed for LGBTQ rights—cannot acknowledge sex differences in athletic ability making competition unfair without being branded transphobic. Trans woman Caitlyn Jenner was asked and gave her view from the vantage of a trans woman and gold-winning Olympian (running as Bruce Jenner years before transitioning). Caitlyn: "This is a question of fairness. It just isn't fair. And we have to protect girls' sports in our schools." Incredibly, this triggered responses like, "Caitlyn Jenner is no friend of the LGBTQ community. Don't call her an [activist]. She's a menace." And another, "Caitlyn Jenner is classically uninformed, wildly privileged, and tragically self-hating," (see for example Gajewski as discussed in eonline.com). Martina Navratilova is considered to be one of world's all-time best tennis players; she holds the standing record of winning Wimbledon nine times in a row. She worked for years for gay and trans rights which included coming out as lesbian in the 1980s (when it was still taboo). She has received the National Equality Award from the largest LGBTQ advocacy group in the USA. And yet Martina does not support trans women competing in women's sports. She wrote a thoughtful, lengthy article expressing her views. For this, and her overall opinion, she has been called the insulting term transphobic and her long history as an advocate and friend of LGBTQ? All cancelled. However, and most importantly, her evidence, the data, and her reasoning are not addressed.

Cardiac output, muscle fiber type, bone length cannot be made to be irrelevant, not even when one experiences the earnest need to present and live as a gender different than the sex they were born as. The data, the science, and the real world still remain: biological sex still matters.

Like the old parable of blind people touching different parts of an unknown object, the partial experiences and differing views only make sense when one can see the whole elephant. One blind person feels a leg: the object is hard pillar. To another, it is a small, pliable, rope-like thing (the tail). To others, the thing is a large unmovable wall. It is an elephant, experienced differently by narrowed exposure. The tragedy for society is that everyone has partial information. Getting information curated for us via social media algorithms is like a permanent blindfold, obscuring the full elephant.

# CHAPTER TEN

# Moon Landing Conspiracy

How can an adult human, with the entirety of scientific information available via the magic glass box in their pocket, believe the moon landing was a hoax? As with most opinions that people have, they are aware of and exposed to information that supports their view. Try considering you, or they, might have been exposed to some enticing but misleading or partial information. When this happens in tandem with a lack of information that fairly explains the other side, the table is set.

This chapter is chosen because it was fun to write, and because it is a great illustration for the overall effect. I would be willing to bet that none out of ten scientists could give a fair accounting of the best arguments for moon landing as a hoax. They are disgusted with, or at least have no tolerance for, polite engagement with those who believe it. That's a shame. People make their opinions about conspiracy theories based on a balance of interest and willingness to question mainstream views. Like everything else, opinions about conspiracies are ultimately largely based on the information and experiences people have.

## Yes, We Landed on the Moon

There is ample information to support a human moon landing.

The idea that the Apollo moon landings were a fraud was instigated by the writings of a single person in the 1970s. The late Bill Kaysing had his own problems. He was an avowed non-conformist with some gentle luddite tendencies. After serving in the Navy and earning a BA (in English, not related to science or technical fields), he worked as a senior level technical writer for Rocketdyne from 1956–1963. He was never an engineer for the company that made the lunar exploration engines, as is sometimes reported. Then he left his job, sold the family TV, cancelled newspaper subscriptions, and eventually left his home to become a nomad. He lived on odd jobs and began working on his book, *We Never Went to the Moon: America's Thirty Billion Dollar Swindle*, self-published in 1976. In his book, he referred to his years at Rocketdyne as having been exposed to inside information—the fact that he left six years before the first manned moonwalk did not seem to matter. The appeal of a good conspiracy is strong and there are always new adherents well prepared for the excitement of a good mystery and to feel privy to inside information. Within the original book, he described (p. 7) how his belief in the hoax arose many years after the landings, as if from a mysterious, near other-worldly hunch.

> From whence did this odd idea come, I wondered. I had not really given the Apollo program much thought in the years since leaving Rocketdyne. I had followed it in a cursory fashion, becoming aware of it only through the more startling developments: the fire on Pad 34, for example. So it is possible that I had simply lost interest in astronautics despite the prospect of a moon landing. But I didn't think so; there was more to it than mere diminishment of interest. Somehow, I seemed to have perceived that the Apollo project has become a gigantic hoax and that nobody was leaving Earth for the Moon, certainly not in July of 1969. Call it a hunch, an intuition; information from some little understood and mysterious channel of communication . . . a metaphysical message. While tenuous and ephemeral at its source, it was strong and vivid in its form. In short, a true conviction.

Mr. Kaysing may have been a deep thinker, brilliant in his own way, and philosophical—yet truly—this is archetypal opposite-science. His thinking that launched a conspiracy on the Apollo missions seems to have, as he himself described it, been a conviction that did not arise from cool headed empirical observations while working at Rocketdyne. No, it originated years later as a feeling, that over time became unshakable. This matters because it adds to the argument his views were, from the beginning, delusional.

Today, believing the manned moon landings did not occur is increasing in tandem with increased reliance on social media for information. Historian Roger Launius, and former Chair of the Division of Space History at the Smithsonian National Air and Space Museum, has written about the history of the moon landing conspiracy. As the landings were happening, less than 5 percent of the population reported doubt that the landings had really happened. When Launius wrote in 2010, he concluded that doubt was beginning to grow, especially among persons under twenty-five. A survey in 2019 found that 10 percent of Americans "don't believe in the moon landing."

All the anomalies that Mr. Kaysing wrote about and that have been modified over the years can truly appear to be evidence the landing was faked. Yet all have either good, or at least reasonable, explanations. Let's begin with that. The photographs have objects with shadows that are not the same length, are not completely parallel, or that have more than one shadow. All of these could be indicative of either a close-by light source (closer than the sun) or multiple light sources. These effects can also be caused by a reflective surface that is not flat. The moon is not flat, every meteor that has hit it has left a crater that has never eroded. The non-uniformity of the moon is visible with a naked eye, and clear via telescopes. Different sizes of shadows and non-parallel looking shadows will appear in snow drift scenes as well.

Moreover, in an effort to definitively determine whether or not this is a possible explanation, in 2008 a set was constructed with reflective sand representing moon dust. The reflective sand and uneven terrain indeed created shadows of different lengths, shadows that appeared non-parallel, and there were semi illuminated areas that were in shadows of large objects. Thanks to MythBusters, August 27, 2008, all the best anomalies that suggest the landing was faked, were explained, recreated, and made available to the public. Thus, besides that fact that experts say the shadows and lighting do not prove the footage was faked, there is modern film (via a 2008 TV show) literally showing the effects being recreated due to light-colored reflective dust and sand, and a single light source. Finally, if one goes out in snow drifts, similar effects are observable in the first person (like if person A's shadow falls on an oddly shaped drift, and person B's falls on flat surface).

A camera shot may not pick up the slight unevenness from drifting snow, yet it causes distortions in shadows. In late afternoon, the low sun deflecting off a vertical side of a snow-white drift can itself cause a secondary shadow. Indeed, the sun shining on the reflective moon can illuminate objects two hundred thousand miles away. Have you never seen a moon shadow? The shadows are interesting and they may cause legitimate questions, but are truly explainable.

There is/has been concern that there are no stars in the sky in any of the photos, but stars would be visible. There is no dispute that stars would be visible to anyone standing on the moon, at any time, because the sky would always be dark even in the day due to the lack of atmosphere. But ask any old school photographer about this. If the foreground is bright, a photograph set to have the bright foreground in focus, will not pick up the comparatively very faint pinpoints of light in the far distance.

Cameras have settings for letting light in, and the "shutter speed" will take light for a brief time for bright objects, or a longer time for dim objects. The setting to collect the distant light would be different, and if used the bright objects in the foreground would be washed out blurry. Put a flashlight on the floor and turn it on, shining right at an apple or something. Put another flashlight in a shoe box with a little pin prick, and put this a few feet behind the flashlight and apple. Turn out the lights in a windowless room. You can switch your eyes back and forth to see both. Try to get a photo that shows both clearly. It's hard. Add movement to the illuminated object and film it. Human eyes adjust automatically, pupil constriction is fast and retuning is a bit slower. But the point is that the lack of stars in the photos of the bright moon surface is expected and normal. Furthermore, if the set was constructed and filmed to pass off as a fake landing, it is not believable that none of the rocket scientists and designers would be aware or remember the sky would have visible stars. It would be trivially easy. If stars should have been in actual moon pictures by the laws of physics, they would have been put on the constructed set too.

The Van Allen Radiation Belt is an area of high radiation that surrounds the Earth, caused by the magnetic field of the planet. There are some things that are not in dispute: it is highly dangerous and passing through it could easily cause lethal radiation poisoning. Deniers of the moon landing correctly point out that humans have not been beyond the belts in fifty years, and that the discoverer of the belts had originally expressed that technology in the 1960s would not allow safe crossing due to the high radiation.

There is an inner and an outer area of the radiation: the inner area starts at around 500 miles and extends to about 8,000 miles from the Earth's surface. The heights of the belts vary as a function of where one is on Earth, the size is smaller at the poles, and larger at the equator. There is a break between the two areas, and the outer radiation belt begins at about 10,000 miles and ends around 25,000 miles out. For perspective, the diameter of the Earth is about 8,000 miles.

The levels of radiation at different heights are not identical, and the radiation varies such that at the poles, it is possible to leave the earth's atmosphere with insignificant exposure to the radiation. However, this angle would have made achieving lunar orbit very difficult. Thank goodness they had actual rocket scientists working out how to do this. The path taken was calculated and the path is available to anyone truly interested, along with pictures and calculations. After illustrations and explanations, astrophysicist Dr. Margarita Safonova writes for the independent news source *The Wire* in 2019 that the Apollo 11 travelled across "the inner zone of the outer belt in about 30 minutes and through the most energetic region in about 10 minutes. On its way back, its trajectory was optimized such that Apollo 11 would steer clear of the belts as much as possible. It approached Earth from the south and was travelling at an even greater inclination and velocity than it had been on its way to the Moon. The astronauts were inside the fringes of the radiation belts for only about 60 minutes."

The net damage from radiation exposure is a function of the intensity of the radiation and time length of exposure. In sum, the exposure did not add up to a lethal dose of radiation. The discoverer of the radiation belts, James Van Allen, lived about two hours south of me, in Mt. Pleasant, Iowa until he died in 2006. A moon hoax documentary categorically stated it would not be possible for living astronauts to cross the Van Allen Radiation Belts, and Dr. Van Allen had reportedly referred to the documentary as an "entertaining assemblage of nonsense" and said that "the claim that radiation exposure during the Apollo missions would have been fatal to the astronauts is only one example of such nonsense."

In 2004, Dr. Van Allen was asked by engineer and Clavius.org web page creator Jay Windley to verify the quote attributed to him. Dr. Van Allen agreed it was accurate and correct in 2004, two years before he died, and signed a letter to that effect. Van Allen's handwritten verification of the quote can be found online, and Mr. Windley has the original. According to Windley, Dr. Van Allen was contacted because Windley (who created and monitored a moon hoax debunking website) was curious if the quote was accurate, and felt it was important enough to verify (personal communication, May 9, 2022). Apparently, Dr. Van Allen thought so too. This was his view of the question of radiation, the rocket path, and the protections against radiation that were employed. The authenticity of the quote, and signature, appears clear.

If interested persons are relying on their smart phones, they have not yet been privy to the totality of the information available. A person who initially and casually becomes interested in the anomalies and the early quotes about radiation might read, like, or share a couple of articles they found of interest. Then, conspiracy articles du jour and moon hoax quotes of confirmatory nature may begin to be served right up whenever they check their social media device.

The rocks are fakes, says their feed, with convincing evidence. Indeed, it is true that *one rock* was found to be a fake. This does not mean that they are *all* fake or that there was no moon landing. If a Rembrandt painting is discovered to be faked, it does not mean Rembrandt did not paint. The rock was in storage for years, then changed hands. Why not assume that at some point, someone stole the "real" rock and replaced with an obvious fake. Or perhaps the story of how the moon rock was acquired was never true in the first place. A rock that was purported to be a moon rock, is not. It is a fake. That is all.

Legitimate moon rocks are composed of minerals that are not common on the Earth (e.g., ilmenite, or anorthite), and lack the minerals that are very common on Earth. Moon rocks do not have large amounts of quartz or mica for example. Unlike getting to the moon, determining if a rock is from earth versus the moon is *not* rocket science. There are plenty of known moon rocks. They are documented and described in methodical, minute detail. An example the detailed cataloguing by NASA for the lunar rocks is in the references. Individual rocks have pages of information about what mineral content is in what millimeter part, different polarized photos of slices, information of the techniques of estimating the age and history of the rocks, information of the stages of processing of the rocks, and the fifty or so references (the names of the dozens of the scientists) who did the work necessary for the quantifying and classification, that is reported within the cataloguing—of each rock.

Besides debunking the landing was an elaborate hoax, there is also some hard evidence it did occur and could not have been faked. First, there would be too many people involved to keep them all quiet and NASA could not pressure so many physicists, who can calculate the formulas and understand rocket physics, to say it was possible if they knew it was not. The point is the level of conspiracy is too great. NASA estimates four hundred thousand persons were involved in one way or another to achieve the Apollo missions. Admittedly, not all of these people would have to be "in on it." But who would? All twelve moon landing astronauts, obviously. Maybe some of their closest colleagues or family.

If the Van Allen Belts are uncrossable, that is a few hundred scientists who well know it and have been convinced (like Van Allen himself) to lie about it. A few dozen master minds and controllers, both at NASA and the White House presumably. If the footage and signals that the NASA employees were monitoring during the missions was faked, then a dozen or so additional engineers were to intercept, design, and feed fake data through the wires simultaneously. If not, then a several dozen more of the NASA employees were in on it, lying about incoming data they were not really seeing. If the footage and pictures were all faked by design, this would involve cinematographers, and set builders and designers. At least a few dozen geologists would need to deny their education and integrity to lie about all the fake rocks. The point here is that whether it was a hundred or a thousand: it is too many to keep quiet. Someone would talk and bring evidence.

In addition to the rocks and pictures and data brought back from the moon, somethings were left behind. Most notable is the laser reflector array. Designed to allow precise measures of the moon distance and location, a laser from Earth is sent out and hits the array, which is basically a two-foot square set of mirrors. It bounces back, and the time to get back is used to calculate distance. It is exact, and it has told scientists that the moon is getting farther from the earth. About four centimeters per year. The array is still used today. According to NASA's website,

> University of Maryland physics professor Carroll Alley was the project's principal investigator during the Apollo years, and he follows its progress today. "Using these mirrors," explains Alley, "we can 'ping' the moon with laser pulses and measure the Earth-moon distance very precisely. This is a wonderful way to learn about the moon's orbit and to test theories of gravity.". . . A key observing site is the McDonald Observatory in Texas where a 0.7 meter telescope regularly pings reflectors in the Sea of Tranquility (Apollo 11), at Fra Mauro (Apollo 14) and Hadley Rille (Apollo 15). . . .

Add the late Dr. Alley (1927–2016) to the long list of people who would have to know and who have been compelled to keep quiet, to keep up the charade.

What about advances in photography and the subsequent lunar missions that have been unmanned? As expected, they have photographed the moon and produced new evidence. The completely unnatural looking disturbed-dust paths left from the footsteps, the lunar rover tracks, as well as the landing sites are clearly visible. The Lunar Reconnaissance Orbiter has taken exquisite photographs, published in 2011. As Noah Petro explains and illustrates in a NASA video available via YouTube, the high resolution is jaw dropping. It was achieved because a new generation of scientists calculated a possible adjustment to the Lunar Orbiter's path. By making it oval-shaped without changing the overall average height, it was able to get closer to the surface, as explained Dr. John Keller, of Lunar Rover Team. Rocket science. Astro Physics. Chemistry. And one might consider that this new generation of scientists, with their own new insights and original ideas, Petro and Keller and others, presumably grew up dreaming of rockets and astronauts. They went to college, then graduate school, and have become the new generation of bona fide NASA rocket scientists.

This new group is now designing and monitoring the spacecraft and photos. They would have to be enticed to go along with the hoax as well. Or perhaps they were pre-selected from an early age and brainwashed. Maybe the NASA rocket scientists with doctorates in astrophysics are too ignorant to see the façade and are actually unwitting fools. But which of these is most likely? Occam's Razor is the principle that when deciding on the best explanation for observations, it is best to shave away dubious scenarios that require many outlandish and bizarre conjectures. It says we must have gone to the moon. The publishers of the chemistry and calculators of the formulas and engineers of the new rockets, they all have access to the data, and have shared it. They are not dupable. They'd have to be lying en masse, in on "it." It just doesn't make sense.

## Moon Landing Never Happened

Evidence it did not happen can be found online, and good questions about the existing evidence against actual manned lunar landings have been provided.

Some of the photographs are *really* odd. The moon has no atmosphere, no air, and thus no wind or air movement. Besides the apparent flag fluttering that appears to be moving in the wind, when an Apollo 15 astronaut hopped by, the flag appears to react without being touched. This movement without touch would be impossible in a vacuum, without air. There is a clip that shows this (for example, representative YouTube share was posted by AstroClownBuster). To explain this, it has to be supposed that something the camera did not pick up, physically hit the flag at the precise same instant the astronaut went by causing it to react as if the movement of air had caused it. To many this appears a leap of faith. "If a guy hops by a flag and the flag waves in the breeze created, is that fake footage?" asks someone who has been served the clip with commentary to confirm the idea the moon landing was faked. Expert physicist says confidently: "Yes, there is no breeze behind you when you walk by if there is no air . . ."

An exchange very much like this occurs with Joe Rogan and Neil deGrasse Tyson at about the twenty-two-minute mark of episode 310, and footage showing this exact thing at about the twenty-four-minute mark. Because it will be effortful and many readers will not take the effort: this is past the residual moving from when flag was planted, the flag is perfectly still, then an astronaut hops by, and then the flag moves. After some back and forth, the explanation comes down to three possibilities: 1. The film clip was faked or got mixed up with the real footage, but the landing still occurred. 2. The astronaut kicked up some matter that somehow hit the flag. 3. The moon landing was faked. The point is: It looks weird, and the weirdness lacks a straightforward explanation. An astrophysicist of excellent reputation admitted that if such a thing were filmed, it indicates fakery. Why is it preposterous that if a person sees this on their social media feed a few times, presented the right way, and are then provided a cohesive conspiratorial explanation, that they could reasonably consider the possibility?

There are other pictures that are really questionable. The dust from the golf club hitting the ball appears to fall faster than the astronaut's feet descend when they hop (not possible, with no air resistance everything falls at same rate). The shadows in some pictures have not been explained, and it isn't just a question of some angles being slightly off: There are pictures that show shadow angles of multiple objects on one side of a picture as nearly 90 degrees different from an object on the other side of the photograph. That's not explainable by a hill or undulation of the landscape. If the light source is far away, like the sun, the shadows are parallel. That fact is not in dispute.

You can place two cans in sunlight about two feet apart. It doesn't matter where they are placed, the shadow is exactly the same direction. The shadows are always parallel. If you turn your phone flashlight on to cast a shadow in darkened room, they are not parallel shadows, and the shadow direction changes if the object is moved. It is because the angle from a close light source is different for different objects so the shadows are not parallel. When shadows are not parallel, the light is not from the sun, only a much closer light source can cause shadows to diverge.

There are multiple variations of photos like that of the figure below. But the point to emphasize is that some people see these pictures, and others are not aware of them. If one starts clicking on moon fake landing links: one will soon be served photos like this with expert commentary. It's not that one photo shows some lack of parallelness, but that multiple objects in various pictures show the different shadow alignment in one area of the photo from another area. The debunking websites do not address the photographs that are considered to be the best evidence and most difficult to explain away; this makes it easy to keep believing the "conspiracy."

Apollo 14 photo courtesy of Flickr public domain images, with arrows added to recreate typical images depicting the shadow controversy.

Here are a few other things that any respectable moon landing doubter will have been made keenly aware of via their media streams. A museum moon rock that was gifted by Neil Armstrong, Michael Collins, and Buzz Aldrin to the ambassador of the Netherlands in 1969, was tested and found (beyond any doubt) to be Earth's own petrified wood. Moreover, it is an incredible fact that just fifty years after the Apollo missions, hundreds of the valuable moon rocks have been "lost or stolen" and remain unaccounted for. Does this not support conspiratorial thoughts? The head of NASA Marshall Space Flight Center, Wernher von Braun, along with other NASA insiders, went to the only area of the world where meteorites from the moon are likely to be reliably found in 1967— and came back with hundreds of pounds of meteorites. In 1967. That can seem a strange coincidence to persons who have already started to wonder, and then find this fact conveniently popping in their media feeds.

It might be a coincidence, but it is a coincidence that makes protestations that no reasonable person could entertain the conspiracy a bit hollow. How about this: All original recordings of the original moon landing have been lost. NASA, who was able to orchestrate safe travel though twenty thousand miles of radiation, land two hundred thousand miles away, take off and come back safely seven times, was *not* able to keep track of the recording. Although there is no actual explanation, NASA has written, "In early 2005, responding to inquiries from NASA retirees and others, NASA began a search for the 14-track data tapes. Ultimately, the agency couldn't find the tapes and determined that they had most likely been erased and used again . . ."

The Wikipedia article on the topic begins, "The Apollo 11 missing tapes were those that were recorded from Apollo 11's slow scan television telecast in its raw format on telemetry data tape at the time of the first moon landing in 1969 and subsequently lost. The data tapes were used to record all transmitted data (video as well as telemetry) for backup." The saga of the lost footage is detailed in various sources (O'Neal, 2009). It is at least possible to imagine how this information could be presented and how it would seem to a person who is already wondering if the moon landings might have been faked when this news is proclaimed across their YouTube feed.

Perhaps the biggest support available for the conspiracy is the undeniable reality that all the six Apollo landings were between 1969 and 1972, by the United States. No other country has sent a human outside of Earth's orbit, and the USA only did so during these four years. The moon skeptic websites of today point out not only that the Van Allen Belt is dangerous to traverse, but that once past it there is little protection from the Sun's radiation. The earth's magnetic field shields the atmosphere and protects life from radiation. This is the kind of information some people are seeing on their news and media feeds:

> What protects the Earth from the sun's cosmic radiation are the Van Allen Belts, named for the scientist who discovered them, James Van Allen. The Van Allen Belts surround the Earth, trapping the cosmic radiation from the sun, so that the radiation doesn't strike the Earth, as one of the phenomena that enable life on Earth to exist. The Van Allen Belts also enable low-Earth orbit, such as that by the numerous satellites in space, like the International Space Station. In order to reach the moon, you must go past the Van Allen Belts, and then traverse at least an additional thousands of miles before reaching the moon. Once you go past the Van Allen Belts, the spaceship, astronauts, and equipment such as video cameras, all become exposed and vulnerable to the sun's destructive cosmic radiation. It is border-line impossible to protect the ship from the sun's cosmic radiation after going beyond the Van Allen belts; certainly, the spaceships used for all the moon landings were not

designed to withstand that kind of heavy radiation. To protect the spaceship, and the astronauts and equipment inside, the spaceship would need to be covered by something like a lead-coating shield; doing this, however, would make the spaceship far too heavy to get off the ground, let alone all the way to the moon." Suspiciously, up until 1968, NASA, and the scientific community at large, sincerely believed in the radiation dangers, such as those pointed out by James Van Allen. (Chandrasekaran, writing for the Liberty Forecast Blog.)

Moon conspirators are constantly reminded that no humans have been able to go above five hundred or six hundred miles from the earth's surface in fifty years. But fifty years ago, they went two hundred fifty thousand miles, landed, and came back again. Six times. Then never again.

One final thing that seems suspicious are the comments and behavior of some key humans. The astronauts seem scripted and tense in the past moon walk press conference. They all retired and avoided public life. Neil Armstrong, the first man on the moon, never gave an interview and made only two public appearances the rest of his life, and always had a reason to avoid any the moon landing anniversaries. There are websites (with links to videos thereof) showing Astronaut Terry Virts talking about the possibility of flying outside of near-Earth orbit. Most people who are interested or open to the moon landing being faked have seen him state, "now we can only fly in Earth's orbit, that's as far as we can go." This sounds like the state of the space program in the early and mid-sixties. As written by Dr. Elizabeth Howell in 2014 for space.com:

"I'd really like to fly Orion to the moon," Virts said to Space.com in a September interview. Orion will undergo its first uncrewed test flight on Dec. 4 when it rockets 3,600 miles (5,800 km) above Earth before coming in for a high-speed re-entry. Crewed missions are expected to follow in the 2020s.

In an interview posted by NASA with International Space Station Crew astronauts Terry Virts and Samantha Cristoforetti, this quote is heard at the sixteen-minute mark.

The plan that NASA has is to build a rocket called SLS (Space Launch System) which is a heavy-lift rocket, it is something that is much bigger than what we have today, and it will be able to launch the Orion capsule with humans on board as well as landers or other components to destinations beyond earth orbit. Right now, we can only fly in Earth orbit, that is the farthest that we can go. This new system that we are building is going to allow us to go beyond and hopefully take humans into the solar system to explore, so the Moon, Mars, asteroids, there are a lot of destinations that we could go to and we're building these building block components in order to allow us to do that eventually.

As a whole, moon landing skeptics receive open derision from the scientific community, and the lack of understanding about the extent of the information the doubters receive breeds contempt. Writing this chapter was eye-opening. Moreover, even though it did not change my mind, it became easier for me to sympathize, to fathom what seemed previously unfathomable. I do not imagine I am unique. As a check, I asked another academic to read the chapter portion explaining the skeptic viewpoint, and a college student as well. Guess what? They were taken aback, and a bit doubtful for a minute that a human moon landing really occurred. Until they read the rest of the chapter.

I mention this because it is important: it is not only fools that entertain "conspiracies," And not all smart people get the same information. In fact, there is no shared information. Information today mostly does not overlap. If you tell me you watch Tucker Carlson, I can guess the information that comes to your feeds, and guess what information you do not have (and it is featured in the next chapter). If you tell me that Rachel Maddow is your favorite source of news, I probably have a good idea of which information you do not have (and it too is in the next chapter).

A truism that bears repeating: you do not know what you don't know. And today, when we get most of our news from a screen's curated gateway, it is standard to only get one side of any debate. This not only makes people think the lunar landings were a hoax, but prevents clear and thoughtful communication about BLM, elections, what children are, and are not, learning in various school systems: information *needed* for debates and for democracy to work.

It is not just others that don't know the information you know. You don't know what they know either.

# CHAPTER ELEVEN

# Election Fraud 2020

*There is a possibility that the 2020 presidential election was a massive fraud, stolen from then-president Donald Trump. There is a possibility that Mr. Trump actually received fewer votes, and that Mr. Biden was the legitimate winner, with Trump seeking to steal the election from President Joe Biden. Both would be serious assaults to our democracy. Both sides claim evidence, and the typical person is largely ignorant of the other side's evidence and viewpoint.*

The election and recounts have long ended, yet President Trump still asserts election fraud occurred and that he is the real winner of the 2020 election. Specifically, he maintains that there was massive fraud and if the votes had been properly and legally counted, he had more votes than Biden in Pennsylvania, Wisconsin, Georgia, and Michigan. Given the dynamics of personalized news and selective reading and viewing, there is important information that a segment of the population probably remains unaware of, in spite of being engaged and reading or viewing a lot of news. Clear and trusted just-the-facts information has been superseded by flexible and ever-confirming algorithms.

## Why People Believe Biden Was the Legitimate Winner

People are receiving and digesting their own personalized streams of curated news information.

After the election results were reported in November of 2020, the then-president and his chosen legal team were stating there was unequivocal evidence that Dominion voting machines had changed votes. Evidence?

"We have mathematical evidence in a number of states of massive quantities of Trump votes being trashed (via computers) and Biden votes being injected." said Trump attorney Sidney Powell on November 19, 2020 (see Rev Transcript Library). The math would prove it. The affidavits and experts would prove it. As one of the attorneys said, they were not proving it that day at the press conference for the unfair media, it was just a summary of the facts they would prove in court, in front of an impartial judge who had taken an oath to be unbiased. Were they right?

## The Thoroughness of the MITRE Report

The math has subsequently been checked. When (some) people encounter within their curated newsfeeds that such allegations have been well investigated and debunked, it refers to analyses like the one carried out by the non-profit MITRE Corporation. The report on data analytics of the 2020 election was published in February of 2021. MITRE used a team of seven experts with experience and advanced degrees in engineering, law, and information security to analyze the data, using math, and publish the lengthy, well-referenced report using the publicly reported vote tallies (the same ones that Trump's attorneys say are frauds). The report considers allegations that Dominion voting results might be fraudulent.

While a short summary cannot do the forty-page document justice, the math relies on county by county, and precinct by precinct, comparisons of the percent of voters who voted (a.k.a. the turnout) to the percent difference in the result for the declared winner versus the loser (a.k.a. Biden's lead). Overall, there should be something like a normal distribution, and outlier results can be further investigated. The basic idea is as that if a county or a precinct switched a lot of votes, or added votes to benefit a candidate, then the results of the location will be oddly in favor of the candidate, compared to other precincts or counties.

This approach is called a fingerprint analysis, and there is a fair amount of expertise and history on this. It easily detects fraud in elections that are fraudulent (Russia in 2012 deviates from the expected very clearly). Essentially, precinct by precinct, it compares expected to actual. To cut to the crux of the matter, in Georgia, the methods ruled out all but six counties immediately, as the results were in near perfect keeping with past history of the voting and the current overall state and national results. Six counties warranted further study: Cobb, Douglas, Fayette, Forsyth, Henry, and

Rockdale because they all showed a bigger than expected jump in percent for the Democratic candidate.

Thus, as experts do, they looked further to determine what had happened, if there was an explanation. Each of the counties had been leaning increasingly Democrat going back to 2004. Demographics change, and some areas become "bluer" and some start to become more conservative. The MITRE report is an extensive document and goes into considerable details, but using the data they amass, and the trends in the election results going back to 2012 are depicted in the figure below.

The 2020 increase in these counties towards the Democratic candidate is in keeping with the long-term trends for these counties. If Dominion machines were switching votes for these counties, they apparently began back in 2012, and kept it up in 2016. With the exact same increase again in 2020. That would be pretty unlikely. But it is actually impossible because Dominion voting machines were *not used* in 2012, or 2016. This is what is meant by "no evidence Dominion switched votes." It is straightforward to check whether expected increases are in line or out of line (there is literally a line plot that shows it). Any spots that look like outliers can be checked more closely for explanation: nothing suggests fraud, and if fraud had happened, it would show up.

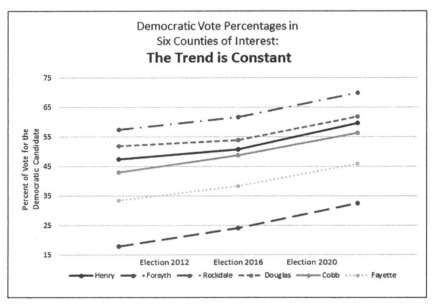

Courtesy of Catherine DeSoto, PhD. Chart created based on data available from MITRE Report.

What about all the addresses with extra ballots mailed to them? They have been investigated: there are charts that show the locations that had more than ten votes delivered. They are RV parks, colleges, various group living environments. No counties show an unusual or unexplainable number of mail-in ballot returns based on years past or current surrounding areas. What about the states that have a mix of Dominion voting machines and other machines, like Wisconsin and Michigan? One can compare the results tabulated by the accused Dominion machines to those by non-Dominion machines. Why hasn't anyone done this to prove the subtracting of Trump votes and addition of hundreds of thousands of Biden votes? They have.

People have compared "Dominion and non-Dominion counties to see if there was any indication of widespread vote manipulation by Dominion in those states. Michigan and Wisconsin had a statistically significant greater increase in Democratic support in counties that did *not* use Dominion machines. In Arizona, only one county (Maricopa) used Dominion machines, but its increase in Democratic support was similar to the increases in some non-Dominion counties."

That quote is found in the MITRE Report, page 19, along with charts and more data, more specifics. If Dominion cheated, they made the counties where their voting machines are used give Trump a few more votes than expected, and not vice versa. But it isn't anomalous. There is no evidence of vote flipping or any other kind of systematic fraud, and it would show up if it happened.

Cheating leaves a trail in the statistics. Sidney Powell was wrong about the math suggesting fraud: Math rules it out. There are reasons the lawsuits have lost in court. Most of the claims are absurd, and the claims that were not absurd have been well investigated. What do persons mean by calling allegations "absurd"? Here is an example of absurd: Trump attorneys Rudy Giuliani and Powell compared the votes cast against total voters registered in the state of Michigan. They declared that over-voting by up to 300 percent had occurred in many places. They asserted candidates were able to buy election insurance from Dominion to guarantee their win. That there were affidavits of precinct workers that swore garbage cans full of at least sixty thousand Biden-only votes were carried in, and then counted two or three times each.

Giuliani said there were places in Wayne County where more than double the number of the entire population votes were cast. First, even if somehow the election workers failed to notice the votes were more than the population, this *would* be the kind of thing that the finger print analysis methods would so easily detect and *would* be clear evidence of fraud. However, the affidavit by the "expert" that was the main proof, was wrong. It actually used the *Michigan* vote tallies against population of *Minnesota*. People and various media quickly checked the numbers: no voter discrepancies were found when the proper population numbers *from* Michigan were used *for* Michigan. Absurd. There are numerous such examples. After a couple of these, you should stop. It gets increasingly absurd.

## Actual Consensus and Power Politics

Individual affidavits are not proof: they are just statements by individuals that are notarized. Trump's attorneys have not only lost their related lawsuits claiming the election fraud, they have been sanctioned for continuing to file frivolous lawsuits, abusing the judicial process, and undermining confidence in legal and fair elections.

Overall, most people know Trump lost. But not most Republicans: most Republicans more or less believe Trump probably should have been declared the winner, because they trust and love Trump, and embrace what he represents. For the rest of the world, it is not just the initial vote that is convincing, it is also the recounts, and the second recounts, and the fingerprint analyses, and the external audits, the inspections of mail-in rosters, the analysis of mail-in return rates, the clear explanations of the stated concerns. Wrong addresses were usually college students with two addresses on file but that voted properly. Yes, a few people voted twice, it happens. Some voted for Trump twice. But that was rare and not the thousands claimed: the initial claims of widespread double voting such as by Secretary of State Brad Raffensberger were later essentially recanted as the investigation found most were quite legitimate (like two people with the same name), and most of the rest were by accident. In no case did it change the election outcome. The vast majority of the dead voters (like Roberto Garcia in Michigan, for example) were typically found alive and well with a little effort.

For many people, it is clear that attempting to overturn a lost election would be just as treacherous as plotting mass election fraud, maybe worse if the losing party refuses to ever accept it and the accusations tear the country apart. People are worried. Overall, allegations of fraud by a losing candidate must be investigated, but there comes a point where claims of cheating and stolen elections ruin the pillars of democracy: faith in elections, respect for rule of law, and peaceful transitions of power. Many look at their news feeds and the data they find, and are surprised and pained by the ruin that is happening.

## Critically Thinking about Consensus

If the election *was* stolen due to plots and cheating and shenanigans in the states Trump claims, one would probably not expect Biden supporters (who presumably conspired to commit the fraud) to admit cheating occurred; Democratic officials would be "in on it" and say the election was fair regardless. In contrast, if the election *was fair* and there was no conspiracy, Democratic officials would of course maintain it was fair and their preferred candidate had won. The point is that what Democratic officials say is not going to be persuasive regarding the question of Democrat cheating. This is because in both scenarios, the behavior of Democratic officials is probably the same. By the rules of logic, if trying to judge between two theories and both sides say X is true: then X being true is not helpful in deciding. Let's not bother noting all the Democrats who state the election was fair.

Conversely, the behavior of the GOP can be considered. If fraud occurred and there was evidence that supported it, we would expect the victims' supporters (here we would mean the GOP) to all acknowledge it, 100 percent. On the other hand, if the loser is *claiming fraud where none exists*, some of his supporters will still go along with the claim for various reasons (they want to keep their jobs, they are afraid, some really believe their leader and that fraud occurred). But we would expect some of his allies, some people who would have definitely preferred Trump had won, to actually look into it, break away, and admit there is no evidence of fraud.

Here is partial list of people who have considered Mr. Trump's claims, looked into the facts, and subsequently gone on record as stating the 2020 presidential election was fair, and that President Biden is the properly elected president. People whose analysis and opinions should count for something are listed, some with a key quote or comment:

- Head of Cybersecurity and Infrastructure Security Agency (CISA) Risk Management, Bob Kolasky (selected in 2018, during Trump's Presidency)
- Department of Homeland Security's Cybersecurity and Infrastructure Security Agency Director, Trump Appointee Bill Krebs
- US Election Assistance Commission Chair, Benjamin Hovland
- Chair of the Committee on November 2020 Michigan Election, Senator Edward McBroom
- National Association of State Election Directors President, Lori Augino

- US Attorney for Northern District of Georgia and Trump Nominee, B. J. Pak
- Escambia County (Florida) Supervisor of Elections, David Stafford
- General Counsel for Secretary of State (Georgia), Ryan Germany
- Election Infrastructure Sector Coordinating Council Chair, Brian Hancock
- Trump's appointed Attorney General William Barr. In the days after the election, Barr had been concerned enough to authorize investigations into allegations of fraud as Attorney General, but the investigations did not point to fraud, instead they resolved the concerns. "To date, we have not seen fraud on a scale that could have effected a different outcome in the election." "If there was evidence of fraud, I had no motive to suppress it." "There had been no discrepancy reported anywhere, and I'm still not aware of any discrepancy."
- GOP House of Representative Conference Chair Liz Cheney, "More than 60 state and federal courts, including multiple Trump-appointed judges, have rejected the former president's arguments, and refused to overturn election results. That is the rule of law."
- South Dakota GOP Senator Mike Rounds, "The election was fair—as fair as we've seen," "We simply did not win the election as Republicans for the presidency."
- GOP Representative from Texas, Dan Crenshaw, former Lieutenant and Navy Seal, when challenged that Biden actually lost, "Five different states? Hundreds of thousands of votes? You're kidding yourself."
- Georgia Secretary of State Brad Raffensberger, "The vast majority of claims are simply unfounded."
- Fox and Friends host and arch Trump supporter, Brian Kilmeade. He said claims Trump won Arizona in the 2020 presidential election is an "outright lie" and Mr. Trump is wasting the time of supporters with "bogus" election fraud claims.
- GOP Governor Brian Kemp. A key and clear quote about claims of widescale election fraud in Georgia, "Their claims would be extraordinary if true, but they are not."

Did Trump respond to the assessments of his allies and the outcomes of the expert investigations with grace and dignity? Nope.

## Objective Assessments of Evidence

In keeping with Mr. Trump's belief there is literally no possibility he could have ever fairly lost, no way more people would choose the other candidate over him, he responds with name calling and threats and firings.

For example, in response to his ally Governor Kemp stating investigations showed his state's election was valid, Trump calls him a disaster. Mr. Trump even opined the Democrat Stacey Abrams "might be better" and went so far as to note that it would be okay with him if she (liberal Democrat Stacey Abrams) took Kemp's place as Governor of Georgia.

He fired his nominee, Cybersecurity and Infrastructure Agency Director, Chris Krebs, who looked into the claims that votes were flipped to Biden by a secret computer program and officially said it was clear such a thing did not happen. Then, one of Trump's attorneys publicly said CISA Mr. Krebs should be taken out and shot for his disloyalty. No wonder many agree, "yes, yes you won."

Trump essentially fired a federal attorney in Georgia that he himself nominated, B. J. Pak, for questioning his narrative. Trump also dismissed his handpicked, amazingly supportive US Attorney General Bill Barr for not agreeing the election was stolen, and called him a "swamp creature." (Was that the second previously loyal attorney General Trump fired for being disloyal?) Either Trump is wrong about the election being stolen, or he is a poor judge of people: he keeps appointing a lot of disaster deep state insiders who plot against him.

## April 2021 and the GOP's Ninja Report

Take a moment, go back in time to Arizona in April, 2021. The GOP Senate in Arizona was insisting on doing yet another audit of the ballots. This was after multiple recounts and checks into the voting machines, all showing that Biden received more votes.

After lawsuits to get access to the ballots, the new count began on April 23, 2021. The Republican-controlled Senate had controversially hired Cyber Ninjas to oversee their recount. This was controversial because the head of the effort for Cyber Ninja, Doug Logan, was a well-known and ardent Trump supporter. He had publicly called for the overturn of election results, and the Ninja team was widely viewed as overtly pro-Trump. When the results were finally released on September 24, 2021, some minor problems were found, but after all the effort, the GOP-selected Trump-supporting members of the audit committee summarized their efforts in their final report: Maricopa County Forensic Election Audit:

> This audit is the most comprehensive election audit that has been conducted. It involved reviewing everything from the voter history for the election, to retallying all 2.1 million ballots by hand, to performing forensic photography and review of the ballot paper, to conducting cyber forensic imaging and analysis of the provided voting equipment. This extensive process involved over 1,500 people who contributed a total of over 100,000 hours of time over the course of more than five months from when setup began, to when this report is completed. This volume of the report serves to outline details of the results from the audit; including all the data and evidence to support the conclusions of this report. The audit included a full hand-recount of all 2.1 million ballots from the 2020 General Election. During this process all original ballots were counted, as well as those ballots returned from duplication. Ballots that were duplicated included various categories of ballots that were not able to be run through the voting machines, such as damaged ballots or Uniformed and Overseas Citizens Absentee Voting Act (UOCAVA) ballots. The tallies from the original ballots sent to duplication, and the ballots received back from duplication were kept separate so that a comparison could occur (page 2).

The Cyber Ninjas found some problems with mail-in ballots based on people moving, and voting from their old address. Small scale stuff that happens, not nearly often enough to have any material impact on the outcome. They found some cybersecurity best practices had not been reliably followed. Nonetheless, the final tally of the GOP-hired and selected Cyber Ninjas, based on their openness to election fraud? *The final tally increased Biden's lead to 45,469 votes.* Biden won Arizona. Said the team of Trump supporters—Cyber Ninja—who took the time to look into the matter.

Did it matter? No, because this information was not clearly and correctly conveyed to all interested parties by an objective and fair source of unbiased facts.

## Legal Cases Are Loud and Clear: Trump Lost Fair and Square

Space obviously prevents consideration of all sixty court cases that have been dismissed, denied, or found Trump's arguments unconvincing. Consideration of some heard by judges appointed by Trump follows.

## Pennsylvania

In Pennsylvania, US Circuit Judge Stephanos Bibas was appointed by then-president Trump in 2017. Bibas wrote the opinion that rejected Trump's claim that the Pennsylvania presidential election was fraudulent and should be declared as such. "Elections are the lifeblood of our democracy. Charges of unfairness are serious. But calling an election unfair does not make it so. Charges require specific allegations and then proof. We have neither here." In another section, "Even if we could grant relief, we would not," going on to mention the lack of reasonable "likelihood of success on its merits." That is from a conservative Trump appointee, a federal judge whose job was to look at the case objectively (see Levi and colleagues, 2021).

## Wisconsin

Trump nominated Brett Ludwig to serve and his confirmation as a US District Judge was September 9, 2020. Three months later, he heard and then dismissed the case brought by Trump that Wisconsin presidential election was fraudulent.

The decision of *Trump v. Wisconsin Election Commission* begins in a startling manner, "This is an *extraordinary* case." The emphasis is original. In brief, Trump alleged the election officials were so egregiously out of line in their decisions and conduct that the election was a failure, and the results must be tossed out. The judge goes through at length the laws and history of voting, how electors are to be chosen, all of which matters to Trump's claim. Readers of the decision find a list of people Trump is accusing of committing open election fraud: the Dane County Clerk, five named members of the State of Wisconsin Elections Commission, the City Clerks of Kenosha, Madison, Racine, and Green Bay, Milwaukee County Clerk, Milwaukee City Clerk, the Milwaukee Country Elections Director, the Executive Director of the City of Milwaukee Elections, the Mayors of all the above cities, the Secretary of State, and last but not least, the Governor of Wisconsin. All cheaters, all scheming against him, the plaintiff, Donald Trump.

Trump requested a recount of Dane and Milwaukee Counties on November 18, 2020. This was done and were completed on November 27 and 29. The results were signed by the governor on November 30, 2020. This requested recount was not accepted, and, the Trump campaign immediately filed a petition against the governor and the Elections Commission. The Wisconsin Supreme Court denied this petition on December 3. Before going on, consider the steps that led to the Ludwig decision because the context matters.

As the election approached, numerous polls showed Trump was behind. When the votes were originally counted, Trump had narrowly lost, as he had narrowly won four years earlier. Trump requested a recount. He did not accept the recount, and promptly sued the governor. This was rejected by the Wisconsin Supreme Court. Trump refiled in the circuit court, and essentially added new people and more claims, with the case landing in the lap of recent Trump appointee, conservative Judge Brett Ludwig. Perhaps Trump took solace in finally having his case heard by a fair and quality judge. Judge Ludwig goes through the claims Trump has made, and the relevant previous court history in cases that are related, as court opinions do.

Reading the document, it is almost as if one can hear the sigh, the stretch, and the "Hold my beer" emanating from the written decision. First, Trump's protests about the election are found by Judge Ludwig to not be material deviations from the constitution, but disagreements over election processing, none of which were illegal. The judge says Trump's arguments are regarding details of administration, and that such complaint is contrary to the plain meaning of the law. Judge Ludwig's written decision stated that Trump was in effect asking that "any disappointed loser in a presidential election, able to hire a team of clever lawyers, could flag claimed deviations from the election rules. . . ." (page 20). It gets worse. The judge wants to be clear. He goes on to clarify that even if the actual manner were in question (and not just the details), Trump would still lose because the "record shows (all the election officials and mayors, etc.) acted consistently with, and as expressly authorized by, the Wisconsin Legislature." There is no fraud.

The decision ends on page 22, and the steely closing paragraph begins by restating the opening sentence for emphasis, "This is an *extraordinary* case. A sitting president who did not prevail in his bid for reelection has asked for federal court help in setting aside the popular vote based on disputed issues of election administration, issues he plainly could have raised before the vote occurred. This Court has allowed plaintiff the chance to make his case and he has lost on the merits. In his reply brief, plaintiff 'asks that the Rule of Law be followed.' It has been."

The next line is the salt in the wound, the stab. The death blow to an already well dead horse. Trump's appointee writes, "DISMISSED WITH PREJUDICE," (all caps are original). Yikes. Legally, this means the case has been dismissed based on the merits of the case, is permanently over, and charges cannot be refiled. Of course, one never knows, but some people say that this is done when a judge thinks the lawsuit's deficiency is such that no cure for the underlying deficiency can be imagined (U.S. Law Essentials).

## The Supreme Law of the Land

At the same time the Wisconsin case was playing out, the Unites States Supreme Court was deciding against Trump, by denying requests to halt the certified electoral vote count (*Texas v. Pennsylvania*). In this case, the state of Texas asserted four states had fundamentally violated election rules. Trump officially supported this particular case, describing the case as, "very strong, ALL CRITERIA MET." And as "the Big One." (Platoff, 2020). However, after reading briefs provided by both sides, the Supreme Court, *with three Trump appointees,* denied the suit (December 11, 2020). Two justices dissented (neither were Trump appointees) writing that they would have at least heard the case, but as they wrote in the dissent, "would not grant other relief." This appears to signal for the record that they were not impressed with the arguments for stopping the certification, regardless.

Did Trump's response (to having his hand-selected Supreme Court justices rule against his very strong case) include reconsidering that maybe more people really did vote for Biden, to accept the Supreme Law of the Land? Never. Inconceivable, no matter what: Trump wasn't wrong, and he didn't lose. The Supreme Court is also a disgrace, it was a "disgraceful miscarriage of justice," sayeth the Donald. Typical response of someone who cannot take a loss. There is no process that will satisfy the Donald, nothing that can convince him. He will forever insist he won.

On January 6, Trump's attorney Rudy Giuliani, said this, "Over the next ten days, we get to see the machines that are crooked, the ballots that are fraudulent, and if we're wrong, we will be made fools of. But if we're right, a lot of them will go to jail. . . . I'm willing to stake my reputation, the President is willing to stake his reputation, on the fact that we're going to find criminality there," (Rev Transcript Library).

Ten days passed. No Democrats in jail. No criminality found. They were wrong. But they do not admit it. Moving targets and ruining of the pillars.

## When a Trusted Politician Won't Accept a Loss

A popular candidate, especially one that a significant portion of the country deeply trusts, repeatedly claiming a legitimate election was full of cheating and not valid presents a major problem. Especially when there is no source of clear just-the-facts reporting readily available to all. There is, in fact, a lot of clear evidence that Trump really lost, that more people actually wanted Biden more than Trump as their president. Essentially every remotely objective entity has been able to confirm this from the statistics and the data and the evidence (including many people who obviously wanted Trump to have won).

What kind of a person would refuse to accept a loss? Past behavior is the best predictor of future behavior. Like many people, Trump is flawed. Often people's best qualities are also their worst qualities. His larger than life confidence, his willingness to speak his mind, to stand up to authority: these make him strong, but also arrogant and brash. When his TV show did not win the Emmy? "I got screwed out of an Emmy," (DJT 2004). He said the Emmys are "dishonest" and "rigged."

The Donald self-righteously, and without any shame or embarrassment at all, stated he had anticipated the win and so had stood up before the winner was announced. From his view, it was so unfathomable he could have lost, there was no shame in expecting to win and standing up to accept the prize when the winner was announced, and then not be named the winner. . . . It must be rigged against him, he was too popular to ever lose, "everybody thought I was going to win it," (DJT 2004, these quotes and associated tweets are widely available online, see for example Pond, 2016).

Trump may still believe he really was the true winner of the Emmy. He may die believing he really won the 2020 election. But some fear that, with the split of information, the country will die over his belief, and the ingrained, unshakable conviction that he is a driver, a winner, and by God, he cannot lose.

## Why People Believe Trump Won the 2020 Election

People are receiving and digesting their own personalized streams of curated news information. Even if the full, entire set of information supports one conclusion, partial information can appear to be a slam dunk for a different conclusion. It is important to understand the evidence that does exist, so that we can disagree without hate.

It is amazing that with polls documenting that only 55 percent of American citizens believe Joe Biden is the validly elected US President, those that are sure he legitimately won have little understanding of why anyone would doubt it. A January 2022 poll shows that 42 percent of the country is either unsure or thinks Biden did not win.

## Georgia on the Mind

There have been several dozen credible witnesses that have gone on record, sworn under threat of perjury that there were problems with the 2020 presidential election. It is important to realize what these people are saying before any dismissing of their claims. Many people are unaware of the testimony, and it can be difficult to locate online.

### VOTERGA.org Founder

Garland Favorito founded an organization to improve his home state of Georgia's election integrity in 2006 and observed problems with the Georgia 2020 election. Favorito is an information technology specialist with forty years of experience in computer programming and internet systems design. Further, by virtue of his organization and presentations to various entities, he has been a long-term advocate for election integrity. This is the reason he closely monitored incoming totals: eighteen years of volunteer work related to election support.

The concerning events occurred on November 5, 2020. Mid-morning Mr. Garland Favorito saw the publicly reported totals were approximately 364,000 votes for Biden and 132,000 for Trump. This was an unexplained change from the earlier morning totals, which he had written down as 344,000 to 133,000. Biden's lead had increased, which is plausible, but Trump's total had actually decreased, as if votes had been subtracted. In response, Favorito contacted the election director, Rick Barron, and also made an open records request for the election results summaries. Having not received any official response after approximately three weeks, and not knowing if this was a more widespread problem that had perhaps occurred beyond what he had directly witnessed, he sought explanation. He eventually joined a lawsuit to obtain the requested records and, by that point, to investigate the election in December of 2020.

In spite of what has been claimed in the media, his original filing specifically noted the subtraction of votes could have been caused by malware in the voting machines that count ballots, or by ballot mismatch and human error. That is, his allegation was not that cheating had occurred, but that votes were subtracted, that this could be a sign of cheating (obviously), but the possibility of reasonable explanation was acknowledged (within the affidavit). The point of real contention was he got no response for a question about an observed subtraction of votes, posed by a person with a clear history of working to improve elections. To many, this seems as suspicious as the subtraction of votes.

## Certified Election Monitor for Fulton County

Serving as certified audit monitor for the recount, Judy Aube stated she personally saw boxes of mail-in ballots that were 98 percent for Biden and that appeared to her to be perfectly and uniformly filled out. They were without deviation in the mark that would normally be present. She felt they looked pre-printed. She said other observers felt the same way, and not knowing what to do, they made a handwritten list of the box numbers that seemed suspicious (appeared too uniform in marking style, different from other boxes). She stated she still possesses the list. Apparently, no one in charge of the elections asked to see the list, or seemed interested in her observation.

## Precinct Poll Manager Who Participated in the Recount

As an experienced poll manager, Susan Voyles was an obvious choice to be recruited to help with the recount that the Secretary of State had ordered to be completed by November 20th. She accepted the work which began at 7:00 a.m. on Saturday, November 14 at the World Congress Center in Atlanta. After a training video, and signing an oath they would be fair, she began the work of hand counting ballots, which involved separating ballots into piles for Biden, Trump, or other, or possibly into a manila envelope if the intent of the voter was not clear or there was a problem with the ballot. Counting the ballots required separating them by stacks of ten and comparing the tally to the original results.

The main concern was discovering what appeared to be uncounted absentee ballots during what was supposed to be a recount. Voyles states that Box 5, Batch Numbers 28–36 had a batch (about 100 ballots) that unlike the other batches did not appear to have ever been handled, had very uniform markings, and contained only two votes for Trump. She, a poll worker for twenty years, said she had never seen ballots that were so similarly marked, giving the definite impression of having been mass printed, rather than filled out by different individuals. She also said that unlike the other batches, the edges were pristine, and had no indication of having been handled as the other batches did, even the crease appeared to have never been folded (as would be needed for an envelope insertion).

## Poll Workers

*Ms. Barbara Hartman* worked as an auditor in the hand count of the Georgia election on November 14 and 15 at the World Congress Center. Her job was to count absentee ballots. She states she was given several stacks, all of which appeared uniform and fresh, as if they had not been previously unstacked or handled. She stated that she could see no creases, as if they had not been folded to fit into envelopes. Moreover, the ballots were all uniformly marked with black ink, perfectly filling in the circles and not overlapping. They seemed to her to be uniformly "stamped." She does not give an estimation of the amount or a percent, but says they were mostly for Biden.

*Rolles.* Sonia Rolle and Gordon Rolle worked as counters in the recount, the same days that Barbara Hartman worked (November 14 and 15). They both had prior experience as both poll workers, and as auditors (counters of ballots). Essentially, they go on record as stating lots of people were not counting according to protocol, that this would make it easy to miscount, that some people were given many more ballots to count than others, and that GOP observers were sometimes not allowed to observe uploading of ballots.

*Michigan Affidavits.* There are about 100 affidavits from poll works and observers in Michigan that came forth with one or more concerns. Most of these concerns might or might not represent fraud, but they are concerns that should be directly answered. For example, Alexandra Seely, Michael Cassin, and Brett Kinney were auditors that all state they saw ballots that were plainly not clear, and that their challenges of assigning the votes were not properly processed according to the official protocol. And that they were all given to Biden.

## The Saga of Antrim

Is it possible that some people do not know even the basic outline of what happened in Antrim County, Michigan? Certainly, the interpretation can differ. To some it is a clear-cut case of being caught red handed cheating and then having to undo the fix. To others it is human error that happened and was corrected. Nonetheless, the basic facts are that Antrim County published results five different times: On November 4, 5, 6, and updated again November 16 and once more on the 21st. Votes for Biden decreased from an original report of 7,769 to 5,960 votes, while Trump's total increased from 4,509 to 9,748.

## Ramsland's Early Report of Alarm

It cannot be surprising that this was a point of concern: early results stated Biden won, then when the mistake was apparent, with lots of attention, a corrected count was published. Biden had still won though. Finally, after more counting and investigation, it was clear Trump had more votes. An example of the concerns this resulted in can be read in *Allied Security Operations Group Report*, by Russell Ramsland. The Allied Group offers computer security services. Ramsland himself is self-described as having an MBA from Harvard University, with cybersecurity experience for the Department of Defense with significant experience in cyber forensic analyses. The report concluded that the events in Atrim County were evidence that Dominion voting machines appeared intentionally designed to allow "systematic fraud," (p,10).

Besides the changed results along with the effort and confusion it took to get the correct count and winner reported, Ramsland said the computer system log system was anomalous. It showed full election logs for prior years, but that the logs for resolving ballot concerns for the 2020 election *were missing* along with all server security logs for the day of the election and the day after the election. The ability of the Dominion machines to connect to the internet was asserted, detailed, and noted by Ramsland to be a "fatal error in security and election integrity." (p, 4). What are people paying attention to this report going to think?

## Halderman's Exhaustive Analysis

A later and even more exhaustive report (Halderman, 2021) concluded the mistake was human and accidental. The author is an expert, an engineering professor at the University of Michigan, who has a long history of expertise in computer forensics and cybersecurity that is extraordinary and impressive, beyond reproach. He explains that the errors were traceable to the use of various ballot designs, some of which changed close to election day. This part is still in some dispute, with some people still thinking the change in vote totals is suspicious, and others, like Halderman, saying it was a mistake that was corrected. This is the point of disagreement, but it is also vital to be clear on points of agreement, which follows a discussion of his report.

To clarify, Professor Halderman firmly believes that it was human error, and he does not think the election was stolen or that there was any plot. A quote: "Local staff performed logic and accuracy testing to ensure that the scanners were working. However, testing was not repeated after the ballot design changes, except in the one township where the memory cards were updated. The county did not test loading scanner results into its election management system, which the state recommends but does not require.

On election day, the scanners appear to have functioned normally for ballots that matched the ballot designs on their memory cards. However, they were not configured to handle the initial and revised ballot designs simultaneously . . ." He thinks it was a mistake. That happened again and again. "To their credit, the county and state quickly understood the technical cause of the major anomalies. However, during the process of correcting the original problems, further human errors occurred that led to additional inaccurate results," (p. 47). Indeed, it *could* have been a series of mistakes.

The report details exactly how he analyzed the election management system and the memory cards from the ballot scanners. He was able to access records and the generated computer logs. In the end, he concludes the fundamental error that caused the inaccurate tally was quickly caught and corrected, and that many initial allegations and concerns from near the time of the errored reporting (such as by the *Allied Report* of 2020) were disproven (see report). This has been widely quoted in the media and in some social media feeds (debunked is the term of the year). But, to be fair, it is often overlooked that some of the things in the Allied Report were substantiated, and not at all disproven. There was disagreement, and agreement. It is crucial to be clear on both.

## Points of Agreement

Halderman's knowledge of cybersecurity was able to get around some password protections. As he wrote, "each election project is individually password protected. However, I circumvented this by creating a new project with a known password, extracting the password hash from the project's database, and copying it into the databases for the other projects," (p. 10). This suggests to some evidence that election systems can be hacked by experts. The attempt to reassure the public regarding this may *not* be reassuring if one suspects election workers can be corrupt enough to alter vote tallies. He continues, "Performing similar steps on the real EMS (election management system) would require physical access to the computer or the hard drive." Halderman is saying this could not be done remotely, but apparently could be done if one had actual physical access. The assurance that controls are in place "to limit" to "authorized personnel" is *not* reassuring if authorized personnel are suspected.

Instead of showing the Michigan voting system is in great shape and that hacking could not happen, there are some quotes (that some media and some feeds include and some leave out) that should be of interest to all: "The (Allied Security Report that questioned the integrity of the voting machines) report is correct that the EMS is missing important Windows security updates, potentially leaving it vulnerable to various methods of attack," (p. 45). "The report (*Allied Report* by Ramsland) is correct that the Windows security event log in the EMS image only contains entries extending back to November 4, 2020, the day after the election." Those are words of the chosen expert who wrote the report that vindicates the machines.

Although *based on the event logs he reviewed,* he says it does not appear that the election system *has* ever been connected to a network, the concerns of Ramsland were correct in that Dominion scanners do indeed have the ability to be connected to external networks. This is the view of the expert hired by the Michigan Secretary of State and Attorney General. Moreover, Professor Halderman wrote, "Some Michigan jurisdictions use this functionality to transmit preliminary results to their (systems) using wireless modems. Connecting scanners or (election systems) to the Internet or other external networks creates significant risks." As he explains (all of these quotes and passages are from p. 45–46 of the report), this makes it possible for unofficial results to be intercepted and changed, a precinct's election system server or individual scanners could be attacked via the network.

Finally, "The report (the *Allied Report* by Ramsland) is correct that the authentication and access control mechanisms on the (election servers) have serious weaknesses. Antrim workers almost exclusively used a single Windows user account that had full administrative privileges over the computer. This account has the necessary privileges *to alter log files and bypass other security controls.* For instance, anyone logged into this account has full access to the SQL server databases that run the election, with no additional authentication required," (emphasis added).

To many who are following these reports and have read reports about election problems, it is unclear why people are so sure the elections are secure and tamper proof. Their feeds are providing them with the actual wording and conclusions of the experts whose work has been touted as proving the election process is safe and secure through the use of different selected quotes. Selective and divisive information pushing viewpoints into factions without overlap.

## Georgia Still on the Mind

People who are skeptical of the 2020 election results are aware of the court cases that have been dismissed, they are also aware that some have been dismissed on technical terms, without looking at the main point of the lawsuit. Georgia is instructive.

As detailed above, numerous experienced election workers came forward with similar stories of significant counting concerns, in addition to Favorito who stated the total sum of votes for Trump had dropped while he was monitoring election results. The deviations from normal counting procedures were accompanied by unusual appearing ballots, described similarly by multiple vote auditors. Why are there paid human vote auditors if, when several go on record with concerns, they are ignored? Consider the outcome of these people's efforts to alert the system of problems.

After contacting election officials and getting no response, they as a group filed an old standby: an open records request. Then, they petitioned the court for help because the open records request had not produced results, thus *Favorito v. Fulton County* came to be. It may be that people make mistakes about how and where to file something so serious, but the underlying issue remains: Why were there pristine ballots in a recount? And why was the recount so poorly done? Was adding and subtracting votes that Favorito saw a widespread problem?

To review, using excerpted words taken from the final October 2021 court decision of *Favorito v. Fulton County* (Words from the court decision are in the block quote below, with my own added author comments in parentheses for clarity.):

> Petitioners claimed that fraudulent ballots had been counted in the General Election. In support, they offered affidavits from individuals who participated in the ballot counting process (who legally swore) that there were large numbers of absentee ballots that looked as if they had been marked by machine rather than by hand (p. 2). Petitioners therefore sought the production of scanned ballot images and physical copies of every mail-in and absentee ballot, (p.2). March 15, 2021 was the initial hearing on the motion to unseal. At this hearing, the Court requested that Petitioners submit a written plan, (p. 2). Then, the Court set a hearing to determine whether the proposed plan should be adopted, (p. 3). Court issued an order on April 16, 2021, directing Fulton County to produce all scanned absentee ballot images in electronic format with the original metadata for each ballot, (p. 3).

On April 20, 2021, the Court entered a final order finding that "Fulton County had violated the ORA (open records request) by failing to give timely and sufficient responses," (p. 3). Basically, this means Favorito's side was winning, and Fulton County was found to be at some fault.

Favorito returns to the court on May 21 with recognized experts in fraud who have reviewed the scanned ballots and say the Fulton County recount was obviously off. From the court decision, "Mr. Sawyer testified that he viewed the information provided on the Georgia Secretary of State's website from the risk limiting audit and compared that data with the scanned ballots provided by Fulton County pursuant to the Court's April 16, 2021 order. He testified that there were 1,539 batches of scanned ballot images produced pursuant to the Court's April 16, 2021 order, but only 1,283 batches were counted in the Secretary of State's count," (p. 4). This means the vote totals did not match.

Following the hearing, the Court granted Petitioners motion to unseal, (p. 5). This means Favorito and his group were winning and would get to see the ballots for themselves.

But respondents (Fulton County) then filed motions to dismiss on May 26, 2021, arguing not that Favorito should not see the ballots. The argument was not that there was no cause for concern, but that *sovereign immunity barred Petitioners state equal protection and state due process claims* (p. 5). This means the court is saying Favorito could not sue the county, he did not have "standing." To some people this might seem like a technicality given the serious nature of the concern brought to the court.

The court granted the dismissal (meaning Favorito lost, on June 24, 2021).

But it wasn't over. Favorito came back by adding more people, apparently hoping the case could then move forward on the merits and they could have access to the ballots to check the counts.

More amended petitions and responses ensued. The final decision includes the judge writing out a summary of the allegations: people counting ballots alone (against the rules) and increasing the possibility of fraudulent ballots getting inserted, and that expert testimony that the recount vote was in blatant error (based on the scanned images provided by the county not matching the totals by the county)—that even if all this were true, it would not matter because the petitioners still lack standing. "Even if the Court construes the allegations in Petitioners' pleadings, including their attached affidavits and exhibits, in the light most favorable to them, the Court is constrained to conclude that Petitioners lack standing to pursue their state equal protection and state due process claims," (p, 10). And on page 11, "regardless of the veracity of these allegations, the Court finds

Petitioners have still failed to allege a particularized injury." Basically, the court ruled Favorito failed to show he had been hurt in any personalized way, which is somehow required for this kind of case to move forward. In sum: Case dismissed. Ballots were not made available.

This is the kind of loss that does not convince. People following the case wanted those ballots to be looked at again, and to see the issues resolved.

## Georgia No Peace I Find

More than a year after the Favorito case dismissal, something new emerges in Georgia.

A private citizen (an all-new person) has painstakingly compared the thousands of publicly available images of the ballots, via the now old open records request, to the official numbers of the recount of absentee ballots (the same ones that the affidavits of Voyles and the others referred were about). This private citizen and an attorney have brought this to Georgia Governor Brain Kemp. Kemp (yes, the very one who elicited Trump's anger and was dubbed a disaster for standing by his state's recount) decides to assign some of his staff to check. Probably he was thinking nothing would come of it. But surprise! The staff finds the same. Essentially, there were multiple instances when the official count gave Trump zero votes, when he clearly had some votes, per the official ballot images. This can be verified by any individual taking the time and expense to duplicate Rossi's work, or by reviewing the governor's November 17, 2021 letter.

It is important to be clear about the nature of the problem. Most of the ballot batches align just fine. But a couple dozen did not. One example (of many) is Batch 22, and the errors appear to be against Trump. Absentee Scanner 2 Batch 22 reports: two hundred votes for Biden, and zero for Trump. The ballot images from the County (the ones the judge made them release) of this batch show there were eighty-five votes for Biden, and twelve for Trump. Governor Kemp wrote to the members of the State Election Board, which was made public during December of 2021. Some people's newsfeeds reported this letter from Kemp to the Election Board, which on March 16, 2022 voted to send the case to Georgia's attorney general.

The analysis was created by (Rossi) and Attorney Jack James who volunteered their own time without compensation to review thousands of ballot images, audit tally sheets, and other data to double check the work of the county. Their dedication to this immense task is commendable. Thirty-six inconsistencies noted by Mr. Rossi are factual in nature, pose no underlying theories outside of the reported data, and could not be explained by my office after a thorough review, details below. The purpose of this letter is to convey the inconsistencies to the board and request them to be explained or corrected. To determine whether it was appropriate to refer Mr. Rossi's claims to you, my office tested the veracity of his work by independently repeating the research Mr. Rossi conducted . . . (they verified the issues, and got the same counts) . . .The data that exists in public view on the Secretary of State's website of the RLA report (the State of Georgia's Risk Limiting Audit Report) does not inspire confidence. It is sloppy, inconsistent, and presents questions about what processes were used by Fulton County to arrive at the result. Though reasons for, or explanations of, Mr. Rossi's concerns may exist, they are not apparent in the RLA report data (Kemp, p 1-2).

One might surmise the reports of sloppy counting that experienced poll workers flagged (Affidavits of Voyles, Hartman, and others) could have been taken more seriously. These concerns were real, but not covered in many media feeds in any form. Nor has the Rossi analysis, governor's official response, nor the associated referral to the attorney general been included in many media feeds. How are people to judge the chance of fraud if they do not know the evidence?

Seventy-five percent of Republicans think that Trump really won the 2020 election. A big part of the problem is information like this, that they know due to their information feeds, and that they see *not* being covered by the legacy media sources. This provokes suspicion as much as the miscounting.

Problems with our election system affect all members of a voting democracy, and everyone should care about having them understood and corrected. To many, given the information they have, it seems like partisanship is preventing legacy media coverage of legitimate, documented concerns, and that complete trust in the election is blind trust. It is perceived as rejection of objective, tangible information, and it breeds suspicions. It is a quick hop to perceive the only goal that matters to "others" is confirming Biden won the election, as if nothing else matters. When legacy media highlights that all concerns have been debunked and only represent the most outlandish conspiracies, they are not viewed as providing a balanced, accurate, facts-only summary by those following the above parts of the ongoing saga. The absolute dismissal of any and all concerns does not reassure, indeed it breeds further mistrust.

Such is the victory of divisive information streams over the fairness needed for a democracy to survive.

# CHAPTER TWELVE

# Tax the Rich

*Tax policy may be an issue that fundamentally divides conservative and liberal approaches to society, but today people have lost sight of reasons people might reasonably disagree.*

Liberal persons may believe that anyone who wants to cut taxes or end social safety net programs must be selfish, cruel, and ignorant. Conversely, conservatives often seem wholly unable to imagine how any government action can ever be a benefit to society, and liberals are often viewed as naïve fools. Some shared knowledge and translation of viewpoints is more essential than ever.

## Why Taxing the Rich Makes Sense to Some People

First, increases in wealth hoarding has not been equal across the top 1 percent. Instead, wealth among the billionaire segment has greatly accelerated. The extent of the shift is clear when one has certain key data streams on their smart device, and it seems alarming. Excessive concentration of wealth within minuscule segments of a population is perhaps universally seen as potentially harmful to a society: the question is at what point wealth hoarding becomes excessive and harmful. The primary data source on privately held wealth in the USA is the Survey of Consumer Finances, published every three years. Moreover, *Forbes* publishes an annual list of billionaires, along with their current, and previous year's net worth.

What does it mean to be exceptionally wealthy in the 2020s? To begin to answer a typical level of wealth needs defining. Median net worth in

USA is currently about $120k and median household income is about $70k: Half the people have more wealth than $120k in assets, and half have less. The median wealth level is so far away from the wealth of the ultra-rich that it is hard for a human mind to comprehend. Humans do not readily grasp really big numbers: a million is a lot, a billion is a lot, so is a trillion. It starts to blend for many people after a million. Not to discount the advantages that come from being born into a family with income in the half million range, a spare vacation home, and the possibility of an Ivy League education assumed, but this is not the demographic that has increased hoarding. It is the top one hundredth of the top 1 percent: the top .01 percent.

To aid in comprehending the enormous numbers of the uber wealthy, we can convert dollars to something for which we are more used to aggregating small and large quantities: time (seconds, minutes, days, years). If the middle amount of wealth represents one year, it would take ninety-thousand years to approach the worth of the least wealthy person on the *Forbes* list of the four hundred wealthiest persons. But consider this: it would take 1.2 million years to approach the wealth of those on the top of the list. The top .01 percent, represents about sixteen thousand families— even within this level of elite wealth there is serious spread. In any event, the real change in the economy is not the one in 100, the often referenced "top one percent." Not the attorney with $500k yearly income, but those whose wealth may be increasing by millions *a day*. The superfluously wealthy.

The decline of taxation for top income brackets coincides with the decline of middle-class wealth. Inequality.org has published many calculations of interest in their article on Inequality and Taxes. As taxation of personal and corporate wealth decreases and extreme wealth amassing is encouraged by tax policy, the overall wealth of middle and working classes decline, "when corporate tax receipts made up 21.8 percent of all federal revenue in 1965, the average CEO-to-median worker pay ratio was 21 to 1. By 2019, corporate tax receipts had fallen to just 6.6 percent of federal revenue and the average pay ratio had risen to 320 to 1."

When average bosses make more than three hundred times the amount of their full-time workers, it becomes trivially easy to argue that wealth hoarding is not incentivizing, and not spurring job growth. Tax cuts will not result in more factories opening, nor more cars, appliances, or yachts, being bought, but does result in less pay for workers. Whether or not a multibillionaire keeps versus pays an extra $10 million in taxes will make *no* difference to their decisions. A $10 million tax bill to Larry Page sounds like a lot (Page is number eight wealthiest in 2021 with $92 billion net worth).

Yet—as a portion of wealth—it is the same as a $13.15 tax bill for a person whose net worth is the median: $121k. Would a $13 change in a bill make a small business owner not open a new business or hire someone? Would it make a nurse not buy a car? Of course not.

Wealth moving and concentrating at the top has not just increased, it is accelerating. According to *Forbes* annual survey or the wealthiest Americans, the top five saw their wealth increase (on average) by 150 percent in 2021 as shown in the figure below. The Covid pandemic, which was devastating to many small and medium-sized businesses, has not been bad for everyone.

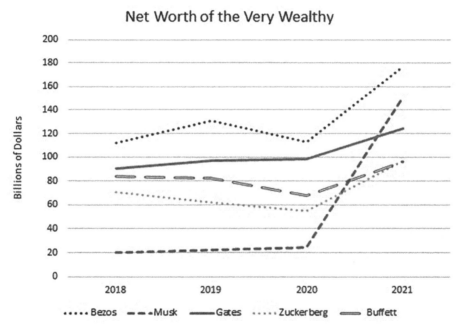

Net Worth of the Very Wealthy

Courtesy of Catherine DeSoto, PhD.

## Liberal Positions

Liberals who want to "tax the rich" do not think all people should have all the same amounts of money. It *is* believed that, in a wealthy society, all people contributing to society should have some minimum standard, regardless of mistakes or talents. It is generally thought that anyone who works full time helping generate the profits of Amazon (even if they are not graced with the fortitude and talent of Jeff Bezos) should share in the wealth the company generates and be able to afford decent shelter, have a child or two if desired, medical care, and food. An annual vacation and paid sick leave seem warranted. This is not happening. Today, working at Walmart or Amazon or JP Morgan may not pay enough to feed families, have a house, and have health care.

Congresswoman Katie Porter did the math and cogently testified with hard numbers. The viral video of Porter was viewed 10 million times, and it is safe to assume most every liberal person was provided the chance to watch this important testimony via their feed. People with the more liberal news algorithms know that millions of working adults receive welfare in the form of Medicaid and/or food stamps (12 million to be exact, with 70 percent of them working fulltime). The data came from the non-partisan Government Accountability Office, using the data regarding actual welfare recipients obtained directly from welfare offices. Most of these working recipients worked for private for-profit companies (as opposed to public sector jobs or charities).

As the Government Accountability Office wrote in the 2020 report, "Each year millions of wage-earning adults participate in federally funded social safety net programs to help pay for basic needs including health care and food assistance." Perhaps if extreme wealth hoarding was less incentivized by the tax structure, private companies would be more incentivized to use profits to pay the workers who are, at least partly, personally responsible for generating the profits. Or perhaps not, but this is the crux of the argument, and the kind of arguments some feeds provide to some users and which shapes viewpoints.

While the chance of success can be a motivator and spur innovations and wealth, it is also true that extreme inequality in wealth and access is not good for societies. It is also bad for incentivizing full-time work when full-time jobs do not guarantee a basic sense of well-being. Some inequality of outcome is fine and good, even needed—but what is the right amount of income inequality, and what is the government's role in monitoring it? This is the question.

## Gini Index versus the Goldilocks Zone

Where is the just-right Goldilocks zone where people work hard for success, but people are not cursed by the odds against them? Progressives think wherever the perfect balance lies—today in the USA it has gone way too far. The Gini Index is a statistic that summarizes a large amount of data regarding who is controlling the capital in a society and consolidates into one number. A Gini Index of zero would mean every person in the population has the exact same amount of wealth as every other person, and an index of one would mean one individual has all (100 percent) of the wealth. A recent overview of the index is provided by Takeshi Kato and Yoshinori Hiroi (2021), but we can summarize and state that a Gini index over about .4 is associated with an increased risk for social unrest, with the USA's index being around .41 in 2016. More to the point, wealth concentration has markedly increased since then.

In 2021, the richest seven Americans owned $830 billion, easily surpassing the GDP of several European countries. Progressive democratic presidential candidate Senator Elizabeth Warren proposed increasing tax in what she called "the ultra-millionaire tax." Republican leadership hated it, and most democrats did not embrace it. She proposed to raise taxes on wealth, starting at wealth above $50 million, and kicking in stronger when wealth exceeds twenty times that amount: at the $1 billion mark. Under the $1 billion mark, people would pay a 2 percent wealth tax (2 cents per dollar). But for each dollar over the $1 billion mark, they would pay six cents. Because there is so much concentrated wealth in the USA, this actually would sum to at least $400 billion a year.

For perspective, this is an amount that would be able to pay for most of the infrastructure repairs. Perhaps this would allow prison systems to rehabilitate and treat mental health, rather than just punish, lowering recidivism. Perhaps excellent addition treatments could be available to every addict who wants it. Perhaps de-escalating and additional training for police could finally become a reality. Maybe low-income family housing could be built and become more available. Perhaps the lack of judges and associated backup in immigration hearings at the border could be solved. Perhaps underfunded school districts in economically blighted areas could uniformly be increased with teachers being offered $250,000 to start (it would be great to see if the best teachers would or would not start to compete for those jobs).

## Musk Time and the Role of Government

In a society with fifty individual states and 334 million people, none of these problems can be solved by the private sector. Are the top 100 billionaires going to collectively decide to hire immigration judges, and institute a national police training program? Will they guarantee a teacher bonus and classes of ten pupils for persons who teach in designated schools that are underfunded with high percentages of low-income students? Philanthropy can be a good thing, but it has limits. So far, the synergy and cooperation has not happened and self-initiated philanthropy is whimsical, targeted, and spotty.

Progressives do not believe that an across-the-board wealth tax starting at about the $1 billion mark will have any impact on decisions to hire, or raise wages, or innovate.

*A million an hour and Musk Time.* Let's go back to using time as a bridge to thinking about superfluous wealth, and create a new unit of measure to illustrate that decisions on hiring or purchasing is unlikely to be affected. We can invent a new unit of measure called Musk Time and base it on one year and $126.4 billion. Mr. Musk's wealth increased from $24.6 billion to $151 billion from 2020 to 2021. Congratulations. That is $126.4 billion increase. Divided by 365 days, and then again by 24 hours equals. . . . Guess the amount. No, not one million dollars an hour, it is $14.4 million an hour. How much per minute? $240,000. About four minutes equals $1,000,000: the time the wealthiest person in the USA took to increase wealth by $1 million across a year is to be called *Musk Time.*

> The wealth gap calls for a new measure. Musk Time is proposed as the average time the wealthiest person in the USA took to increase wealth by $1 million in a given year. In 2021, one unit of Must Time equaled four minutes. Every four minutes, he was another one milling dollars wealthier.

Musk Time is a way of quantifying big number uber-wealth in terms of time. It means that for someone who saw wealth increased $126.4 billion in a year, every four minutes was associated with another $1 million. It's not that it is bad, not that he *should* not be allowed to have it. The question is pragmatic: Will paying six cents on the dollar after the $1 billion mark make a material difference to such an earner? $6 billion in taxes is about seventeen days. If six cents on the dollar after the $1 billion mark were the tax policy for him and all his colleagues—there is a lot of potential benefit to his country. It seems unclear to persons whose news feeds encourage them to consider this, why a profit of $126 billion versus $120 billion would stimulate the economy more than making the sum available as grants to hire more teachers and pay them better.

The downside of lowering taxes for highest wealth is that it makes hoarding easier. Corporations, no matter the size of the profit, must continue to make decisions that continue to maximize profits. That is our law.

Some think this can harm society if there is no upper limit, no restraint. It is possible that the drive for never-ending profits may cause societal harm in myriad ways, that should be part of the calculations.

## Layered Harms of Incentivizing Wealth Hoarding

A clear rise in addiction and overdoses began around 2013, with an increase in heroin beginning to be discernable as early as 2010. By 2016, overdoses from synthetic and semi-synthetic opioids had surpassed heroin overdoses. Families Against Fentanyl reports on the aggregate effects of fentanyl and along with the CDC reports that overdose deaths now top 100,000 annually. This is the leading cause of death among persons ages 18–45, surpassing suicide (about 20,000 deaths a year), and Covid-19 (around 10,000 deaths in 2020). The increasing numbers are coming from synthetic and semi-synthetic opioids (like Fentanyl, Tramadol). What caused the increase? Was part of it the lure of big profits?

The Sackler Family ran Purdue Pharma, and this company was the first to start advertising to doctors that the problem of painkiller addiction was overblown, and they should be freer to prescribe opioids to appropriately treat patient-reported pain. Many pharmaceutical companies agreed, and the trend in the medical community was to prescribe more opioids. I remember this happening at the time; there was new talk regarding why it was so important to thoroughly treat pain, fear of addiction should not keep doctors from treating chronic pain appropriately.

Dr. Nora Volkow summarized in NIH's 2014 report on America's Addiction to Opioids, "The number of prescriptions for opioids (like hydrocodone and oxycodone products) have escalated from around 76 million in 1991 to nearly 207 million in 2013, with the United States their biggest consumer globally, accounting for almost 100 percent of the world total for hydrocodone (e.g., Vicodin) and 81 percent for oxycodone (Percocet)." Indeed, from 1991 to 2011, the number of opioid prescriptions in the USA almost tripled.

As an odd quirk of history, the Vicodin brand as well as Percocet became much less available in the USA based on a close, 17–20, vote by the FDA in June, 2009. The FDA voted to take them both off the market. The vote and the safety concern were not based on the danger of hydrocodone ingredient, but for the danger of acetaminophen overdose (Vicodin was a combination of opioid and acetaminophen). Oxycodone was available without acetaminophen: acetaminophen-free Oxycontin had become available in 1996.

The pharmaceutical company who manufactured and marketed Oxycontin is the one facing the nearly two thousand lawsuits for deceptive marketing and contributing to the current opioid crisis. Some readers may have seen the Hulu drama *Dopesick,* based on the *Forbes* 400 Sackler family and Oxycontin. The concern for acetaminophen is real, but the result of making Vicodin and Percocet taboo was not just to decrease liver damage from acetaminophen. Dependent people, nor people in pain, did not just stop taking opioids when the prescription readiness was shifting. Presumably, they switched to something, anything, available.

In 2010, heroin overdoses began to increase. In 2013, came the rise of fentanyl. As Dr. Volkow wrote in the 2014 NIH report on addiction, *"Growing Evidence suggests that abusers of prescription opioids are shifting to heroin as prescription drugs become less available or harder to abuse."* It is complicated and causes and effects overlap, but it can be seen that Oxycontin and other oxycodone drugs had indeed been decreasing as heroin increased.

Are the Sackler's any more or less greedy than other corporations? Certainly, some are saying so, but all corporations are expected to increase profits. The Sackler's did have some research that did show the potential for addiction from oxycodone was relatively low. Once Purdue started the message, other pharmaceutical companies joined right in. Is punishing capitalists for being capitalists sensible? Progressives, with segregating news feeds sense that incentives to hoard wealth and increase profits beyond a certain point are potentially harmful.

From 1951 to 1964 the federal tax rate for income (and unearned capital gains was included, but had a cap) was 91 percent for wealth above an income that would be equal to about $2 million today (and as always, taxable income was below actual income). The middle class grew with this shocking tax rate, the economy grew, and debt did not balloon. Today the top tax rate is 37 percent, and worse, the top tax bracket begins at the household income of $628,000, or individual income of $520,000: The same maximum rate for incomes 250,000 times apart. Worse yet, the ultra-rich find ways to keep the tax bill low.

Incredibly, as many studies document, for the first time since the early 1920s, the people on the *Forbes* list of billionaires now actually pay a lower tax rate than do people in the middle class. Not since the roaring 1920s has this happened. How did that inequality work out? History unlearned is bound to repeat. There was a reason taxes on the ultra-rich were high in the 1950s and 1960s. People had not forgotten the 1930s and 1940s. Capitalism can work, does work, but it needs restraint and reason.

Progressives want people to get help when they need it. Their news feed helps them visualize people with tragic backgrounds and disadvantages who could not keep up with their rent when wealthy developers started flipping houses, enriching themselves while displacing neighborhoods. Moreover, inhabitants of major cities see homeless men with PTSD and mental health issues, living in tents, surrounded by violence and drug use. Progressives believe some of these souls were caught in addiction that at least partly was made easier by some long ago ultra-rich pharmaceutical executives sending beautiful representatives out to practicing doctors, touting the non-addictive nature of the new opioids.

At some point, many addicts seek treatment, perhaps they go to a rehab center . . . and are told there are a few grants, but the waiting list is long. Unemployed and without insurance, a homeless man is offered weekly out-patient meetings. The point is addiction and homelessness are societal problems, exacerbated by pharmaceutical products and the long-ago advertising campaign to doctors regarding the need to lower pain. Perhaps the unrestrained drive to hoard wealth complicates homelessness in indirect ways.

It is in society's interest for help to be there: Inpatient treatment to get them out of the drug culture is probably a must for a long-term homeless addict. But there is no funding. Every program that helps the problems of poverty needs funding. From lead water pipes, to improving schools, to mental health and addiction help. Newsfeeds that highlight the need for dollars to tangibly improve human lives, juxtaposed on the unimaginable individually held wealth make it hard to understand opposition to tax reform.

The wealth gap is truly astounding. The average cost for a one-month in-patient program is about $20,000. In 2020 Musk Time, four minutes could fund a month of rehab for about fifty people. One full day of 2020 Musk Time? Six months inpatient treatment for almost 2,876 people.

Tax the rich.

## Why Some People Think Wealth Accumulation

## Is Good for Society

It would be a wonderful thing if giving every person $25,000 a year would eliminate poverty, reduce crime, and end homelessness. However, history and current observations tell us this is unlikely to work. It is understandable to see suffering and want to fix it. But it is possible that the best way to help society as a whole is to reward individuals who have the talent to improve the world, and let them.

## California Dreaming

Progressive income taxing, welfare to individuals, and government attempts to manage the economy have not solved social problems. Some media streams emphasize this and document the state of California's various worsening social problems. The California Senate has been under control of the Democratic Party since 1970. Same for the eighty-member house State Assembly, except for two years (1995 to 1996). Currently, the majority has a large enough majority of the seats there is no chance of veto, regardless of who is governor. Nonetheless, the executive branch in California has been in Democratic Party control since 2011, more than a decade.

The mayor of Los Angeles has been Democrat since 2011, and San Francisco has not elected a non-Democrat since 1964. The US Senators from California have both been from the Democratic Party for three decades. Progressive policies have ruled, and California has the highest income tax rate in the United States. California has a problem with affordable housing, crime, drug use, job creation, and above all, homelessness. Numbers can be spun without telling the whole truth, and Lies of Omission matter. The full picture makes it clear: compared to US as a whole, job growth in California has not kept up in the past ten years (defined as starting in 2012, ten years ago) and in spite of myriad initiatives, affordable housing continues to plague the state.

Based on Census Data as reported by the California Budget and Policy Center, California has the highest number of residents living in poverty, and the highest per capita poverty rate. Workers' earnings have risen (as it has across the USA as a whole), but the median cost of rent has grown faster than earnings have risen each year, making the housing crisis continually worse, not better as continually promised. For about 20 percent of people living in California, shelter costs exceed 50 percent of their household income. California, which claims 12 percent of the US population, claims 53 percent of the unsheltered homeless.

If one has not visited the beaches and boardwalks, plenty of videos are available of the open drug use, miles of tents and boxes, excrement and litter. But only some of the population sees these videos. If one navigates to YouTube and begins to search and click on offerings related to "Venice

Beach Homelessness," which populate many feeds, one may also be presented news footage of the extent of the problem, such as KTVU Fox 2 Channel's, "Rainy Weather Raises Concerns Around Santa Cruz Homeless Encampment." Images that put the extent of the problem directly in a person's focus, but that some feeds don't typically show, are served based on algorithms' discretion. It is possible to see some disturbing images.

California is an example, but similar problems are happening in Philadelphia and many other places. Something is wrong in America, and some are seeing evidence and being offered reasons and solutions for the problems.

Everyone wants to fix it. No one wants to see suffering, addiction, or homelessness. But how to fix it? This is why California as a state is sometimes focused upon: it is seen as a modern case study in letting progressive policies work. According to Adam Summers, columnist for the Orange County Register, writing in November of 2021, while billions are spent on the problem, homelessness and crime get worse.

The predominant approach (favored by the federal government and California) is called Housing First. This emphasizes immediately placing those experiencing homelessness in "permanent" housing, with the idea that access to supportive services will follow. It also includes a harm reduction philosophy, which allows people to continue to abuse substances. While Housing First may work for some, it is certainly not a one-size-fits-all solution. Yet, that is the approach California has taken. In 2016, the state made it official policy to only fund Housing First programs. Now, for example, a program that requires residents to remain drug-free is ineligible for state grants and put at a competitive disadvantage.

There are other approaches to homelessness that may appear cruel, but seem to work better. Furthermore, if it was your child who was homeless and addicted—what would you do for them? Would you pay for their apartment, where they could come and go as they wish, not work, and let them continue daily heroin use within a hardcore drug scene? Would you think that would be best for them?

Housing First, besides being terribly expensive, provides permanent housing, allows drug use, and then afterwards seeks to offer counseling addiction help, but *not* as a prerequisite to the housing. There is no real-world evidence the approach has lessened homelessness, as the homeless problem has gotten much worse. Why not require nightly shelter and require treatment that is needed? Cities do not have to allow people to openly use drugs and defecate in the streets.

Even progressives are starting to see failures of the progressive approach and to advocate for more personal responsibility, and less victim comforting. The reason is not a lack of compassion, but a desire for what will work in reality. Essentially, enforced abstinence from drugs, with in-patient treatment, and then reward for progress as it comes. It makes no sense to provide a nice apartment to a hard-core addict suffering from untreated schizophrenia and paranoia. They are not ready for the responsibility.

Author Michael Shallenberger, a former progressive policy advocate, explained why he has come to understand that handouts and free apartments have not, and will not, work during an October 21, 2021 meeting of the American Enterprise Institute. A different approach, which has been employed with some success, was detailed and advocated. It emphasizes shelter first, while noting individualized housing is too expensive to offer to everyone right off the bat. Persons who view this video are often persuaded that apartments and responsibility should be earned, not given as a handout, just like for the non-homeless. Homes require work. This approach makes the reward valuable not only to society, but to the individual earning it. And this approach can give back something that handouts never will: pride in the hard work of staying clean. After contrasting his current views to those he held earlier in his life, when he "was part of the radical left," Shellenberger tells of his own family and friends who have been homeless. He then examines the problem with California's Housing First approach, and then discusses a solution, which includes mandatory shelter.

> Everybody has to be sheltered, so that's a shelter-first policy. You're saying: You need to be in shelter because it's not safe on the street...Then, when you're in shelter, you would get some evaluation if you need medical care, including psychiatric care, so it's also treatment-first. Housing is something that would be earned . . . people who would be like, "I want my own room." And (the social worker) would say, "You can have your own room, but you're not taking your meds." Or, "You can have your own room, but you're not showing up for your job that we arranged for you and we need you to show up for your job." So the housing is earned. Shelter-first. Treatment-first. Housing is earned. That's the right way to do it. (American Enterprise Meeting, 2021)

Conservative Chistopher Rufo's self-made documentary is delivered to millions via many social media algorithms to users looking for documentation regarding the extent of the homelessness problem. As he says, and which shows in his video, the mayor of San Francisco's policies really do sound good. The approach sounds compassionate and well-intentioned, but the "polices have caused widespread chaos," with homeless encampments multiplying, and long-term residents describing scenes of open drug use, gun and knife violence, nudity, and even nonconsensual sex in visible, public places.

A member of the local (Democratic) government is interviewed who is deeply concerned about the problem, which is then traced to big tech wealth not paying taxes and pricing low income residents out of the housing market. The government official's plan? Pay for hotel rooms, have no stipulations, and even provide drug paraphernalia, and, if the self-made documentary is to be believed—offering free alcohol. This video places blame squarely on the progressive policies that have been and continue to be in place. If your social feed does not contain information like this, you are not going to understand the viewpoint, indeed the approach will sound cold and unfeeling, which is not the vibe the documentary actually gives.

California experienced a net decline in its population in 2020, which has never happened before. There were seven hundred thousand people who moved out, and this was not replaced by either the birth rate or people moving in: 180,000 fewer people living in California at the end of 2020 than at the beginning. On one side of the information divide, users encounter documentation that the progressive approach has not worked.

## Tax the Rich? Please Don't

The lure of small-town main streets is a lovely Americana image from the 1950s. Generation X's memories of mega malls similarly so. Certainly, conservatives like Americana culture and as a group dislike change. But reality has to replace nostalgia at some point. Miners, telephone operators, typists, and travel agents have all become rare. Things change and people must adapt. It is easy to feel jealousy or disgust with the wealth some individuals hold. Jeff Bezos's wealth compared to his workers is unsettling to grapple. He is like pharaoh, or a king. There is nothing Bezos cannot buy. The excess is a bit nauseating to contemplate, especially if one is struggling to pay health care for an ill family member, or one's rent was just increased.

On the other hand, Bezos took a risk, and it worked. We can look for a product not available at any store nearby, check the price, order it, and it will come. It will come quickly, in a day or two, and intact. As an entrepreneur, one can have their products available to millions of people, something not possible even five years ago. Amazon did that. The world is changed, some things are worse, but it's also better in many ways. A new set of fast thinking business people can think of new ideas and new businesses. Wealth is shifting. People who were not wealthy can think of ways to become wealthy.

One example of many is Greg Mercer, who left his normal job and started a career on Amazon. He quickly replaced his old salary, then grew beyond it. Mercer founded a new business called Jungle Scout to help other sellers figure out how to sell products on Amazon. In 2020, Mercer was named Ernst & Young's Entrepreneur of the Year, and has raised more than $110 million in funding for a business he started in 2015. There are real world cases of entrepreneurial rising tides lifting other boats. Boats that a serf living under a king, no matter how bright or buoyant, could never see rise.

It is not disputed that inequality is hard to fathom. And it should not be doubted that societies have inequality. But the income inequality in a capitalist system comes from innovation, risk taking, and new advances shake things up and allow new wealth to develop. Conservatives are not blind to unfairness, but generally they see nothing that works better. Free capitalism is as good as it gets, and it should be protected.

## Power and Jealousy

Who resents the power of the billionaires, really? A 2021 poll by Data for Progress asked "Do you think the fact that there are some people in this country who have personal fortunes of a billion dollars or more is a good thing, a bad thing, or neither a good nor a bad thing for the country?" Eighty-two percent said it was either good, or, neither good nor bad. Less than one in five (about 20 percent) thought it was bad for the country. These results are in keeping with other polls. Pew results which found about 75 percent of people thought personal fortunes over a billion dollars were either good, or neither good nor bad.

A similar question asked if people "should be allowed to become billionaires." Here, only one in eight thought it should not be allowed to happen. The survey separated respondents by race (and it didn't matter), but not by income. There is little evidence that most people spend their time worrying about the wealth gap (*Pew Research Center Poll on Inequality*, 2020).

What matters more than vast income, is vast happiness. Bezos and Musk may be a hundred thousand times wealthier than their workers, but are they a hundred thousand times happier? Happiness level does seem to be associated with GDP growth, and the distribution of happiness can be measured by asking people how happy they feel. The difference found between happiness levels can be referred to as "happiness inequality." Does income inequality hurt society? In fact, the relationship is surprising: The more income inequality, the more the happiness gap lessens (as long as gross domestic product keeps increasing). As Clark and colleagues demonstrated in their careful analysis in 2014, the evidence was clear.

> Economic growth is systematically correlated with a more even distribution of subjective well-being. This correlation for the most part holds despite the associated rise in income inequality, does not seem to be the result of any statistical artefact, is found in almost all domains of satisfaction, but is not found in placebo tests on other subjective variables. We suggest the extension of the provision of public goods as one likely candidate explanation for the lowering of happiness inequality. (p. 406)

What they are saying, in science-speak, is that they spent a lot of time collecting data and using math to analyze it. Income inequality does not lead to unhappiness in a society. They are saying they checked for all sorts of explanations, and the data mean that economic growth is associated with happiness, and inequality does not matter.

Other than causing jealousy, where is the actual evidence that income inequality harms society? In terms of the problems that matter, such as drug addiction, health care, homelessness, education system, most conservatives have news feeds that point out how badly the government is doing solving these things. They think Gates, Bezos, and Musk and others of their ilk, or other up and comers who think outside the box, are the ones most likely to solve these problems.

Let them keep their wealth.

# CHAPTER THIRTEEN

# My Research on the Pandemic as the Prime Divider

From a variety of evidence (as discussed below and in chapter 2), it seems clear that the pandemic has intensified political divisions. Perhaps spending more time at home, indoors, and with the divisive news content ever-present to further parse citizens into factions, a sharpening of boundaries between us and them grew. Yet with a pandemic there is something novel—the others' politics seem to suddenly impact autonomy over our bodies and our very ability to stay safe. It feels like life and death. Moreover, the mask is an easy to recognize marker of one's views. As noted in chapter 2, polls support the contention that divisiveness has accelerated over the past two years, and is reaching a breaking point.

In August of 2021, I observed my state (Iowa) open schools with an edict from Governor Reynolds that prohibited public schools and universities from requiring either masks or vaccination. This was a personally enlightening experience. In sharp contrast to the previous semester, where students were spaced at least six feet apart *and* masks were required, I was now required to teach a class of over 100 students, with students sitting right next to each other for an hour at a time, 90 percent maskless. At the time, it felt surreal after a year of pandemic restrictions. And I was mad. I remember my thoughts and words. I thought it might make sense not to require masks for classes if people could sit far apart, or for children, or maybe even a teacher who could crack open windows and lecture several feet away from other humans and whose facial expressions or clear diction might help students with comprehension. But there were no windows, these were adults, some with health problems, and seating was like a crowded theater. I was pretty sure there would be a deadly outbreak. But there wasn't. Moreover, Iowa's Covid rates were not higher than neighboring states that required masks in schools. I was wrong about it. Although I was paying attention to data, Covid is after all a novel virus, and my assumptions about the use of face masks, in hindsight, were seemingly not correct, as shown in the figure below. That is what happened; it is the story watching the cases tells.

Overall, estimating Covid risks based on available data is related to what we scientists like to call "scientific literacy." My own interest was originally piqued when I began to hear (in reality, read) conversations (via social media) that were fraught with high anxiety for children. Anxiety that seemed a bit out of proportion to what I was reading in the scientific literature. For example, "I can't imagine sending my children to school during this pandemic." I bit my tongue (nay, paused my fingers) and asked, "Are you concerned for their safety, or, that they would catch Covid and spread it to your elderly relatives or friends?" I was truly interested, because the rates in children had been very low (in May of 2021 there had been only three Covid-related deaths in children for the state of Iowa, and two had severe underlying illnesses and died with Covid, according to Iowa Department of Health). "Both," she responded. "We don't know enough about the disease and I'm not taking any chances with my children's lives." Hmm.

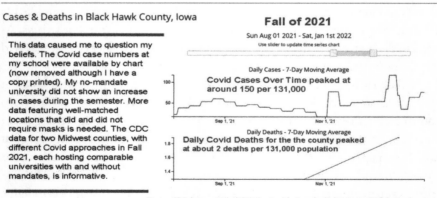

The population of Black Hawk County is 131,000. At the highest point in fall/winter of 2021, the case rate was below one in 1,000; the daily death rate remained below two, approximately 1.5 deaths per 100,000. No masks were required, and most students did not wear masks at the university. Masks were optional at most public locations. The reported infection rate at the university did not spike, but remained below .05 percent throughout the fall semester.

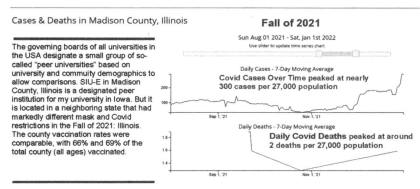

Cases & Deaths in Madison County, Illinois

**Fall of 2021**

The governing boards of all universities in the USA designate a small group of so-called "peer universities" based on university and community demographics to allow comparisons. SIU-E in Madison County, Illinois is a designated peer institution for my university in Iowa. But it is located in a neighboring state that had markedly different mask and Covid restrictions in the Fall of 2021: Illinois. The county vaccination rates were comparable, with 66% and 69% of the total county (all ages) vaccinated.

Sun Aug 01 2021 - Sat, Jan 1st 2022
Use slider to update time series chart

Daily Cases - 7-Day Moving Average
Covid Cases Over Time peaked at nearly 300 cases per 27,000 population

Daily Deaths - 7-Day Moving Average
**Daily Covid Deaths** peaked at around 2 deaths per 27,000 population

Source: CDC. Accessed May 2022. https://covid.cdc.gov/covid-data-tracker/#datatracker-home

SIU-E, in the neighboring state of Illinois, in Madison County, is an (officially) designated similar institution to UNI based on populations and style of the universities. The population of Madison County is approximately 27,000 (less populous than Black Hawk). At the high point in Fall/Winter of 2021, the case rate in the county surpassed five cases per 1,000; the daily death rate often exceeded five deaths per 100,000. Being in Illinois, masks were required at all times at the university, and in the community.

Responses like this made it clear fellow moms feared their otherwise healthy children might die from Covid, and this is a *possibility*. But it was a rare possibility. Was the mom accurate in her guess at the amount of risk? If her goal is to keep her children alive and healthy, was keeping them home from school really going to make that more likely? Social norms prevented my curiosity from further query (I was tempted). Alas, I will never know what she would have alleged the risk of death from infection to be if I had inquired. What would she have guessed regarding how many eight-year-olds might die if all 207 in her son's grade caught the plague of SARS-COVID-19?

It's a tricky thing to be both curious and polite. But it was conversations like these that made me delve into the research process, note the increasing polarization of information received on yet another topic, and helped motivate me to write this book. Where were people getting their information? And how were they understanding it so differently? As someone who had published something loosely related to Covid immunity, and as a psychologist with a side interest in the cognitive biases that lead to faulty judgement, thoughts of availability heuristics were dancing in my head. What follows is an analysis of what happened as evidence regarding Covid unfolded, and why Covid beliefs are now leading the greater divide.

## Common Language and Data

Let us begin with a brief dive into the data regarding risk of death from Covid. The Infection Fatality Ratio is the percentage of persons who *become infected* and then die from the infection. It is based on mortality counts, case counts, and data on the number of people who contract the disease, but don't see a doctor and take a Covid test. There is some "wiggle room" given: epidemiologists use the available data to include ranges, with their best guess for the true number. For example, if the ratio is calculated as 1.1 percent, it means eleven deaths are expected per one thousand infections. The epidemiologist who calculated the number includes a range, such as .96 percent to 1.3 percent, meaning they are pretty sure it is somewhere in this range, based on the data, with the best guess being just over one in a hundred would die: 1.1 percent.[6]

But mortality estimates come in two varieties: the IFR (as above) and the Case Fatality Ratio (CFR). The CFR is a more straightforward calculation, it does not seek to estimate total number of infections, but instead is based *only on known cases*, cases that were tested and reported. CFR misses some infections (if a person does not go the doctor for example) and so an IFR is always lower than a CFR. Mortality estimates have varied since the virus first began spreading among humans. For example, way back in February of 2020, the overall fatality rate among identified *cases* in China was estimated to be 2.9 percent, with variation by region and age group. More recent meta-analysis using all available published estimates places the overall CFR among the general population to be 1 percent (see Alimohamadi, 2021). Current estimates on the IFR are readily available on CDC website.

As of the September 10, 2020 update, near the time the data presented below was collected, the IFR for adults under 40 was .0002. For adults between the ages of 70 and 80, it was .054. To make this clear, it means that in 1,000 infections of adults aged 20–40, no deaths are likely to occur (in 10,000 infections, two are expected). However, for persons in their 70s the educated guess is 54 deaths in 1,000 infections. Reread that, let it sink in. Go to the CDC website and look until you find the data. Because, based on my research, I know that many readers will be skeptical. Good, but don't stop with your skepticism, and definitely don't wait for the information to appear in your news feed. If it has not already, it isn't going to. Look it up, and if needed to settle the question, find it from the CDC.

---

6  Case Fatality Ratio is always higher than Infection Fatality Ratio. They are similar, but CFR is *only* considering medically diagnosed cases, rather than representing total amount of infections in a community. IFR includes estimations of the total amount of infections. CFR includes only people who qualify for, or seek out, medical testing. Thus, it is assumed to miss most mild or asymptomatic cases, and be weighted towards more severe cases.

## Data on Overestimating Risk in 2020

In late 2020, my lab queried university students at my typical, medium-sized Midwestern university about their estimate of the number of persons who would die if 1,000 retirees were found to be infected with Covid. The exact wording was as follows, *"Imagine there is a Covid outbreak at a retirement community where everyone was tested. One thousand (1,000) people were positive. If all 1,000 residents were between the ages of 65 and 80, how many would you expect to die?"* The wording makes it clear that there is an outbreak in a retirement community, and 1,000 persons have tested positive.

Survey responders were asked to estimate the expected number of deaths. The number 1,000 was used to make the comparisons of the guesses to actual IFRs straightforward. Of 272 respondents, 149 guessed a whopping 500 or more deaths. Within these 149 persons guessing half or more would die, no less than 74 persons estimated that 760 or more would die, and 29 (11 percent) of the respondents thought that 90 percent to 100 percent of elderly people would be expected to die if they were to catch Covid. If the previous paragraph sunk in (recall you were told to pause and reread it), you will realize this is off by an order of magnitude (the average estimate from the survey was not twice as high as reality, not five times as high: it was ten times too high).

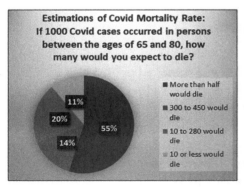 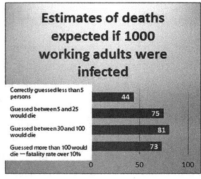

In 2021, university students at a medium-sized Midwestern university were asked to guess how many persons would die if 1000 people were infected. The results for two age groups are shown above. The left chart is shown as a pie chart of percentages. The right chart, which is estimates for working age adults, is shown as a frequency distribution of the number of persons who made various kinds of guesses. Estimates were way too high.

Figure originally published by DeSoto, 2021 in *North American Journal of Psychology*, republished with permission.

It gets worse (if worse means inaccurate risk assessments). A similar question was posed regarding adults aged twenty to forty years. Respondents were asked to imagine that "there is a Covid outbreak at a workplace and everyone was tested. One thousand (1,000) people were positive. If all 1,000 workers were between the ages of 20 and 40, how many would you expect to die?" First, it is encouraging that there was a realization that the risk of death was lower compared to an elderly sample. But did they realize the magnitude of the difference? Remember you were invited to stop and pause after reading the actual IFR estimates. Note that the difference in the CDC best estimate fatality rate for the elderly is not two times more than for younger adults, not five times more, not ten times more . . . it is more than 200 times higher in the elderly group (270 times to be exact).

Surprisingly, and incorrectly, approximately 40 percent of persons guessed that more than 100 people would die in the case of 1,000 working adults all becoming infected. Only 56 students guessed a number in the single digits. One way to quantify this is to say that 80 percent of students made a guess that was at least 10 times over the actual estimated risk according to experts. Guessing above 10 deaths is a substantial over-estimation of risk. Based on available data, the best guess per peer-reviewed literature (with summary tables available) is that none would die. That's the data. That is the expert consensus. But it seems to have been commonly unknown, at least in 2020.

## The Psychology of Cognitive Biases

How was this possible with so much media coverage on the disease? And is this a concern? Is overestimating risk a bad thing? Afterall, a healthy fear of a deadly disease is going to promote taking needed precautions, that is not a bad thing. Is there a down side to over-estimating risk? Decades of study into human thought processes have made some things clear: We are not the logical assimilators of incoming data we imagine ourselves to be. Analyzing data is hard and we take short cuts. There is a branch of psychology that studies heuristics and cognitive biases. There is considerable knowledge regarding common types of errors in decision making.

First, there is the availability heuristic. Human beings tend to overestimate risk of things that are ubiquitous in the media or that are so emotionally salient they are not easily forgotten. The classic example used in Introduction to Psychology classes is the risk or flying. People overestimate the danger of flying, and under-estimate the danger of car crashes. Air travel is actually very safe, especially compared to riding in a car. Why do humans get this wrong? It is because when plane crashes occur it is big news, emotion provoking stories ensue, and it's not forgotten. If something can come to mind easily, it must be common. Everyone can easily recall lots of stories of young and old alike, dying alone, of Covid. It is heavily covered by media, ergo it must be common.

I have the data: People were seriously overestimating the risk of death. What will happen as experience with the disease begins to factor in? Was it predictable? Specifically, as Covid spread across the world and friends personally known become sick and got diagnosed, and people believed (as did the survey respondents) that half of the people will die but—she didn't, then he didn't. Then Joe, Emma, Dan, Lyn, Sasha, Ann, Sam . . . all recovered.

A psychological concept called cognitive dissonance comes in to play. Cognitive dissonance is the uncomfortable feeling of having conflicting beliefs: "I believe about 30 percent will die, but I can see 30 percent are not dying." At some point, some people are going to change their minds. What happens now? Watch out for the combination of source confusion and feelings of betrayal. Maria Zarazoga first documented memory attribution errors in the early 1990s. People may possess the distinct impression that 30 to 50 percent will die, but who told them this?

Actually no one. Ever. No estimate has ever been this high, even using the higher case fatality ratio. People were never actually *told* that 50 percent will die, but that dang availability heuristic: it *seemed* like it was true, and after hearing this and thinking it over, it is predictable for humans to become confused about the source of the belief, and to misattribute the source of the belief to an authority or a media source. Even though no one said it, it was assumed, and people will remember having been told this. That is source misattribution bias. There is an entire body of research on this phenomenon (see Daniel Schacter's the *Seven Sins of Memory* for an overview). This misattribution, the faulty memory, becomes more likely when people have strong attitudes and emotional responses as they seek to retrieve related memories.

What will people do? Psychology is sometimes useful when trying to understand real human behavior which can be somewhat predictable. A feeling of betrayal occurs when personal expectations are violated, and will reliably result in sorrow, frustration, and feelings of mistrust, especially when a person has sacrificed for the sake of the trust. Is quarantining a sacrifice? To sum: Availability heuristic + Cognitive dissonance + Misattribution + Personal Sacrifice = Sense of betrayal. People *feel* like they have been lied to, even if they haven't been.

Next, the human tendency towards dichotomous thinking becomes relevant. This is the human tendency to think of things as black or white without gray, as good or bad without nuance, or as safe or dangerous period. Importantly, this tendency increases under stress, or when things get complex. If Johnny believed that Covid was dangerous, and he believes that authorities told him this, and now he can tell the illness isn't behaving like he expected: along with the surprise, cognitive dissonance, and sense of betrayal the high-danger can go to no-danger like a switch . . . if not the epitome of best-coping, it can be forgiven as classically human and predictable.

The survey was collected across several months. There was tendency for persons who took the survey in October and November to report a lesser risk (average guess was 435 deaths among elderly) compared to people who took survey earlier (average guess of 503 deaths). This may represent the earliest observations and cognitive dissonance as the pandemic spread and people observed the effects first hand. The average of estimation of risk of death fell over time, but as noted in the original publication, it became more politicized.

Studying human behavior has its perks. By thinking about cognitive biases and what is known about decision making and behavior, the irrationality of people can make more sense. Accepting our humanity means accepting we are subject to groupthink, to confirmation bias, to the availability heuristic, to misattribution errors, feelings of betrayal, and all sorts of errors in logic. This is what it means to be human.

## Follow-Up Data: Hints at Why Vaccines Are Refused

In late 2021, a few more students were asked in more detail about their thinking regarding Covid, vaccination, and other issues. The goal was to get a snapshot of how college students were feeling about Covid and related issues after nearly two years of the pandemic.

As noted above, Iowa, where the data was collected, is a state that did not require vaccination nor masks for either public school or college attendance for the 2021/2022 school year. Nonetheless, most students were vaccinated at a rate close to the national average for the age group (that national average being 62 percent, and sixteen out of twenty-four in the sample reported they had taken the Covid vaccine). The survey participants were queried regarding why they thought people might refuse the vaccine. Most students thought fear of side effects was probably a reason (more than half thought this was probably the main reason). Was this accurate? It was. Side effects was indeed tied for the top reason that those who had *not had* the vaccine self-reported as their reason for not having done so.

The methods of the survey were like this: Students were first asked in an open-ended way to state why they thought people were refusing the vaccine. Then, *for those who were not vaccinated,* they were asked to consider a list of possible reasons, and then select reasons that mattered for their choice. Next, they were asked to look back at their reasons, and list the top three. In this way, information about what the vaccinated thought were the reasons, as well as information about actual reasons were discovered. Two choices were selected far more often than other reasons. Here was the exact question and the possible responses, with the top two answers (there was a tie for the top) in bold. The bold responses indicate the two most common reasons young adults, who have refused the vaccine, gave for their choice.

Looking at your response to above—check all that apply as reasons for not having had the vaccine

- I have had Covid and already have antibodies to protect me
- **I think my risk of getting seriously sick is low**
- No one I know who has had Covid has been sicker than a case of the flu
- I am concerned about the possibility of a microchip being injected into me
- **Risk of serious side effects (e.g., paralysis, heart inflammation, blood clots)**
- Risk of "minor" side effects (missing work or feeling sick from the shot)
- Don't like authority telling people in America what they have to do
- Mistrust of pharmaceutical companies
- I think the CDC is acting to help the vaccine companies more than my health
- Anthony Fauci has changed his story and lied about things
- Because Joe Biden wants me to
- I think Covid-19 is not a real disease
- mRNA vaccines might change my immune system in non-helpful ways
- I have no risk factors for serious Covid
- The vaccine loses effectiveness within a year
- There is no individualized recommendation or dosage
- Vaccination is against my deeply held personal or religious beliefs
- The suppression of information makes me not want the vaccine
- My friends or family tell me not to

- I try to know and follow science
- People who get the vaccine are following misinformation

Some answers were never selected. Even when asked to select all that apply, none of the not-vaccinated selected the possibility of a microchip, and none indicated they thought Covid-19 was not a real disease.

This was a small sample, a larger sample would probably capture some less common responses, and research is ongoing, but I wanted to include preliminary results in the book because it is actually surprising that there is not good information on the actual reasons the so-called "vaccine-hesitant" hesitate. As I suspected, neither fear of microchips, nor believing Covid wasn't real, appear to be common reasons.

### "They Don't Understand Science"

There is another question that yielded interesting results. What did the vaccinated students guess about why some do not get the vaccine? A sub-group of respondents who wrote negative things regarding reasons people are not getting vaccinated can be considered separately. This sub-set wrote variations of, "they don't understand science," "misinformed (because they) get information from Facebook," "misinformed, selfishness," or "(they) believe in conspiracies rather than science." Given the division on the issue that we have seen in 2022, the beliefs of people on this issue are worth trying to understand, if the goal is to bridge the disinformation gap and to repair our union.

Ironically, respondents who wrote things like above, were themselves far from consensus science and accuracy in guessing. For example, most greatly overestimated the number of children who had died in their state, with half estimating over fifty. In reality, there had been three. All thought at least 6,000 children in the USA have died of Covid, and half of them estimated more than 30,000 (actual experts, including CDC estimate it be closer to 600). At the same time, they underestimated the actual risk from the most well-known serious side effect from vaccination. The question was worded as follows.

Millions have had the Covid vaccine without any side effects. What is your best guess for a 17-year-old male to experience heart problems (heart inflammation, myocarditis) as a result of receiving a two-dose Covid vaccine series?

- One myocarditis for every 5000 vaccinations
- One myocarditis for every 30,000 vaccinations
- One myocarditis for every 500,000 vaccinations
- Less than One myocarditis for every 1,000,000 vaccinations

Before going on, glance back at chapter 7. For young men and adolescent boys, the risk of myocarditis a few days after the *second* dose of an mRNA vaccine could reasonably be estimated at either one in 5000 (the most recent data) or, one in 30,000 is definitely supportable. I would consider both of these reasonable guesses, based on the data. The irony is that the guess of the subgroup who endorsed "they do not understand science," guessed (as a group) the chance was one in a million. Experts publishing in this area would not agree the risk is that low. The people who *were not vaccinated* were more accurate in their risk assessment, and several said that side effects were the reason they hesitated.

## Why Do We Collect Data?

I sat back and I paused after I wrote that. It still stuns me. And I thought, "Can I publish this?" It is taboo. There is fear that publishing such words will validate the vaccine hesitant. But yet, this *is* the data. College students who had refused the vaccine listed side effects as a top reason, and they were comparatively accurate in their guess of the frequency of at least one severe side effect. Moreover, I believe that in any open, scientific debate, the data supports vaccination for most people, but it probably doesn't support universal two-dose (or three-dose) vaccination for every human over age five. Insisting that this is what science supports requires suppressing some of the data, some of the arguments. This may backfire in the long run, undermining trust in our health institutions. Even if not, it is going to divide people because some people will get some data via their portal's media feed, others will get other data. I might not be able to fix the problem, but I can choose to not add to the problem. It would be cowardly of me to omit the above data from this chapter.

As my students well know, I define research as the systematic collection of data in an effort to try to discover what is likely to be true. We should, I think, all want to know if our opinions are supported by data, or if they might be need revision. It is nice to be correct, but it can be harmful to cling to beliefs that are not in keeping with reality. The point of science is to use math and logic and our collective intellect to learn what is most likely to be true. Given this, all data collection and all data reporting does not qualify as *Research*. What else is there?

When data is collected, analyzed, and reported in a way that is *not* an effort to discover truth, but is instead publicized with an intent closer to attempting to use statistics to try and corral people's opinions, it is not research, and it is not the standard scientific process. Instead, it becomes an attempt to use selected information to persuade people to agree to support a policy. The name for that is propaganda. That may or may not be happening, but we want to remember the definition for this term, and be on guard to avoid it. The algorithms, the lack of knowledge about opposing information, and chasm between viewpoints are making the distinction between propaganda and data (which is often debatable and blurry) markedly different depending on the vantage point.

## Being Wrong with Gusto

My findings about overestimation of risk are not in isolation. The general overestimation of Covid risk has been well replicated by various experts, using various approaches (by Dr. Lapado, UCLA School of Medicine Professor, and colleagues; by Dr. Niforatos, Professor at Johns Hopkins Medical School and colleagues; and by Dr. Ronald Brown, an expert in infections disease Epidemiology). People have demonstrably been misinformed about this topic of import to their lives. That is the real story, the story science tells.

Does confidence in one's own opinion compared to others' opinions correlate with being more informed—or less informed? I suspect it's a negative correlation. David Dunning and colleagues documented something like this a couple of decades ago. The general tendency for the less informed to be surer of themselves has come to be called the Dunning-Kruger effect. Believing you are smart, and others are not, predicts being less competent.

The general effect was demonstrated with data: students were asked how well they believed they had scored on an exam they had just completed. Their estimations were then compared to the actual performance. Students who performed *really* badly greatly overestimated their performance. While conversely, those who outperformed, who were in reality the actual top performers on the exam, tended to underestimate their knowledge. My data set is too small to be classified as good data. But it hints at the Dunning-Kruger effect.

I hope to collect more data, but with the small data so far, this is the summary:

1. A presumed reason as well as the actual reason for *not* being vaccinated was fear of serious side effects.
2. Most respondents were not accurate estimating the most common and most publicized serious side effect: myocarditis/heart inflammation.
3. Most respondents overestimated the number of children who have died from Covid.
4. Of interest, the subgroup of people who believed the other side did not understand science were the least accurate.

A young office worker caught Covid on the job before vaccines were available, got sick, recovered, and was not vaccinated in the spring of 2021. She is yelled at by her boss for not wearing a mask when alone in the office. Another worker is fully vaccinated and wears a cloth mask when alone, physically blocked off from others. Moreover, she loudly states that unvaccinated people deserve to die if they get sick. We have Red Ants ready to secede from the union, and Blue Ants wishing unvaccinated protesters would die. Who is shaking the jar?

Sometimes I wonder if "following the science," which is of course a slogan, is only a slogan? Or does it have actual meaning: Can scientific observation guide us to alter our conclusions so they better match reality? Or, is all that eighteenth-century enlightenment talk to be discarded in favor of the affirmation of the algorithm bubbles? The algorithms, without conscious awareness, methodically exploit those who care about an issue, driving them on to more extreme positions. Get angry. Click on me. You are right. They are idiots. Feel the dopamine.

Ants are insects, they are small, and not very people-like. But if we could thoughtfully imagine, in a David Attenborough sort of way, the following observation. Ants are working on their lives, moving sand grains across their terrarium, carefully collecting food and moving it, piece by piece. All is well. Then something happens, their terrarium falls off the shelf. The sadness of watching the ants form sides, assume the enemy is the other ants, start to fight, and kill each other.

Look at the chapter titles and beware. It is not just others who are being lied to by omission; you can keep your opinions, which you know, but it is unlikely anyone with a smartphone today can fairly articulate an opposing viewpoint. And why is that? Who is shaking the jar? Fairness in media was universally accepted as an elementary ingredient, fundamental and indispensable for a democracy until the prior generation. Today's algorithms would sicken the FCC and Supreme Court of yesteryear, for they would clearly grasp what it portends for democracy.

Read this book, read any book. Put your personalized portal away as a news source. Whether it is the 2020 election, BLM protests, or mask mandates, peacefully work against the militant ignorance that is becoming endemic in modern society. Read a physical book or a hard copy newspaper. Remember the ants.

# Appendix A: Test Yourself

T or F: Jacob Blake had an outstanding felony warrant for alleged sexual assault, from the same address the officers were called to.

T or F: The woman residing at the address (the one who called for police) said he had again taken the keys to her car and shouted to police, "My kids are in the car!"

T or F: It is in dispute whether or not Blake had a knife in his hand during the altercation (that is, Jacob Blake consistently denies he had a knife in his hand).

Evidence he had the knife in hand includes

  a. Photographic evidence showing something in Blake's hand shaped like an open knife.
  b. Police officers shouting for him to drop the knife during the incident, with their commands audible and recorded on video.
  c. The investigating DA states the knife in his hand was part of the reason he has been able to resist arrest by three officers attempting to subdue him.
  d. Blake saying (with his attorney present) he had his knife in his hand, but he believes it was closed (p. 23 of the DA report).
  e. All of the above.

Assume Blake was seen putting a child into the vehicle. Assume the woman who called police yelled, "Those are my children and he took the keys to my car!" With an outstanding arrest warrant for a sexual assault at the same address, police policy would

   a. Require police to ask the perpetrator to stop, but not use force to
      stop him
   b. Stop the perpetrator using deadly force if needed

The car Jacob Blake was in the process of taking was

   a. Owned by the woman at the address and Blake did not have
      permission to use it
   b. A vehicle he had driven to work many times
   c. A vehicle he had driven earlier that same day
   d. B and C both

The children in the car Jacob Blake tried to drive away with

   a. Were his children
   b. Were children he was visiting with the mother's full permission
   c. Lived at the address where the car was parked and where he had
      stayed the night prior
   d. All of the above

T or F: Blake testified that when the mother started fighting with another
       woman, he wanted to take the children and leave because it was his
       son's birthday.
T or F: The woman who called and sought police help has not given a full
       interview and has not cooperated with police (at the time of writing).

**Thought-provoking question**: What are some features of the case of
Michael Brown ("Hands up don't shoot") in Ferguson, MO, that made it
more covered by the media than other cases of white police killing Blacks,
such as the case of Elijah McClain?

* * *

On April 8–9, 2020, the leading surveyor of physicians and health-care data
(Sermo.com) surveyed over 6,200 physicians and reported that among doctors who had treated Covid patients,

   a. 44 percent of doctors had prescribed hydroxychloroquine for
      Covid-19.

b. 83 percent of doctors had prescribed ivermectin for Covid-19.
c. 35 percent of doctors surveyed in New York City were recommending Vitamin D for Covid-19
d. A and C both.

European Centers for Disease Control official recommendation during the pandemic read

a. "In primary schools, the use of face masks is recommended for teachers and other adults when physical distancing cannot be guaranteed, but it is not recommended for students."
b. "The use of face masks is recommended for students, teachers, and other adults when physical distancing cannot be guaranteed, as is typical in classroom settings."

European Centers for Disease Control report (July 2021) on Covid-19 regarding children in school settings contains which quote?

a. "Cases of SARS-CoV-2 in younger children appear to lead to onward transmission less frequently than cases in older children and adults."
b. "Children who do require hospitalization often have symptoms of long SARS-CoV-2 that persist many weeks."

Regarding CDC data for the state of California, published January 19, 2022: Being unvaccinated but having had Covid-19 (that is unvaccinated but with natural immunity) were _____ to be hospitalized with Covid-19 during the time Delta variant became widespread, compared to unvaccinated without natural immunity.

a. Equally likely
b. 55 times less
c. 10 times less

**Thought-provoking question**: What are the reasons Germany's health organizations might give for counting natural immunity as exempt from Covid vaccination requirement?

* * *

Which of the following were written by hand-selected Trump appointed US Attorney General, William Barr?

   a. "It is possible that Trump got more votes, but that has not been proven."
   b. "President Trump's legal team was feeding his supporters a steady diet of sensational fraud claims, without anything resembling substantiation."

President Trump has said thousands of ballots in boxes, that were heavily for Biden, were brought into Detroit in the early morning hours after the election. Which is true?

   a. Detroit has 600 precincts and they transport all ballots to a central location for counting
   b. Boxes of ballots always arrive during the night in every presidential election
   c. The total number of votes was not higher than the total number in other elections
   d. Trump, not Biden, got a higher percentage of the Detroit vote than he did in 2016.
   e. All of the above

Who has agreed there are dozens of unresolved inconsistencies in their State's voting results favoring Biden that "could not be explained," and asked the State Election Board (Nov. 17, 2021) to swiftly act?

   a. William Barr
   b. Attorney Matthew DePerno
   c. Governor Brian Kemp

**Listing question to consider:** How many former Trump loyalists, that were appointed and selected by Trump, have turned on him (Trump feels betrayed and angry)?

* * *

Regarding a 2020 Poll by Reuters/Ipsos on Critical Race Theory: persons were asked whether it was true that "Critical Race Theory was first established forty years ago," which is true about the results?

    a. 19 percent of Democrats knew it was True
    b. 16 percent of Republicans knew it was True
    c. 41 percent of Democrats knew it was True
    d. A and B both
    e. A and C both

Regarding a 2020 Poll by Reuters/Ipsos on Critical Race Theory: what percent of Republicans support "teaching high school students about racism and its impacts"? (11 percent said they didn't know)

    a. 19 percent
    b. 34 percent
    c. 58 percent
    d. 69 percent

Regarding a 2020 Poll by Reuters/Ipsos on Critical Race Theory: what percent of Republicans agree that critical race theory is being used to erase white heritage? (28 percent said they didn't know)

    a. 19 percent
    b. 34 percent
    c. 57 percent
    d. 69 percent

**Thought-provoking question**: What are some possible explanations for a survey that finds a majority of Republicans are simultaneously against critical race theory and think CRT erases white history, but also support teaching about racism and its impacts on modern society's inequalities?

For answers and quick links to references, please refer to book web page at www.drcatherinedesoto.com.

# Appendix B: Fact Checker Exchange

---

On Thu, Aug 12, 2021 at 2:32 PM Catherine Desoto <█████████████
██▶ wrote:

Hi Jason,

I just read your fact check about Covid-19 infection mortality. Your headline referred to people who contract covid: If the "survival rate is not over 99%" - what is the infection survival rate – and what references are you using?

Here is a great source and some info to get you started
Mortality Risk of COVID-19 - Statistics and Research - Our World in Data
(and please do check their funding, where they get their data – I have. It is good data for the CASE fatality ratio by age, but does not purport to represent the chances of surviving the infection. They make this clear.)

I am sure (I'm assuming) we all understand the IFR (Infection Fatality Ratio, is the indicator of surviving the infection). The Hopkins number you referred to is the CASE fatality ratio – that is the number of medically diagnosed cases that end in death. The link above explains it if you are looking for more information.

Even if you aren't going to post it - I am very interested in what you state the IFR is, by age (since there is at least a 1000 fold difference by age, it doesn't make much sense to group them all together).

YOUR source and numbers please? It has been 18 months post COVID - unlike in early 2020, there is now plenty of data on CFR and IFR available, You state their IFR is wrong – what is it?

I am very nice, motivated by the desire to have fact checkers respected and trusted, and appreciate good fact checkers (so needed). I would love to hear back from you on this.
Catherine

Catherine DeSoto, PhD

Co-Director of Psychoneuroendocrinology Research Lab
Professor
Department of Psychology
University of Northern Iowa
Cedar Falls, Iowa 50614-0505
Bartlett 2062

---

On Thu, Aug 12, 2021 at 3:26 PM Jason Asenso ◁▮▮▮▮▮▮▮▮▮▮▮▮▷ wrote:

Hi Catherine, thanks for reading.
My article specifically addresses the social media post that claims COVID-19's survival rate was as follows:

- 0 – 19 years, 99.997%
- 20 – 49 years, 99.98%
- 50 – 69 years, 99.5%
- 70+ years, 94.6%

The data was misused to make this chart, it was supposed to be used to create models. The post also implied that you could weigh your own chances by looking at national statistics, which is wrong.

I refrained from using the words IFR or CFR to avoid getting too technical for readers. However, I do think I could have been clearer in distinguishing between the two and why I didn't give an IFR in light of your email.

My article says: "Of roughly 35.2 million **confirmed** COVID-19 cases in the United States, around 614,300 people, or 1.7%, have died, according to Johns Hopkins University's mortality data as of Aug 6." This was how I acknowledged that the Hopkins stat was the CFR. I avoided making the distinction between CFR and IFR for brevity and to avoid confusing readers with a distinction that didn't affect the factual inaccuracy of the post's central claimed.

I also purposefully didn't mention what the IFR is because it has not yet been released by a health org like the CDC. When I searched this up just now, the first page of results were mostly studies and estimates, nothing definitive enough to make an assertion about what this number is.

When I spoke to Dr. Etzioni for this story, she called the IFR the least known number in the pandemic. This was because of the general belief that COVID deaths are being undercounted and the difficulty in calculating a survival rate during a pandemic. She also said the IFR likely wouldn't be known for a while and that any calculation we do with current data wouldn't capture the full picture. This is likely why the IFR hasn't been released by the CDC.

This PolitiFact article also does a good job further explaining why survival rates are difficult to estimate, and you should take a look at it too.

Thank you for this email though, I've gotten a few asking me what the IFR/survival rate is already, and they show I should have clearly stated why this number is unknown.

Jason Asenso

---

On Thu, Aug 12, 2021 at 4:04 PM Catherine Desoto <██████████████████ ██> wrote:

Hello,
Thanks so much for responding back!
There is plenty of published info on the IFR, I am surprised you could not find it.

Levin and Colleagues (From Dartmouth, Harvard and the Center for Economic Policy Research-UK) determined age-specific infection fatality rates for COVID-19. Their exhaustive meta-analysis included 113 studies, (and 34 geographical locations). Age-specific IFRs were computed using the prevalence data – and importantly as you referred to in your fact check – they reported fatalities 4 weeks after the midpoint date of the study (to address any delay in fatalities and reporting). The estimated age-specific IFR was 0.002% at age 10; and 0.01% at age 25. The IFR increases progressively to 0.4% at age 55, 1.4% at age 65, 4.6% at age 75, and 15% at age 85. They go into detail about the importance of not listing a single number since it is so varied by age. Take a look at their pub:

Levin, A. T., Hanage, W. P., Owusu-Boaitey, N., Cochran, K. B., Walsh, S. P., & Meyerowitz-Katz, G. (2020). Assessing the age specificity of infection fatality rates for COVID-19: systematic review, meta-analysis, and public policy implications. *European journal of epidemiology, 35*(12), 1123–1138. https://doi.org/10.1007/s10654-020-00698-1

Another review (Meyerowitz & Katz, 2020, "A systematic review and meta-analysis of published research data on COVID-19 infection fatality rates"). They found 24 published estimates of the Covid-19's infection fatality ratio included in the final meta-analysis published between February and June 2020. They gave an overall estimate (across ages, which is problematic, but it does address the headline of the fact check most clearly) They point estimate of overall IFR was 0.68% (CI 0.53%-0.82%). I am sure you follow, but this is less than 1% and thus actually 99% surviving.

Meyerowitz-Katz, G., & Merone, L. (2020). A systematic review and meta-analysis of published research data on COVID-19 infection fatality rates. *International journal of infectious diseases : IJID : official publication of the International Society for Infectious Diseases, 101*, 138–148. https://doi.org/10.1016/j.ijid.2020.09.1464
I could give more, say more, but you get the idea. Be careful out there. Fact checking is an important (nearly sacred) job.

With my sincerest best and hope that this is helpful. Feel free to write back anytime.

Catherine
Catherine DeSoto, PhD

Co-Director of Psychoneuroendocrinology Research Lab
Professor
Department of Psychology
University of Northern Iowa
Cedar Falls, Iowa 50614-0505
Bartlett 2062

On Aug 12, 2021, at 4:28 PM, Jason Asenso ◄▬▬▬▬▬▬► wrote:

There are definitely a ton of studies and estimates on IFR out there, but we wanted something more definitive like from the CDC. Also in light of the delta variant, I think it was the right call to hold off on writing about some of these estimates. The situation has changed so much since these studies were published, and likely will continue to throughout the pandemic.

I really appreciate readers like you that challenge our work. There are a lot of editorial decisions that aren't reflected in articles, and I hope this helped give a look into what some of them were.

If I ever need an expert on Psychoneuroendocrinology I'll definitely know who to call
Take care,
Jason

---

Catherine Desoto wrote: Fri, Aug 13, 2021. 3:41 pm

Hi Jason,
Catherine DeSoto again here. I read your last response, and read some more about your background. (I'm also originally from Illinois :) I'm just so curious about all this, and how it's unfolding. Please forgive my repeat emails, and I am (honestly) glad you are willing to take the time to write back. That conveys your commitment to and some pride in your work.

But, given the published data.... there are at least two formal meta-analyses and dozens of individual studies (not by yocals, by experts from eminent universities, representing national policy institutes, peer reviewed, etc etc). How can you justify calling it "false" when existing published research (the meta-analyses I sent) supports it? If you could find something that disproves it to cite, but you didn't: you referred to case fatality rate. "The IFR is always lower than the CFR for respiratory viruses." Vermund & Pitzer, 2021, Yale epidemiologists who also estimate the IFR as between .1 and 1% (99% infection survival). I don't think there is any disagreement that CFR is lower than IFR (or that IFR is the one about how many survive infection).

You said the 2020 references might be old, fair enough. But do you have data to support that the fatality has changed? Please share it. I just looked and cannot find a good published analysis. or is this just a hunch? clearly Delta is more contagious, but that is (or course) not the same. but on the other hand, one can look at the UK data or the USA data on WHO website where one can see the case state and the death rate side by side. There are three distinct waves over the past 18 months, the last one was the Delta Variant. I do not see a reason to say the calculated infection fatality rate (from the published Meta Analyses) must be wrong now because the virus is far more lethal... look at the data through yesterday <u>The United Kingdom: WHO Coronavirus Disease (COVID-19) Dashboard With Vaccination Data | WHO Coronavirus (COVID-19) Dashboard With Vaccination Data</u>

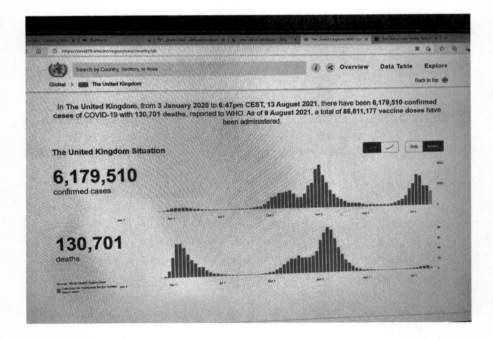

Here is an (speculative) article Medpage today "Why the US Delta Wave Could be Far Less Deadly" https://www.medpagetoday.com/special-reports/exclusives/93955 – published just this week. They are reporting preliminary evidence of likely less deaths (which, as they say, may be due to the most susceptible/older being vaccinated).

Here is a journal article from april 2021 documenting the global fatality rate has lessened:

Hasan, M. N., Haider, N., Stigler, F. L., Khan, R. A., McCoy, D., Zumla, A., Kock, R. A., & Uddin, M. J. (2021). The Global Case-Fatality Rate of COVID-19 Has Been Declining Since May 2020. *The American journal of tropical medicine and hygiene, 104*(6), 2176–2184. Advance online publication. https://doi.org/10.4269/ajtmh.20-1496

So here we are: a greater than 99% survival rate is the same as an IFR of less than 1% (which is **not** the same as CFR) .The numbers flagged as false information are not outside the published record, and you don't have a published reference that disproves it.

How do you see this? I think your headline banner of your fact check….(sorry) is actually itself kind of false (based on the refs I sent, and I could send more). Why do I care? BECAUSE I WANT FACT CHECKERS TO BE RESPECTED. As a scientist, I want facts to matter.

Would you be open to clarifying that published IFRs are in keeping with a 99% survival rate? I think this will increase your credibility. Clarify that indeed, experts and published science converge and do say less than 1% of those infected with Covid succumb (die)? That IS the truth. Again, fact checking is hard, but I'm sure I'm not the only one who was surprised by your headline and article on this. It's so important for fact checkers to stay credible. I hope you'll consider some clarification.

Let me know if you would find more references or any help, but I think the two meta—analyses are clear.

Take care,
Catherine

---

Sent from my iPhone
No response.

# Epilogue

Given the polarization of these issues, perhaps it is only fair for me to disclose my own personal prejudices. I sincerely hope they were not obvious, I hope I have done a sufficiently excellent job of truly presenting the views so that one could not easily tell where I really stand. (Does she think the moon landings were faked?)

I was taught this truth by my late father who was an English professor: one does not really understand any issue until you can credibly give an accounting of the opposing side. As the saying goes, "If you can't intelligently argue for both sides of an issue, you don't understand the issue well enough to argue for either." That is a good litmus test. Truly, how can a person seriously contend they understand an issue if they lack any understanding of the opposing side?

In any case, I will disclose my views, if this is of interest.

*Critical Race Theory* is an interesting and important conceptualization of society whereby everything exists to keep the downtrodden groups down. My understanding of this view: It is the nature of humans to try and keep power, whites have power, society has been set up to keep it this way. This insight, or conceptualization of society, leads directly to efforts to undo the systemic racism that permeates society, which is a major undertaking. It is assumed it is not accomplishable via any piecemeal approach. It is all or nothing. This thinking is what the 1619 Project is born from, and what racially centered curriculum guides are designed to address.

I support teaching children, in age-appropriate ways and through formal lessons, how history connects to the present. I believe that students must be taught that some of today's most blighted neighborhoods have causal roots that trace back to extreme racism and slavery. It is important to me that children in USA grow up knowing about the people who lived in

Greenwood, the murder of Emmett Till, the horrible unjustness of the Trail of Tears, how fear made us turn on Japanese citizens. The stories of these people should be told along with other troubling aspects in our history. If this history is lost, we do not learn from mistakes, and they will surely be repeated. On the other hand, in my view, lessons that imply people of color are always the victim, and whites always the aggressor are obviously historically wrong. To the extent this happens, it should end.

At this point, I believe some weird, off-the-rails lessons have existed in some classrooms that would make most parents unhappy. But it may not be common. More like some teachers will go too far. Not all teachers are deep thinkers, with grace and nuance. I learned some things for this chapter. I do not agree that, in general, expecting standard correct answers in math is harmful to minorities, although a great teacher will see that sometimes this might be needed and make sense. Some of the disinformation of the 1619 Project troubles me just enough that I cannot fully support it. And that itself troubles me. I am sometimes angry at being put in the position of not being able to fully support an attempt to better teach history that needs teaching. I ponder why this came to be.

*Covid mandates.* This is a hard one. Overall, I will disclose I was against my seventeen-year-old daughter getting vaccinated. This is because of her age and the fact she already had it (full case with two days of high fever, loss of smell, the whole thing). When she took the vaccine to allow her to go on a school trip (where two-dose vaccination was required regardless of anything else), it had been under six months since she had recovered, and I did not support it, but understood it. However, if she had been a boy, due to the well-documented difference in myocarditis risk, all other things being equal, I might have fought it. That is the data stubbornly guiding me. On the other hand, I am fully vaccinated. I feel strongly that my mother should be vaccinated. Her 4 percent mortality risk if/when she catches Covid means I want her to have the protection from serious outcomes that vaccination provides. That too is well-documented. Yet, I am against mandates.

Overall, from my reading of the data as it exists today (and I have read about a hundred scientific articles by now as well as published a couple), I think not counting natural immunity is a cardinal sin. I think at some point there is a dividing line based on age where everyone, regardless of health conditions or history, ought to be vaccinated if they really understand the data. (This age, is probably somewhere around age fifty, as a rough guess). When someone states to me that they aren't getting vaccinated, and they are thirty and thin, I do not think so badly of them. It could be a reasonable choice for so many individualized reasons.

Fun fact: Extreme fear of needles, trypanophobia, affects about one in ten Americans. Still, if they are sixty and have never had Covid? I think they are confused by the messaging and politics; they are taking a real risk. I feel sorry for them and wish I knew a way to help. And I get angry about the CDC's one-size-fits-all stance. By not admitting hesitancy for some groups is within reason, they have made their entire message suspect. I ponder why this came to be.

Based on the data today, my view is common, disposable, surgical mask–wearing when community spread is high, *may* help. The respirator style mask (N95) *does* help prevent spread, but they are uncomfortable to wear long term. Cloth masks *do not seem* to be much, if any, help. Wearing a mask outside alone (or when others are not close) does nothing to prevent Covid, and this is an example of something that has been well-documented for some time.

As a scientist who understands research designs, I can see some of the data that is cited for supporting masks is low quality, that it has serious shortcomings that normally prevent strong conclusions. Some of the flaws include being based on individual recollection and report of mask wearing, being correlational without controlling the independent variable, which is a no-no for making cause and effect statements. Findings that support mask wearing are weak if they do not control for other behaviors that likely go along with mask wearing (like general concern about Covid might also make people avoid crowded areas as well as self-report they "always wear a mask"). I see the very small response rates. I ponder why research so obviously flawed like this is getting published, and I wonder why there are no cluster randomized trials published by the CDC. I feel like that is a real question. I ponder why this came to be.

After a full read of the facts and watching most of the trial, I find myself sympathetic to *Kyle Rittenhouse*. As far as the Second Amendment, my dad was an excellent shot who kept a rifle, but I think the last time he shot it was when requested to do so by a police officer in the case of a small, rabid animal in a residential area. The officer thought he himself could not make the shot. My dad grew up in a different world: he hunted as a child, it was food in the 1940s. Gun ownership seems normal to me. I am disgusted at the ease that people can acquire all manner of guns without background checks at gun shows. I support universal background checks, every time, and I support purchasers being required to obtain a license in advance to buy or own a gun. I ponder why these non-divisive kinds of restrictions, that gun owners and non-gunowners typically agree upon, are not enacted. I ponder why this came to be.

*Transgender and biological sex.* I am able to see both sides on the issue of sports participation. I can imagine times when it is definitely fair and appropriate for transgender athletes to participate as the gender they are; and also times when it isn't. I sincerely do not know where or how to draw the line. My education provides a firm foundation for saying there is overwhelming evidence that physical sex is bimodal, and that the male body is different from the female body. Many of these differences are highly relevant to sport performance. I think some awkwardness and growing pains may be understandable as a society loses its prejudice and sorts out new issues. It seems to me that some boys by birth who become transgender women, and begin to live as women in their late teens or twenties might find that for them, sport competition as a woman is simply not competitive, and they will realize this on their own. Overall, I don't have an answer on this one.

*Lunar landing* happened. I do feel confident humans have landed on the moon.

*Trump lost.* It was reasonable to look into it, but he lost. He got fewer popular votes in the 2016 election, but still had more electoral votes for the win. His poll numbers, in 2020, were down from 2016. He lost. That said, it seems much more concern is warranted about vote tampering: *look at what the reports say.* I also fear that if too many people think it was done to them (even if it wasn't), they will feel justified in "doing it back." The reports show it could be done by an expert with access to the machines. If it happens, it is likely to be detectable (that is follow up will show evidence of fraud), but what a mess that would be.

Imagine if in 2024, if Trump becomes the nominee, initial results show Trump got more votes, but recounts and audits really do show truly anomalous results and odd patterns. How would this play out? This would be a problem. Security of our voting could be improved. Tit for tat: there could be a lot of people who feel justified in actual cheating. Cheating uncovered that does change an election outcome would tear our country apart. The factions that exist within the USA seem dangerous regarding this issue. I ponder why this came to be.

*Tax policy.* I don't know. Probably current tax rate on the uber rich is too low in my view. But overall, this is one of the areas I truly learned some things by writing the chapter. I supported Bernie Sanders, so that tells you something, perhaps. But I also saw things in Ron Paul I liked. I think an authentic person who knows history, loves the country and the citizens, and supports the constitution (which requires understanding it) matters more than every stated policy position. Talk is cheap, individual politicians cannot get most of their positions enacted anyway, and stated policy positions are calculated to get donations.

If curious about my politics, my number one issue that marks me a peacenik liberal is war. Always war. War profits corrupt, and it never profits the soldiers fighting. Its horrors are never justified. Mass murder of civilians, mass orders to force humans to kill other humans under threat of death or imprisonment are deep evil. In my view, war itself is always a war crime. War begets war. A candidate's record on war, with preference for those who have seen combat, will probably always guide my vote.

# References

Abel, Martin, Tanya Byker, and Jeffrey Carpenter. 2021. "Socially Optimal Mistakes? Debiasing COVID-19 Mortality Risk Perceptions and Prosocial Behavior." *Journal of Economic Behavior & Organization* 183 (March): 456–480. https://doi.org/10.1016/j .jebo.2021.01.007.

Alimohamadi, Yousef, Habteyes Hailu Tola, Abbas Abbasi-Ghahramanloo, Majid Janani, and Mojtaba Sepandi. 2021. "Case fatality rate of COVID-19: a systematic review and meta-analysis." *Journal of Preventive Hedicine and Hygiene* 62, no. 2 (2021): E311. https://doi.org/10.15167/2421-4248/jpmh2021.62.2.1627.

Ahmad, Farida B., Jodi A. Cisewski, Arialdi Miniño, and Robert N. Anderson. "Provisional mortality data—united states, 2020." *Morbidity and Mortality Weekly Report* 70, no. 14 (2021): 519. https://doi.org/10.15585/mmwr.mm7014e1.

American Enterprise Institute Meeting. 2021. "Why Progressives Ruin Cities." October 21, 2021. American Enterprise Institute Auditorium. www.aei.org/events/why-progressives -ruin-cities/.

Anderson, Craig A., Mark R. Lepper, and Lee Ross. "Perseverance of social theories: The role of explanation in the persistence of discredited information." *Journal of Personality and Social Psychology* 39, no. 6 (1980): 1037.

Armstrong, Rebecca Lee. 2019. "New Survey Suggests 10% of Americans Believe the Moon Landing Was Fake." July 10, 2019. https://www.satelliteinternet.com/resources/moon -landing-real-survey/.

Associated Press. 2020. "Teen in Wisconsin Protest Deaths Used Pandemic Funds for Gun." November 19, 2020. https://apnews.com/article/shootings-police-trials-police -brutality-crime-ed50f249636234311ca585e2463f9320.

"AstroClownBuster." 2010. "Apollo 15 Flag, facing Air Resistance; Proving Fraud." May 6, 2010. https:// www.youtube.com/watch?v=Gn6MTrin5eU.

Ausar, Devendra. 2022. "Google Algorithm Update 2022." January 18, 2022. https://www .divineinfosec.com/google-algorithm-update-2022/.

Bakshy, Eytan, Solomon Messing, and Lada A. Adamic. 2015. "Exposure to ideologically diverse news and opinion on Facebook." *Science* 348, no. 6239 (2015): 1130-1132. https://www.science.org/doi/10.1126/science.aaa1160.

Barda, Noam, Noa Dagan, Yatir Ben-Shlomo, Eldad Kepten, Jacob Waxman, Reut Ohana, Miguel A. Hernán, et al. 2021. "Safety of the BNT162b2 MRNA Covid-19 Vaccine in a Nationwide Setting." *New England Journal of Medicine* 385, no. 12 (August): 1078-1090. https://doi.org/10.1056/nejmoa2110475.

Bernal, Jamie Lopez, Nick Andrews, Charlotte Gower, Eileen Gallagher, Ruth Simmons, Simon Thelwall, Julia Stowe et al. "Effectiveness of Covid-19 vaccines against the B. 1.617. 2 (Delta) variant." *New England Journal of Medicine* (2021). DOI: 10.1056/NEJMoa210889. Brooks, John T., and Jay C. Butler. 2021. "Effectiveness of Mask Wearing to Control Community Spread of SARS-CoV-2." *JAMA* 325 (10): 998-999. https://doi.org/10.1001/jama.2021.1505.

Brossart, Marissa. 2009. "Sarah Gronert Sparks a Whole New Gender Dispute in Pro Sports." March 20, 2009. *Trendhunter.*

Brown, Frank. 1976. "Open Volleys Hot Potato." August 12, 1976. Page 10. *Camden News* Sports Section.

Brown, Ronald B. 2020. "Public health lessons learned from biases in coronavirus mortality overestimation." *Disaster Medicine and Public Health Preparedness* 14, no. 3 (2020): 364-371. doi:10.1017/dmp.2020.298

California Department of Education. 2021. "Mathematics Frameworks Guidelines." Update June 2,, 2021. Accessed March 1, 2022. www.cde.ca.gov/ci/ma/cf/mathfwcfccguidelines.asp.

Callo, Joey. 2021. "The 10 Biggest Pfizer Company Lawsuits in Company History." Lawyer Inc. December 5, 2021. https://lawyerinc.com/biggest-pfizer-lawsuits/.

CBS San Francisco Bay Area. 2021. "Steven Taylor Shooting: Judge Denies Motion to Dismiss Manslaughter Case against Former San Leandro Officer." *CBS*, October 12, 2021. https://sanfrancisco.cbslocal.com/2021/10/12/steven-taylor-shooting-judge-denies -dismissal-san-leandro-officer-jason-fletcher/.

Centers for Disease Control and Prevention. 2010. "Update: Influenza Activity-United States, 2009-2010 Season" July 30, 2010. *Morbidity and Mortality Weekly Reports*, 59 no. 29. 901-908.

Centers for Disease Control and Prevention. 2020. "Estimated COVID-19 Burden." Centers for Disease Control and Prevention. February 11, 2020. https://www.cdc.gov /coronavirus/2019-ncov/cases-updates/burden.html.

Centers for Disease Control and Prevention, National Center for Health Statistics. 2021. "Underlying cause of death data 1999-2020, CDC WONDER Online Database." Accessed February 6, 2022. http://wonder.cdc.gov/ucd-icd10.html.

Centers for Disease Control and Prevention. 2020. "Drug Overdose Deaths in the US Top 100,000 Annually." November 17, 2021. https://www.cdc.gov/nchs/pressroom/nchs _press_releases/2021/20211117.htm.

Centers for Disease Control and Prevention. "10 Leading Causes of Death, United States, 2020." Downloaded May 2, 2022 from WISQARS Data Visualization (cdc.gov). https: //wisqars.cdc.gov/data/lcd/home.

Centers for Disease Control and Prevention. 2022. "Provisional Covid-19 Deaths: Focus on Ages 0-18 Years." May 4, 2022. https://data.cdc.gov/NCHS/Provisional-COVID-19 -Deaths-Focus-on-Ages-0-18-Yea/nr4s-juj3

Chandrasekaran, Krishna. 2021. "The Moon Landing Didn't Happen: Here's How and Why." *Liberty Forecast Blog*, July 14, 2021. https://libertyforecast.com/the-moon -landing-didnt-happen-heres-how-why/.

Cho, Jaeho, Saifuddin Ahmed, Martin Hilbert, Billy Liu, and Jonathan Luu. 2020. "Do search algorithms endanger democracy? An experimental investigation of algorithm effects on political polarization." *Journal of Broadcasting & Electronic Media* 64, no. 2 (2020): 150-172. https://doi.org/10.1080/08838151.2020.1757365.

Cintron, Sonia, Dani Wadlington, and Andre ChenFeng. 2021. "A Pathway to Equitable Math Instruction Dismantling Racism in Mathematics Instruction." https://equitablemath.org/wp-content/uploads/sites/2/2020/11/1_STRIDE1.pdf.

Clark, Andrew E., Sarah Flèche, and Claudia Senik. 2016. "Economic growth evens out happiness: Evidence from six surveys." *Review of Income and Wealth* 62, no. 3 (2016): 405-419. DOI: 10.1111/roiw.12190

Conover, Chris. 2022. "What Is Your Risk of Dying from Covid-19?" *Forbes,* October 6, 2020. https://www.forbes.com/sites/theapothecary/2020/10/06/what-is-your-risk-of-dying-from-covid-19/?sh=7e3f68046159.

CNN. 2021. "Transcript State of the Union with Jake Tapper." November 14, 2021. https://transcripts.cnn.com/show/sotu/date/2021-11-14/segment/01

Crafa, Andrea, Rossella Cannarella, Rosita A. Condorelli, Laura M. Mongioì, Federica Barbagallo, Antonio Aversa, Sandro La Vignera, and Aldo E. Calogero. 2021. "Influence of 25-Hydroxy-Cholecalciferol Levels on SARS-CoV-2 Infection and COVID-19 Severity: A Systematic Review and Meta-Analysis." *EClinicalMedicine* 37 (July). https://doi.org/10.1016/j.eclinm.2021.100967.

Cyber Ninjas. 2021. Maricopa County Forensic Election Audit Volume III: Result Details. Septermber 24, 2021. https:// thenewamerican.com/assets/sites/2/cyber-ninjas-report-vol.-iii.pdf.

Dagan, Noa, Noam Barda, and Ran D. Balicer. 2021. "Adverse Effects after BNT162b2 Vaccine and SARS-CoV-2 Infection, according to Age and Sex." *New England Journal of Medicine* 385, no. 24 (October): 2299. https://doi.org/10.1056/nejmc2115045.

Deift, Percy, Svetlana Jitomirskaya, and Sergiu Klainerman. 2021. "America Is Flunking Math: We Need to Get Racial Politics Out of the Equation Before It's Too Late." *Persuasion,* May 17, 2021. https://www.persuasion.community/p/why-america-is-flunking-math-education?

DeSoto, M. Catherine, Robert T. Hitlan, Rory-Sean S. Deol, and Derrick McAdams. 2010. "Testosterone fluctuations in young men: The difference between interacting with like and not-like others." *Evolutionary Psychology* 8, no. 2 (2010): 147470491000800203. https://doi.org/10.1177%2F147470491000800203

DeSoto, M. Catherine. 2009. "Ockham's Razor and Autism: The Case for Developmental Neurotoxins Contributing to a Disease of Neurodevelopment." *Neurotoxicology* 30, no. 3 (May): 331–337. https://doi.org/10.1016/j.neuro.2009.03.003.

DeSoto, M. Catherine. 2020. "Regional differences in use of immune-modulating catechins should be investigated regarding COVID-19." *Brain, Behavior, and Immunity* 89 (2020): 526. http://www.doi. 10.1016/j.bbi.2020.07.012

DeSoto, M. Catherine. 2021. "Overestimating Covid-19 Mortality: Differential Findings Based on Support for Trump versus Biden." *North American Journal of Psychology* 23, no. 2 (June): 273–282. https://scholarworks.uni.edu/facpub/61/.

Di Pierro, Francesco, Somia Iqtadar, Amjad Khan, Sami Ullah Mumtaz, Mohsin Masud Chaudhry, Alexander Bertuccioli, Giuseppe Derosa, et al. 2021. "Potential Clinical Benefits of Quercetin in the Early Stage of COVID-19: Results of a Second, Pilot, Randomized, Controlled and Open-Label Clinical Trial." *International Journal of General Medicine* 14 (June): 2807–2816. https://doi.org/10.2147/ijgm.s318949.

Dolan, Kerry, Jennifer wang, and Chase Peterson-Witham. 2021. "The Richest in 2021." www.forbes.com/billionaires.

Doung-Ngern, Pawinee, Rapeepong Suphanchaimat, Apinya Panjangampatthana, Chawisar Janekrongtham, Duangrat Ruampoom, Nawaporn Daochaeng, Napatchakorn Eungkanit et al. 2020. "Case-control study of use of personal protective measures and risk for SARS-CoV 2 infection, Thailand." *Emerging Infectious Diseases* 26, no. 11 (2020): 2607. doi:10.1001/jama.2021.1505.

Ellison, Sarah. 2020. "How the 1619 Project Took over 2020." *Washington Post*, October 13, 2020. https://www.washingtonpost.com/lifestyle/style/1619-project-took-over-2020-inside-story/2020/10/13/af537092-00df-11eb-897d-3a6201d6643f_story.html.

Entrenas Castillo, Marta, Luis Manuel Entrenas Costa, José Manuel Vaquero Barrios, Juan Francisco Alcalá Díaz, José López Miranda, Roger Bouillon, and José Manuel Quesada Gomez. 2020. "'Effect of Calcifediol Treatment and Best Available Therapy versus Best Available Therapy on Intensive Care Unit Admission and Mortality among Patients Hospitalized for COVID-19: A Pilot Randomized Clinical Study.'" *The Journal of Steroid Biochemistry and Molecular Biology* 203 (October). https://doi.org/10.1016/j.jsbmb.2020.105751.

Epstein, Robert. 2016. "The New Censorship How Did Google Become the Internet's Censor and Master Manipulator, Blocking Access to Millions of Websites?" *U.S. News*, June 22, 2016. https://www.usnews.com/opinion/articles/2016-06-22/google-is-the-worlds-biggest-censor-and-its-power-must-be-regulated.

European Centers for Disease Control. 2021. "COVID-19 in children and the role of school settings in transmission - second update." July 8, 2021. http:// www.ecdc.europa.eu/en/publications-data/children-and-school-settings-covid-19-transmission.

European Centers for Disease Control. 2021. "Questions and Answers on COVID-19: Children aged 1-18 Years and the Role of School Settings." Page last updated September 8, 2021. http:// www.ecdc.europa.eu/en/ covid-19/questions-answers/questions-answers-school-transmission.

Francis, John L., George J. Palmer, Rebecca Moroose, and Alane Drexler. 2003. "Comparison of Bovine and Porcine Heparin in Heparin Antibody Formation after Cardiac Surgery." *The Annals of Thoracic Surgery* 75, no. 1 (January): 17–22. https://doi.org/10.1016/s0003-4975(02)04349-7.

Franklin, Nikki. 2020. "Sermo Doctors Reveal Global COVID Treatment Patterns." *Sermo*, April2,2020.https://www.sermo.com/press-releases/largest-statistically-significant-study-by-6200-multi-country-physicians-on-covid-19-uncovers-treatment-patterns-and-puts-pandemic-in-context/.

Gajewski, Ryan. 2021. "Caitlyn Jenner Faces Backlash for Opposing Transgender Girls in School Sports. May 02, 2021. www.eonline.com/ca/news/1265097/caitlyn-jenner-faces-backlash-for-opposing-transgender-girls-in-school-sports.

Gartrell, Nate. 2021. "Judge Upholds Manslaughter Charge Against Sam Leandro Cop inWalmart Killing, but Says No Way in the World a Jury Will Convict." June 30, 2021. MercuryNews.com. https://www.mercurynews.com/2021/06/30/judge-upholds-manslaughter-charge-against-san-leandro-cop-in-walmart-killing-but-adds-theres-no-way-in-the-world-a-jury-will-convict/

Gazit, Sivan, Roei Shlezinger, Galit Perez, Roni Lotan, Asaf Peretz, Amir Ben-Tov, Dani Cohen, Khitam Muhsen, Gabriel Chodick, and Tal Patalon. 2021. "Comparing SARS-CoV-2 Natural Immunity to Vaccine-Induced Immunity: Reinfections versus

Breakthrough Infections." *MedRxiv*, (August). https://doi.org/10.1101/2021.08.24.21 262415.

Geary, David C. 2021. "Male, Female: The Evolution of Human Sex Differences." Washington, DC: American Psychological Association.

Geldsetzer, Pascal. 2020. "Use of Rapid Online Surveys to Assess People's Perceptions during Infectious Disease Outbreaks: A Cross-Sectional Survey on COVID-19." *Journal of Medical Internet Research* 22, no. 4 (April). https://doi.org/10.2196/18790.

Google. 2009. "Personalized search for everyone." December 4, 2009. Downloaded April 29, 2022. https://googleblog.blogspot.com/2009/12/personalized-search-for-everyone.html.

Government Accountability Office. 2020. "Federal Social Safety Net Programs: Millions of Full-Time Workers Rely on Federal Health Care and Food Assistance Programs." October 19, 2020. https://www.gao.gov/products/gao-21-45.

Grio. 2022. "Ex-Office Faces $10 Million Lawsuit Related to Fatal 2020 Shooting Inside Walmart." April 20, 2022. *The Grio*. https:// thegrio.com/2022/04/20/ex-officer-faces -10m-lawsuit-related-to-fatal-2020-shooting-inside-walmart/.

Griffith, Keith. 2021. "Two top FDA Regulators Resign in Fury at White House for Politicizing COVID Boosters." The Daily Mail. September 1, 2021. www.dailymail. co.uk/news/article-9947445/Two-FDA-vaccine-regulators-RESIGN-clashing-WH -COVID-boosters.html.

Groh, James. 2020. "Aerial Footage Shows Aftermath of Unrest in Kenosha." *TMJ4*. August 25, 2020. https://www.tmj4.com/news/local-news/aerial-footage-shows-aftermath-of -unrest-in-kenosha.

Gunaydin, Lisa A., Logan Grosenick, Joel C. Finkelstein, Isaac V. Kauvar, Lief E. Fenno, Avishek Adhikari, Stephan Lammel, et al. 2014. "Natural Neural Projection Dynamics Underlying Social Behavior." *Cell* 157, no. 7 (June): 1535–51. https://doi.org/10.1016/j .cell.2014.05.017.

Halderman, J. Alex. 2021. "Analysis of the Antrim County, Michigan, November 2020 Election Incident." March 26, 2021. www.michigan.gov/documents/sos/Antrim_720623 _7.pdf.

Harris, Leslie. 2020. "I Helped Fact-Check the 1619 Project. The Times Ignored Me." March 6, 2020. https://www.politico.com/news/magazine/2020/03/06/1619-project -new-york-times-mistake-122248.

Howard, Phillip. 2016. "Bots and Automation Over Twitter During the Third U.S. Presidential Debate." *Oxford Internet Institute,* October 31, 2016. https://www.oii. ox.ac.uk/news-events/news/bots-and-automation-over-twitter-during-the-third-u-s -presidential-debate/.

Howell, Elizabeth. 2014. "Space Station-Bound Astronaut Eager to Fly NASA's Orion to the Moon." *Space* November 21, 2014. https://www.space.com/27820-nasa-astronaut -orion-spacecraft.html.

InanlooRahatloo, Kolsoum, Grace Liang, Davis Vo, Antje Ebert, Ivy Nguyen, and Patricia K. Nguyen. "Sex-based Differences in Myocardial Gene Expression in Recently Deceased Organ Donors with No Prior Cardiovascular Disease." *PloS one* 12, no. 8 (2017): e0183874.

Inequality.org. "Inequality and Taxes." Downloaded April 2, 2022. https:// inequality. org/facts/taxes-inequality-in-united-states/?msclkid=83f0103dcfa911ec940bcd586cb 20a70.

Isidore, Chris. 2021. "Pfizer Revenue and Profits Soar on Its Covid Vaccine Business." *CNN*, November 2, 2021. https://www.cnn.com/2021/11/02/business/pfizer-earnings /index.html.

Jackson, Jon. 2021. "Johns Hopkins Doctor Marty Makary Accuses CDC of 'Sitting on Data' to Suit Their Narrative." *Newsweek* , June 14, 2021. https://www.newsweek.com/johns -hopkins-doctor-marty-makary-accuses-cdc-sitting-data-suit-their-narrative-1600545.

Joe Rogan Experience. 2013. Number 310 Neil NeGrasse Tyson. https://open.spotify.com /episode/3kvqMVgf68IWbUzZi2t7jw.

Kale, Sirin. 2021. "The Life and Tragic Death of John Eyers – a Fitness Fanatic Who Refused the Vaccine." *The Guardian.* November 30, 2021. https://www.theguardian.com/society/2021 /nov/30/life-tragic-death-john-eyers-fitness-fanatic-who-refused-covid-vaccine.

Kato, Takeshi, and Yoshinori Hiroi. 2021. "Wealth disparities and economic flow: Assessment using an asset exchange model with the surplus stock of the wealthy." *PloS one* 16, no. 11 (2021): e0259323. https://doi.org/10.1371/journal.pone.0259323

Kaufman, Elliot. 2019. "The '1619 Project' Gets Schooled." *Wall Street Journal*, December 16, 2019. https://www.wsj.com/articles/the-1619-project-gets-schooled-11576540494.

Kaysing, Bill, and Randy Reid. 1976. *We Never Went to the Moon: America's Thirty Billion Dollar Swindle*. Washington: Health Research. Assessed March 9, 2022. https://www .futile.work/uploads/1/5/0/1/15012114/we_never_went_to_the_moon.pdf.

Kemp, Governor Brian. 2021. "Brian Kemp Georgia Letter Joe Rossi 11.17.2021" November 17, 2021.Accessed March 7, 2022. www.scribd.com/document/544350830 /Brian-Kemp-Georgia-SEB-Letter-Joe-Rossi-11-17-2021.

King, Laura. 2021. *Experience Psychology*. McGraw Hill: New York.

KTVU Fox 2 San Francisco. 2021. "Rainy Weather Raises Concerns Around Santa Cruz Homeless Encampment Already Flooded Out." http://www.youtube.com /watch?v=aKsbo9dGKJo.

Kozol, Jonathan. 1991. *Savage Inequalities*. New York: Crown Pub.

Lamminmäki, Annamarja, Melissa Hines, Tanja Kuiri-Hänninen, Leena Kilpeläinen, Leo Dunkel, and Ulla Sankilampi. 2012. "Testosterone measured in infancy predicts subsequent sex-typed behavior in boys and in girls." *Hormones and behavior* 61, no. 4 (2012): 611-616. DOI: http://doi.org/10.1016/j.yhbeh.2012.02.013

Ladapo, Joseph A., Jonathan T. Rothwell, and Christina M. Ramirez. 2021. "Association of COVID-19 Risk Misperceptions with Household Isolation in the United States: Survey Study." *JMIR Formative Research* 5, no. 8 (2021): e30164.Launius, Roger. 2010. *Denying the Apollo Moon Landings: Conspiracy and Questioning in Modern American History*. 48th AIAA Aerospace Sciences Meeting Including the New Horizons Forum and Aerospace Exposition. https://doi.org/10.2514/6.2010-1131.

Leonhardt, David. 2021. "U.S. Covid Deaths Get Even Redder." *The New York Times*, November 8, 2021. https://www.nytimes.com/2021/11/08/briefing/covid-death-toll -red-america.html.

Levi, David F., Amelia Ashton Thorn and John Macy. 2021. "The Courts Held." *Botch Judicial Institute at Duke Law* 105, no. 1. https:// judicature.duke.edu/wp-content /uploads/2021/04/TheCourtsHeld_Spring2017.pdf.

Levin, Dan, Gil Shimon, Maggie Fadlon-Derai, Liron Gershovitz, Amiram Shovali, Anat Sebbag, Shakib Bader, Noam Fink, and Barak Gordon. 2021. "Myocarditis Following COVID-19 Vaccination – a Case Series." *Vaccine* 39 no. 42 (October): 6195–6200. https://doi.org/10.1016/j.vaccine.2021.09.004.

Liggins, Greg. 2020. "Police Identify Man Shot and Killed by Officers inside San Leandro Walmart." *KTVU FOX 2*, April 19, 2020. https://www.ktvu.com/news/police-identify -man-shot-and-killed-by-officers-inside-san-leandro-walmart.

Luo, Huabin, Haiyan Qu, Rashmita Basu, Ann P. Rafferty, Shivajirao P. Patil, and Doyle M. Cummings. 2021. "Willingness to Get a COVID-19 Vaccine and Reasons for Hesitancy among Medicare Beneficiaries." *Journal of Public Health Management and Practice* 28, no. 1 (June): 70-76. https://doi.org/10.1097/phh.0000000000001394.

Machman, Gerald. 1976. "Transsexual for Tennis?" September 22, 1976, Page 22. *Oakland Tribune*.

Mitchell, Amy, Jeffrey Gottfried, and Katerina Eva Matsa. 2015. "Facebook Top Source for Political News among Millennials." *Pew Research Center*, June 1, 2015. https://www.pewresearch.org/journalism/2015/06/01/facebook-top-source-for-political -news-among-millennials/.

MITRE Corporation. 2021. "Data Analytics to Enhance Election Transparency." February, 2021. https://www.mitre.org/publications/technical-papers/data-analytics-to-enhance -election-transparency.

Mevorach, Dror, Emilia Anis, Noa Cedar, Michal Bromberg, Eric J. Haas, Eyal Nadir, Sharon Olsha-Castell et al. 2021. "Myocarditis after BNT162b2 mRNA vaccine against Covid-19 in Israel." *New England Journal of Medicine* 385, no. 23 (2021): 2140-2149.

Moms for Liberty. 2021. "Quisha King, Moms for Liberty - Duval County, FL Destroys Critical Race Theory." Youtube. June 13, 2021. 2:02. https://www.youtube.com /watch?v=GiGjZY6JrkI.

Montgomery, Jay, Margaret Ryan, Renata Engler, Donna Hoffman, Bruce McClenathan, Limone Collins, David Loran, et al. 2021. "Myocarditis Following Immunization with MRNA COVID-19 Vaccines in Members of the US Military." *JAMA Cardiology*, 6, no. 10 (June). https://doi.org/10.1001/jamacardio.2021.2833.

NASA. 2011. "New Images Offer Sharper View of Apollo Sites." September 5, 2011. https://www.nasa.gov/mission_pages/LRO/news/apollo-sites.html.

NASA. 2011. "Noah Petro Explains New LRO Images of Apollo 12, 14, and 17 Sites." Youtube. September 6, 2011. 1:28. https://www.youtube.com/watch?v=_WZ26s4ik2w.

NASA. 2015. "ISS Crew Discusses Life in Space." Youtube. March 14, 2015. 21:32. https://www.youtube.com/watch?v=3gJ0DfULLGU#t=11m0s.

NASA. Apollo 11 Lunar Sample Information Catalog JSC: 12522. Sample Description 10094. Accessed March 7, 2022. https://curator.jsc.nasa.gov/lunar/catalogs /apollo11/10094.pdf.

National Institute of Health. 2021. "Vitamin D." COVID-19 Treatment Guidelines. Last modified April 21, 2021. https://www.covid19treatmentguidelines.nih.gov/therapies /supplements/vitamin-d/.

New York Times Archives. 1976. "No Jersey Bar on Dr. Richards." August 14, 1976, p. 34.

New York Times Archives. 1976. "Rival Play in Richards Rift." August 20, 1976, p. 3.

Newsweek. 2021. "Watch Black Father Blast Critical Race Theory at Board Meeting in Viral Video." Youtube. June 18, 2021. 2:39. https://www.youtube.com /watch?v=m66rcHzWaPU.

Niforatos, Joshua D., Edward R. Melnick, and Jeremy S. Faust. 2020. "Covid-19 fatality is likely overestimated." *BMJ: British Medical Journal (Online)* 368. Accessed March 7, 2022. http://web.archive.org/web/20200511040649id_/https://www.bmj.com/content /bmj/368/bmj.m1113.full.pdf.

Nomura, Shuhei, Akifumi Eguchi, Daisuke Yoneoka, Takayuki Kawashima, Yuta Tanoue, Michio Murakami, Haruka Sakamoto, et al. 2021. "Reasons for Being Unsure or Unwilling Regarding Intention to Take COVID-19 Vaccine among Japanese People: A Large Cross-Sectional National Survey." *The Lancet Regional Health. Western Pacific* 14 (September). https://doi.org/10.1016/j.lanwpc.2021.100223.

Owermohle, Sarah. 2021. "Biden's Top-down Booster Plan Sparks Anger at FDA." *Politico*, August 31, 2021. https://www.politico.com/news/2021/08/31/biden-booster-plan -fda-508149.

O'Neal, James. 2009. "Search for Missing Recording Fails." August 6, 2009. *TV Technology*. https://web. archive.org/web/20131019101737/http://www.tvtechnology.com/feature -box/0124/search-for-missing-recordings-ends/202982.

Parker, Sean. (2017). Interview with Axios Mike Allen. Downloaded May, 2022. Available at www.axios.com/2017/12/15/sean-parker-facebook-was-designed-to-exploit-human -vulnerability-1513306782.

Pal, R., M. Banerjee, S. K. Bhadada, A. J. Shetty, B. Singh, and A. Vyas. 2021. "Vitamin D supplementation and clinical outcomes in COVID-19: a systematic review and meta -analysis." *Journal of Endocrinological Investigation* (2021): 1-16. https://doi.org/10.1007 /s40618-021-01614-4

Payne, Daniel C. 2020. "SARS-CoV-2 Infections and Serologic Responses from a Sample of U.S. Navy Service Members — USS Theodore Roosevelt, April 2020." *MMWR. Morbidity and Mortality Weekly Report* 69, no. 23 (June): 714-721. https://doi .org/10.15585/mmwr.mm6923e4.

Picower, Bree. 2009. "The Unexamined Whiteness of Teaching: How White Teachers Maintain and Enact Dominant Racial Ideologies." *Race Ethnicity and Education* 12, no. 2 (June): 197–215. https://doi.org/10.1080/13613320902995475.

Platoff, Emma. 2021. "U.S. Supreme Court Throws Out Texas Lawsuit Contesting 2020 Election Results in Four Battle Ground States." December 11, 2020. *The Texas Tribune*.

Polack, Fernando P., Stephen J. Thomas, Nicholas Kitchin, Judith Absalon, Alejandra Gurtman, Stephen Lockhart, John L. Perez, et al. 2020. "Safety and Efficacy of the BNT162b2 MRNA Covid-19 Vaccine." *New England Journal of Medicine* 383, no. 27 (December): 2603-2615. https://doi.org/10.1056/nejmoa2034577.

Pond, Steve. 2016. "How Donald Trump Became the Emmy's Sorest Loser." August 15, 2016. The *Wrap*. https://www.yahoo.com/entertainment/donald-trump-became -emmys-sorest-loser-173105205.html.

Porter, Katie. 2019. "Lawmaker Challenges Big Bank CEO by Showing Him Math." April 16, 2019. Accessed March 7, 2022. www.youtube.com/watch?v=yh4nhkuvuFc.

Poynter Institute PolitiFact (2021). "Why the Survival Rate for COVID-19 is not over 99%." Downloaded May 23, 2022 from www.politifact.com/factchecks/2021/aug/06 /instagram-posts/why-covid-19-survival-rate-not-over-99/.

Public Broadcasting System Amanpour and Company. 2019. "Jonathon Haidt explains how social media drives polarization." December 4, 2019. www.pbs.org/wnet/amanpour -and-company/video/jonathan-haidt-explains-how-social-media-drives-polarization/

Pulitzer Center. 2019. "The 1619 Project Curriculum." Accessed March1, 2022. https: //pulitzercenter.org/lesson-plan-grouping/1619-project-curriculum.

Ramsland, James. 2020. "Allied Security Antrim Michigan Forensics Report, revised preliminary summary, v2." December 13, 2020. Accessed January 15, 2022. https: //www.depernolaw.com.

*Red Lion Broadcasting Co. v. FCC*, 395 U.S. 367, 89 S. Ct. 1794, 23 L. Ed. 2d 371 (1969).

Reuters/Ipsos. 2021. "Reuters/Ipsos Poll: Critical Race Theory." *Reuters/Ipsos,* July 15, 2021. https://www.ipsos.com.

Rev. 2020. "Rudy Giuliani Trump Campaign Press Conference Transcript November 19: Election Fraud Claims." November 19, 2020. https://www.rev.com/blog/transcripts/.

Rev. 2020. "Rudy Giuliani Speech Transcript at Trump's Washington DC Rally: Wants Trial By Combat." January 6, 2021. https://www.rev.com/blog/transcripts/.

Rimm, David and John Somervill. (1976). Abnormal Psychology. Academic Press: New York.

Robertson, Elaine, Kelly S. Reeve, Claire L. Niedzwiedz, Jamie Moore, Margaret Blake, Michael Green, Srinivasa Vittal Katikireddi, Michaela J. Benzeval. 2021. "Predictors of COVID-19 Vaccine Hesitancy in the UK Household Longitudinal Study." *Brain, Behavior, and Immunity* 94 (March): 41-50. https://doi.org/10.1016/j.bbi.2021.03.008.

Rothwell, Jonathon and Sonal Desai. 2020. "How Misinformation Is Distorting COVID Policies and Behaviors." *Brookings*, December 22, 2020. https://www.brookings.edu /research/how-misinformation-is-distorting-covid-policies-and-behaviors/.

Rudacille, Deborah. 2005. The Riddle of Gender: Science, Activism, and Transgender Rights. Pantheon Books: New York.

Rufo, Christopher. 2020. "Chaos by the Bay: The Truth about Homelessness." August 3, 2020. http://www.youtube.com/watch?v=uw8MACDZ3RI

Safonova, Margarita. 2019. "How NASA Worked Around Earth's Radiation Belts to Land Apollo 11 on the Moon." *The Wire.* June 9, 2019. https://thewire.in/the-sciences/apollo -11-van-allen-radiation-belts-translunar-injection.

Scarella, Mike. 2022. "U.S. Court Revives Lawsuit against Pfizer, Others on Iraq Terrorism Funding Claims." *Yahoo! News,* January 4, 2022. https://news.yahoo.com/u-court -revives-lawsuit-against-193221732.html.

Schacter, Daniel L. 1999. "The seven sins of memory: insights from psychology and cognitive neuroscience." *American Psychologist* 54, no. 3: 182.

Sharff, Katie, David M. Dancoes, Jodi L. Longueil, Eric S. Johnson, and Paul F. Lewis. 2021. "Risk of Myopericarditis following COVID-19 mRNA vaccination in a Large Integrated Health System: A Comparison of Completeness and Timeliness of Two Methods." *medRxiv* (2021). https://doi.org/10.1101/2021.12.21.21268209

Scully, Marie, Deepak Singh, Robert Lown, Anthony Poles, Thomas Solomon, Marcel Levi, David Goldblatt, Pavel Kotoucek, William Thomas, and William Lester. 2021. "Pathologic Antibodies to Platelet Factor 4 After ChAdOx1 NCoV-19 Vaccination." *New England Journal of Medicine*, 384, no. 23 (April): 2202-2211. https://doi.org/10.1056 /nejmoa2105385.

Search Engine Journal. n.d. "Google Algorithm Updates & Changes: A Complete History." Accessed March 8, 2022. https://www.searchenginejournal.com/google-algorithm -history/.

Shah Alam, Mohammad, Daniel M. Czajkowsky, Md. Aminul Islam, and Md. Ataur Rahman. 2021. "The Role of Vitamin D in Reducing SARS-CoV-2 Infection: An Update." *International Immunopharmacology* 97 (August). https://doi.org/10.1016/j .intimp.2021.107686.

Sherman, Eli and Ted Nesi. 2022. "COVID Positive Health Care Workers Called into Work in Rhode Island." *WPRI,* January 3, 2022. https://www.wpri.com/target-12/covid -positive-health-care-workers-called-into-work-in-rhode-island/.

Silverstein, Jake. 2020. "On Recent Criticism of the 1619 Project." *The New York Times*, October 16, 2020. https://www.nytimes.com/2020/10/16/magazine/criticism-1619 -project.html.

Simoneau, Jean-Aime, and Claude Bouchard. (1989). "Human variation in skeletal muscle fiber-type proportion and enzyme activities." *American Journal of Physiology-Endocrinology And Metabolism* 257, no. 4 (1989): E567-E572. 10.1152/ajpendo.1989.257.4.E567

Sørvoll, Ingvild Hausberg, Kjersti Daae Horvei, Siw Leiknes Ernstsen, Ingvild Jenssen Lægreid, Svetlana Lund, Renathe Henriksen Grønli, Magnus Kringstad Olsen, et al. 2021. "An Observational Study to Identify the Prevalence of Thrombocytopenia and Anti-PF4/Polyanion Antibodies in Norwegian Health Care Workers after COVID-19 Vaccination." *Journal of Thrombosis and Haemostasis* 19, no. 7 (July): 1813–1818. https://doi.org/10.1111/jth.15352.

Southern Poverty Law Center. 2018. *Teaching Hard History : A Framework for Teaching American Slavery*. Montgomery, Alabama: Southern Poverty Law Center. www.splcenter.org/sites/default/files/tt_hard_history_american_slavery.pdf.

Steffensmeier, Darrell, and Stephen Demuth. 2006. "Does gender modify the effects of race–ethnicity on criminal sanctioning? Sentences for male and female white, black, and Hispanic defendants." *Journal of Quantitative Criminology* 22, no. 3 (2006): 241-261.

Stern, Jeremy. 2021. "State Civics and U.S. History Standards Are Less Politically Biased Than Before." August 8, 2021. https://fordhaminstitute.org/national/commentary/

Stern, Jeremy A., Alison E. Brody, José A. Gregory, Stephen Griffith, and Jonathan Pulvers. 2021. "The State of State Standards for Civics and US History in 2021." *Thomas B. Fordham Institute*.

Stern, Jeremy A., and Sheldon Stern. 2011. "The State of State Standards for Civics and US History in 2011." *Thomas B. Fordham Institute*.

Summers, Adam B. 2021. California Needs a New Approach to Homelessness." *Orange County Register*. November 21, 2021. https://www.ocregister.com/2021/11/22 /california-needs-a-new-approach-on-homelessness/The Heritage Foundation. 2020. "New York Times Quietly Edits '1619 Project' after Conservative Pushback." *The Heritage Foundation*, September 26, 2020. https://www.heritage.org/american -founders/impact/new-york-times-quietly-edits-1619-project-after-conservative -pushback.

Thorbecke, Catherine. 2020. "Colorado Police Officers Fired for Recreating Chokehold in Photos at Elijah McClain Memorial." *ABC News*, July 3, 2020. https://abcnews .go.com/US/colorado-police-recreated-chokehold-photos-elijah-mcclain-memorial /story?id=71600727.

Travis, Justin, Scott Harris, Tina Fadel, and Ginny Webb. 2021. "Identifying the Determinants of COVID-19 Preventative Behaviors and Vaccine Intentions Among South Carolina Residents." *PLOS ONE* 16, no.8 (August). https://doi.org/10.1371 /journal.pone.0256178.

Trenchard, Lorraine, and Hugh Warren. 1984. *Something to Tell You: The Experiences and Needs of Young Lesbians and Gay Men in London*. London Gay Teenage Group.

Trump v. The Wisconsin Elections Commission et al, No. 2:2020cv01785 - Document 134 (E.D. Wis. 2020). Assessed February 5, 2022. https ://law.justia.com/cases/federal /district-courts/wisconsin/wiedce/2:2020cv01785/92761/134/.

U.S. Department of Health and Human Services. Centers for Disease Control and Prevention. 2010. "Update: Influenza Activity - United States, 2009-10 Season." *Morbidity and*

*Mortality Weekly Report* 59, no. 29 (July): 901–908. https://pubmed.ncbi.nlm.nih
.gov/20671661/.

U. S. Department of Justice Civil rights Division. 2014. "Investigation of the Cleveland
Division of Police by US Attorney General's Office of Northern District of
Ohio." December 4, 2014. www.justice.gov/sites/default/files/opa/press-releases
/attachments/2014/12/04/cleveland_division_of_police_findings_letter.pdf

UK Office for National Statistics. "Coronavirus COVID-19 Latest Insights: Deaths." n.d.
Accessed December 2021. https://www.ons.gov.uk/peoplepopulationandcommunity
/healthandsocialcare/conditionsanddiseases/articles/coronaviruscovid19latestinsights
/deaths#deaths-by-vaccination-status.

UK Health Security Agency. 2022. "COVID-19 Vaccine Surveillance Report Week 16."
April 21, 2022. https://assets.publishing.service.gov.uk/government/uploads/system
/uploads/attachment_data/file/1070356/Vaccine-surveillance-report-week-16.pdf

Volkow, Nora D. 2014. "America's addiction to opioids: Heroin and prescription drug
abuse." *Senate Caucus on International Narcotics Control* 14 (2014): 1-16.

Wikipedia Contributors. 2019. "Death of Sandra Bland." Wikipedia. Wikimedia Foundation.
November 17, 2019. https://en.wikipedia.org/wiki/Death_of_Sandra_Bland.

Williams, Christina L., Allison M. Barnett, and Warren H. Meck. (1990). "Organizational
effects of early gonadal secretions on sexual differentiation in spatial memory." *Behavioral
Neuroscience* 104, no. 1 (1990): 84-97. 10.1037//0735-7044.104.1.84

Williams, Nia, Trisha Radia, Katharine Harman, Pankaj Agrawal, James Cook, and Atul
Gupta. 2020. "COVID-19 Severe Acute Respiratory Syndrome Coronavirus 2 (SARS-
CoV-2) Infection in Children and Adolescents: A Systematic Review of Critically Unwell
Children and the Association with Underlying Comorbidities." *European Journal of
Pediatrics* 180, no. 3 (March): 689–697. https://doi.org/10.1007/s00431-020-03801-6.

Wang, Yu, Huaiyu Tian, Li Zhang, Man Zhang, Dandan Guo, Wenting Wu, Xingxing
Zhang et al. "Reduction of secondary transmission of SARS-CoV-2 in households by
face mask use, disinfection and social distancing: a cohort study in Beijing, China." *BMJ
global health* 5, no. 5 (2020): e002794. http://dx.doi.org/10.1136/bmjgh-2020-002794

Weiss, Bari. (2022). Honestly Podcast "Why the Past 10 Years of American Life Have Been
Uniquely Stupid." April 12, 2022. Available at https://podcasts.apple.com/us/podcast
/honestly-with-bari-weiss/id1570872415.

Wheatley, Courtney M., Eric M. Snyder, Bruce D. Johnson, and Thomas P. Olson.
"Sex differences in cardiovascular function during submaximal exercise in
humans." *Springerplus* 3, no. 1 (2014): 1-13.

Wood, Gordon. 2019. "Historian Gordon Wood Responds to the New York Times' Defense
of the 1619 Project." World Socialist Web Site, December 21, 2019. https://www.wsws
.org/en/articles/2019/12/24/nytr-d24.html.

WPRI News. 2022. "COVID Positive Health Care Workers Called Into Work in Rhode
Island." January 3, 2022. www.wpri.com/target-12/covid-positive-health-care-workers
-called-into-work-in-rhode-island/.

Zaragoza, Maria S., and Sean M. Lane. 1994. "Source misattributions and the suggestibility
of eyewitness memory." *Journal of Experimental Psychology: Learning, Memory, and
Cognition* 20, no. 4 (1994): 934.

Zatz, Marjorie. 1984. "Race, Ethnicity, and Determinate Sentencing: A New Dimension
to an Old Controversy." *Criminology* 22, no. 2 (May): 147-171. https://doi
.org/10.1111/j.1745-9125.1984.tb00294.x

# Index